T0305476

F. A. Hayek and the Epistemology of Politics

F. A. Hayek and the Epistemology of Politics is an exploration of an important problem that has largely been ignored heretofore: the problem of policymaker ignorance and the consequences of limited political knowledge. Scott Scheall explores the significance of the fact that the possibilities for effective political action are constrained by policymakers' epistemic limitations. The book offers an explanation for why policymaking often fails and why constituents, whatever their political affiliations, are so often disappointed with political leaders.

In this philosophical examination of his work, Hayek's ideas are not merely discussed, analyzed, and contextualized, but extended; the book both draws and defends previously unrecognized implications from the Hayekian canon.

The book will be of interest to scholars of the works of F. A. Hayek and his intellectual adversaries, to policymakers, and to those of all political, philosophical, and social-scientific persuasions.

Scott Scheall is Assistant Professor and Director of Graduate Studies in the Faculty of Social Science in Arizona State University's College of Integrative Sciences and Arts, as well as Project Director for the History of Economic Thought in Arizona State University's Center for the Study of Economic Liberty. He has published extensively on topics related to the history and philosophy of the Austrian School of economics. Scott is co-host of *Smith and Marx Walk into a Bar: A History of Economics Podcast*.

Routledge Studies in the History of Economics

The Political Economy of the Han Dynasty and Its Legacy
Edited by Cheng Lin, Terry Peach and Wang Fang

A History of Utilitarian Ethics
Samuel Hollander

The Economic Thought of Michael Polanyi
Gábor Biró

Ideas in the History of Economic Development
The Case of Peripheral Countries
Edited by Estrella Trincado, Andrés Lazzarini and Denis Melnik

Ordoliberalism and European Economic Policy
Between Realpolitik and Economic Utopia
Edited by Malte Dold and Tim Krieger

The Economic Thought of Sir James Steuart
First Economist of the Scottish Enlightenment
Edited by José M. Menudo

A History of Feminist and Gender Economics
Giandomenica Becchio

The Theory of Transaction in Institutional Economics
A History
Massimiliano Vatiero

F. A. Hayek and the Epistemology of Politics
The Curious Task of Economics
Scott Scheall

For more information about this series, please visit www.routledge.com/
series/SE0341

F. A. Hayek and the Epistemology of Politics

The Curious Task of Economics

Scott Scheall

Routledge
Taylor & Francis Group

LONDON AND NEW YORK

First published 2020 by Routledge

2 Park Square, Milton Park, Abingdon, Oxon OX14 4RN
605 Third Avenue, New York, NY 10017

Routledge is an imprint of the Taylor & Francis Group, an informa business

First issued in paperback 2021

Publisher's Note

The publisher has gone to great lengths to ensure the quality of this reprint
but points out that some imperfections in the original copies may be apparent.

British Library Cataloguing-in-Publication Data
A catalogue record for this book is available from the British Library

Library of Congress Cataloging-in-Publication Data
Names: Scheall, Scott, author.
Title: Hayek, economics, and the epistemology of politics / Scott Scheall.
Description: Abingdon, Oxon ; New York, NY : Routledge, 2020. |
    Series: Routledge studies in the history of economics; 228 | Includes
    bibliographical references and index.
Identifiers: LCCN 2019048881 (print) | LCCN 2019048882 (ebook)
Subjects: LCSH: Hayek, Friedrich A. von (Friedrich August), 1899–1992. |
    Policy sciences—Philosophy. | Political science—Philosophy. |
    Economics—Philosophy.
Classification: LCC HB101.H39 S34 2020 (print) | LCC HB101.H39
    (ebook) | DDC 330.15/7—dc23
LC record available at https://lccn.loc.gov/2019048881
LC ebook record available at https://lccn.loc.gov/2019048882

ISBN: 978-1-138-28995-6 (hbk)
ISBN: 978-1-03-217443-3 (pbk)
DOI: 10.4324/9781315266732

Typeset in Bembo
by Apex CoVantage, LLC

For Larry, this man's best friend.

"The curious task of economics is to demonstrate to men how little they really know about what they imagine they can design."
— F. A. Hayek, The Fatal Conceit: The Errors of Socialism (1988)

"God, grant me the serenity to accept the things I cannot change, the courage to change the things I can, and the wisdom to know the difference."
— The Serenity Prayer (attributed to Reinhold Niebuhr)

Contents

Preface   ix
Acknowledgments   xii

Introduction   1

PART I
The problem of policymaker ignorance   11

1   **Policymaker ignorance: the first problem of politics
    and political inquiry**   13

Some terminological clarifications 15
*The logically ancillary nature of the problem of policymaker
    incentives 15*
The logical priority of the epistemic 19
A taxonomy of ignorant policymakers 27
Reflection and foreshadow 29

2   **Beyond the socialist oasis: Hayek's extensions of Mises'
    calculation argument**   34

*The insurmountable epistemic burden of the administrator of a pure
    and isolated socialist oasis 35*
Hayek's epistemology – a first pass 37
The epistemic burdens of socialist administrators in other contexts 41
*The epistemic burdens of countercyclical economic policymaking
    and Keynesian demand management 54*
*The generality of the reasoning underlying the Austrians'
    political-epistemological approach 63*
Reflection and foreshadow 65

3   **Liberalism and the problem of policymaker ignorance**   75

    The epistemic burdens of realizing an effective liberal order: the problem
       of the epistemic requirements of liberal transitions 77
    The epistemic burden of policymaking within liberal environments 96
    The epistemic burden of policy inaction 98
    Reflection and foreshadow 99

PART II
Hayekian political epistemology   105

4   **The epistemological aspects of Hayekian political**
    epistemology   107

    Hayek versus Mises on matters epistemological, part one 107
    Hayek as theoretical psychologist and epistemological naturalist 112
    Reflection and foreshadow 129

5   **Political order and disorder as epistemic phenomena**   137

    Knowledge, planning, social order, and epistemic mechanisms 137
    Further epistemic requirements of social order 140
    How prices tell you what to do 142
    How reputation signals tell scientists (and others) what to do 146
    Political order and disorder 151
    Reflection and foreshadow 155

6   **Hayekian political epistemology as a science of the limits**
    of deliberate political action   158

    Hayek versus Keynes yet again 159
    A constitutional approach to the problem of policymaker ignorance 170
    Functional omniscience and omnipotence 174
    Reflection 176

    Reflection and foreshadow: what the argument is and what
      the argument is not   178
    Bibliography   183
    Index   196

Preface

I have always been fascinated by and, I must confess, have never really understood, peoples' political beliefs. Now, do not get me wrong on this point. I do not mean that I cannot understand why people hold political beliefs different from my own. Even if I disagree with their particular concerns, I am usually sympathetic enough to understand why people want the world to be certain ways; why they have worries about various aspects of society, the environment, what have you; and why they want this problem or that problem solved, or at least mitigated. What I have never understood is why people think, if perhaps only unconsciously, that politicians are knowledgeable and capable enough to contribute much to the mitigation of many problems. It is obvious, I would think, that politicians are nothing like all-knowing and all-powerful gods. Indeed, it is no less obvious – I would think – that politicians are just human beings and so basically like all other human beings in their limited knowledge and constrained capabilities. If we were to gather hundreds of everyday average people at random, give them access to and control over the apparatus of government, and tell them to solve the world's problems, they would not suddenly become uniquely knowledgeable and capable, individually or collectively, to effectively address these problems. Yet somehow, these obvious facts are often forgotten in political discourse. People across the political spectrum, people of all political stripes, assume on some (again, perhaps only unconscious) level that politicians are at least knowledgeable and capable enough to effectively address their personal political predilections. Political beliefs – beliefs about what actions policymakers should take, what policies they should pursue, what goals they should try to realize – seem to imply an assumption that policymakers are sufficiently epistemically equipped to effectively take on the relevant task. At least, few people advocate for policies that they consciously recognize policymakers to be only knowledgeable and capable enough to bungle.

The present book considers the question: what if the assumption that policymakers are epistemically equipped to make successful policies is mistaken, either in some particular case or in general? What if policymakers are too ignorant to make much of a positive contribution to the mitigation of a particular problem or, more generally, to many problems at all? What if policymakers are sufficiently knowledgeable and capable to mitigate only a limited range of only relatively unimportant problems? How does recognition of their ignorance in some particular case affect policymakers' incentives to pursue various policies? What are the consequences of policymaker ignorance for politics, for society, and for political and social inquiry?

One scours the annals of thousands of years of political thought in vain for an argument that justifies the widely held assumption that policymakers are knowledgeable and capable enough to make a positive contribution to the solution of society's ills, for all intents and purposes, come what may. For whatever reason, political thinkers and writers, philosophers, theorists, political scientists, economists, and pundits throughout history have only rarely been interested in the question of the limits of limited policymaker knowledge and the consequences of these limits for political behavior and the success, or failure, of political action.

There is one significant exception to this neglect of the problem of policymaker ignorance, however. Beginning with Ludwig von Mises' ([1920] 1935) argument against the epistemic feasibility of central economic planning, economists associated with the Austrian School of economics, F. A. Hayek most famously and successfully, have persistently pushed against the notion that the wisdom and capacities of politicians are so well established as to be assumed as a universal axiom. Whether the problem is how to make socialism effective, how to ensure a consensus concerning a plan for society's future, how to promote economic development in developing countries, or how to avoid recessionary episodes in modern industrialized economies, Austrian economists have steadfastly questioned policymakers' capacities to deliberately bring about desired (or desirable) outcomes.

The present work is the product of a lifetime of thinking about the nature of political beliefs, my own and of others, and about 20 years of hard (and occasionally deep) thinking about the Austrian School. I originally discovered the writings of the most famous Austrian economists as an undergraduate economics student deeply unsatisfied with the material I was being made to study. Like many young students of economics, I was attracted to the social sciences by a desire to "make the world a better place." Yet beyond the principles of basic economic reasoning that I learned in introductory microeconomics, it was not apparent how my undergraduate training in economics could possibly serve to improve the world or, really, prepare me for anything other than a boring, albeit perhaps well-paid, desk job or advanced, graduate-level, abstract navel-gazing. It is possible that the real problem was my own lack of imagination, but complaints about the worldly insignificance of economics education were legion then and remain so now, so I am inclined to think that my own admitted lack of ingenuity explains little of this ennui. In any case, I soon realized that, though the Austrian approach seemed far more useful to someone interested in the usefulness of economics, I was less interested in doing Austrian economics myself than in clarifying what Austrian economists did, understanding why they did what they did in the way that they did it, and figuring out what it all meant for liberal politics, broadly construed. It was thus my interest in the methodology and politics associated with the School that led me to pursue a Ph.D. in philosophy, specializing in epistemology, and the history and philosophy of science, rather than a graduate degree in economics proper. In other words, I took the plunge for some serious abstract navel-gazing.

Yet I would like to think that the philosophical woolgathering that takes up much of the present work serves a highly practical purpose in the end. If perhaps unlikely to make the world a better place, it is at least an attempt to keep it from getting worse. Policymaker ignorance is the first problem of politics and political inquiry. It is the ultimate restriction on what can be deliberately achieved via political action. Beyond the limits of policymaker knowledge lie policy goals that can be realized, if at all, only if spontaneous forces intervene. Without the assistance of such non-deliberative forces, policymaking beyond the limits of policymaker knowledge cannot succeed. To the extent that we value the effectiveness of government, whatever its scale and scope, it is important that we acquire a better understanding of the limits of policymaker knowledge and the spontaneous forces that can occasionally help us to eclipse them.

I was inspired to write the book by a dawning recognition of affinity between my long-held political skepticism and Austrian worries over the narrow possibilities for effective policymaking implied by the limits of political knowledge. I eventually realized, however, that, for all their apparent skepticism about government intervention, the Austrians' political pessimism was rather selective and did not extend as far as it should. In particular, it seemed to me far from obvious – and, in any case, not established in the academic literature – that the Austrians' own preference for political liberalism was immune to epistemic objections analogous to those they had long leveled at socialists and defenders of other forms of government intervention. The Austrian penchant for liberalism is, like so many political beliefs, founded upon an unspoken and unjustified assumption about the knowledge and capabilities of policymakers, namely that politicians are knowledgeable and capable enough to deliberately create an effective liberal government. At the same time, I came to see Hayek's epistemology and philosophy of sciences of complex phenomena, not to mention the Hayekian theory of social order, that is, the Hayekian analysis of various mechanisms that facilitate the making of successful plans by serving to coordinate the knowledge of individuals within and across various domains of society, as relevant to the investigation of policymaker ignorance and the mitigation of its effects in the real world. The book is an attempt to substantiate these claims.

Although the focus is mainly on Austrian economists and their intellectual rivals, the book should be of interest to scholars and intelligent laypeople of all political, philosophical, and social-scientific persuasions. The problem of policymaker ignorance that is at the heart of the story is not unique to any particular political party; neither has it been seriously contemplated in either the philosophical or social-scientific literatures heretofore. Mitigating, if not solving, the problem of policymaker ignorance is a pressing matter for anyone, whatever their political preferences, concerned with the effectiveness of policymaking.

Acknowledgments

I first started thinking about writing a book on Austrian economics and political epistemology during the 2013–2014 academic year while a research fellow with Duke University's Center for the History of Political Economy. Several ideas developed over the course of my time at Duke and published in subsequent years figure in the book's argument. The project has benefited from discussions with the HOPE Center's faculty, associates, and staff, Bruce Caldwell, Kevin Hoover, the late Craufurd Goodwin, Roy Weintraub, Neil de Marchi, Marina Bianchi, and Angela Zemonek.

I spent the following academic year, 2014–2015, as a postdoctoral fellow with the F. A. Hayek Program for Advanced Study in Philosophy, Politics, and Economics at the Mercatus Center at George Mason University, writing a rough, ultimately abortive, first draft of the book. The quality of the final version of the book has been greatly improved thanks to the feedback that I received from participants in a workshop on the rough-draft manuscript held at the Mercatus Center offices in Arlington, Virginia, June 18–19, 2015. I would like to thank Peter Boettke, Karen Vaughn, Claire Morgan, Paul Dragos Aligica, Neera Badhwar, Erik Angner, Ted Burczak, Richard Creath (who also happens to be my much-revered dissertation director), Jayme Lemke, Richard Ebeling, Solomon Stein, Lynne Kiesling, and Christopher Morgan for their contributions to the Mercatus workshop.

I spent part of the summer of 2017 and all of the summer of 2018 working in the Hayek archives at Stanford University's Hoover Institution. Although I ultimately decided to save much of the material that I discovered in the Hayek papers for other projects, I would like to nonetheless thank Jennifer Burns, director of the Hoover Library & Archives Workshop on Political Economy, and acknowledge the valuable assistance of the Hoover Library and Archives staff, especially Sarah Patton, David Sun, and Bronewyn Coleman.

Thomas McQuade, Leslie Marsh, Andrew Farrant, Paul Dudenhefer, and Michael Gifford read and offered helpful comments on the completed manuscript. Ross Emmett, Bill Butos, Parker Crutchfield, Nathanael Colin-Jaeger, and Pavel Kuchar read and commented upon parts of the manuscript. The book is markedly better for various discussions that I have had over the years with several colleagues that I am fortunate enough to call friends, especially

Shawn Klein, Christopher Burrell, Steve Elliott, Henry Thomson, Helen Baxendale, Luca Fiorito, Carlos Eduardo Suprinyak, Gerardo Serra, Reinhard Schumacher, Spencer Banzhaf, Tyler DesRoches, Alex Gill, Michelle Saint, Gerald Marsh, the late Greg Fitch, Angel Pinillos, Peter de Marneffe, Zach Horne, Shyam Nair, Andrew Khoury, Mauro Boianovsky, Sandy Peart, David Levy, Maria Pia Paganelli, Erwin Dekker, Stefan Kolev, Nick Cowen, David Harper, Mario Rizzo, Roger Koppl, Gary Mongiovi, Eric Schliesser, Andrew Hamilton, Peter French, and Brad Armendt.

I would like to acknowledge the support of the faculty, staff, and administration of Arizona State University's College of Integrative Sciences and Arts, especially Duane Roen, Nicholas Alozie, Barbara Lafford, Irene Rodriguez, Kelli Haren, Jane Laux, Myrna Hanaoka, Bee Tran, Keith Hollinger, Eva Brumberger, Laverne Dacosta, Robert Benoit, Jesse Chanley, Larry Gesell, Wael Hassinan, Cynthia Hawkinson, Josh Kane, Anique John, Nura Mowzoon, Sara Moya, Yolanda Rodriguez, Mark Simpson, Kathy Thomas, Katrina Walls, and Alden Weight. I would also like to thank Melissa Castle-Kirincic, Mason Hunt, and Steve Slivinski of ASU's Center for the Study of Economic Liberty for their collegial support and assistance.

Some previously published material appears in the text, as noted where appropriate. I would like to thank the publishers and editors of *Journal of Institutional Economics*, *Cosmos + Taxis*, *Erasmus Journal for Philosophy and Economics*, *History of Economic Ideas*, *Review of Austrian Economics*, and *Journal of Economic Methodology* for permission to reprint material from my previously published works.

The book could never have been completed without the generous support provided by grants from the Charles Koch Foundation and ASU's College of Integrative Sciences and Arts.

The final draft of the book was written primarily in various coffee shops, wine bars, and coffee shop/wine bars in and around Phoenix, Arizona, and Palo Alto, California. I would be remiss if I did not acknowledge the friendliness of the owners, staffs, and clienteles of Lux Central, The Henry, Cartel Coffee Lab, and Provision Coffee in Phoenix, and The Wine Room, Coupa Café, and CRU Wine Bar in Palo Alto. I would also like to acknowledge the hospitality of Sofie Petersson and family, who put me and my smelly old dog, Larry, up in accommodations too luxurious for either of us during our summer-long stay in Palo Alto in 2018.

My friends Mike Nordeng, Lauren McCaw, Mohammad Safarzadeh, and Andrea Geissler provided much-needed and much-appreciated emotional support at various points in the development of the project. Finally, I would like to thank my family, my parents, Bonnie, John, and Judy, and my sister, Cindy Scheall. Their contributions to the present work extend far beyond my ability to express gratitude in words.

As much as I would like to blame one or more of the aforementioned people for whatever errors and misstatements surely remain in the text, the responsibility, alas, is all my own.

Introduction

The present work is a plea for inquiry into an important, but heretofore largely neglected, problem. The *problem of policymaker ignorance* is the simple fact that the success of purposeful political action is necessarily limited by the nature and extent of policymakers' ignorance and their capacities to learn. We cannot *deliberately* realize policy objectives beyond the ken and control of our political representatives. In order to realize goals with regard to which policymakers are to some degree ignorant, unconscious, non-deliberative, or *spontaneous* forces must intervene to lend a hand. Policymakers are not both omniscient and omnipotent. There are potential policy goals that they cannot deliberately realize, goals that can be realized, if at all, only if spontaneous forces intervene. Policymaker ignorance is the ultimate barrier that we cannot breach in our attempts to deliberately reform society and "make the world a better place" (in whatever sense of "better" might be relevant to one's personal political preferences). An improved understanding of the nature and extent of policymaker ignorance and its consequences, both in general and in particular political decision-making contexts, would help us determine the limits of effective policymaking and thus could only make our efforts at social reform more effective.

I argue that several of the tools, concepts, and arguments of the modern Austrian School of economics are potentially pertinent to the development of this research program. Indeed, I argue that a previously unnoticed research program in political epistemology more or less falls out of Ludwig von Mises' and F. A. Hayek's arguments against centrally planned socialism and various forms of economic policymaking. This research program concerns the limits that policymaker ignorance places around the goals that can be deliberately achieved via political action and the consequent need for the intervention of spontaneous forces to realize goals with respect to which policymakers are to some extent ignorant. Hayekian political epistemology investigates (*inter alia*) the limits of deliberate political action as determined by the nature and extent of policymaker ignorance and the concomitant need for spontaneity to contribute to the realization of objectives beyond these limits.

The book should be read primarily as an exercise in the philosophy of Austrian economics rather than its history. It is important to emphasize the philosophical nature of the project, as it might otherwise be easy to confuse my purpose as primarily historical. Although the argument is built on a swath of historical material, the book's main theses are philosophical. My goal in the present context is more to contribute to the future of Austrian economics than to a better understanding of its past. With a few relatively minor exceptions, I do not mean to establish novel historical propositions in the book. It is not my view, for example, that Mises or Hayek either intended to develop, or recognized that their arguments led naturally to, a research program in political epistemology. Given the philosophical rather than historical nature of the project, I take myself to be rather unconstrained by the existing Austrian canon and the various historical circumstances in which it was developed and over the course of which it has evolved. I try to be true to the spirit of this literature and, of course, I try to avoid saying anything historically inaccurate, but, when necessary, I freely modify, correct, and fill in lacunae in various aspects of the Austrian literature that are relevant to the project. Hayekian political epistemology is thus not entirely Hayek's intellectual property, but it is *Hayekian*, that is, inspired by Hayek.

I aim to establish six main theses (and a host of related sub-theses), one in each of the six core chapters of the book.

In the first chapter, I argue that the problem of policymaker ignorance is logically prior to the problem that has traditionally, but erroneously, been thought of as the primary problem of politics, namely the problem of policymaker incentives. As traditionally conceived, what matters for "good" politics is the extent to which policymakers are rightly oriented relative to their constituents' interests and properly motivated to pursue policy goals associated with these interests. However, the problem of policymaker incentives cannot be the *fundamental* problem of politics because, even if it were solved, another problem would remain, namely the problem of policymaker ignorance. Even if policymakers were motivated to pursue only their constituents' interests, nothing would ensure that they know either what these interests are or how to realize goals associated with them. If they cannot acquire the necessary knowledge, even the most altruistic policymakers cannot deliberately realize altruistic goals but must either rely to some extent on spontaneous forces for the realization of constituent-minded objectives or *pursue other, less altruistic, goals*.

The extent to which policymakers are constituent minded is determined, at least in part, by the nature and extent of their ignorance. Whether policymakers know enough to realize some policy objective affects their incentives to pursue it. Policymakers who take themselves to be ignorant of either their constituents' interests or of means adequate to realize policy goals associated with these interests face no incentive to pursue related policies. The nature and extent of policymakers' ignorance serves to determine whether and to what extent they are incentivized to make constituent-minded policies. But the opposite is not true: incentives cannot mitigate or otherwise affect ignorance; an incentive to pursue some policy end cannot change the knowledge that policymakers possess with regard to it. In short, solving the problem of policymaker incentives would leave the problem of policymaker ignorance unsolved, but solving the ignorance problem would at least serve to mitigate, if not solve, the incentive problem. For hundreds, if not thousands, of years, political thought has been focused on the quite ancillary problem of policymakers' motivations, while inquiry into the fundamental and determinative problem of policymakers' ignorance has lain fallow.

I offer two arguments in Chapter 1 for the logical priority of epistemic to other normative considerations in political – indeed, in all – decision-making. The first argument is based on introspection. Reflection on our own intellectual processes shows that the options from which we choose in any given decision context have been pre-sorted for our ignorance. Courses of action about which we take ourselves to be irremediably ignorant do not enter our incentive structures. More generally, options with regard to which we take ourselves to be relatively ignorant rarely, if ever, rank in our initial incentive structures above options with regard to which we take ourselves to be relatively knowledgeable. Some epistemic work must occur, if only at a pre-conscious level, before other normative (e.g., moral/ethical, prudential, pecuniary) considerations can be applied to a menu of options and a decision made. Ignorance brackets the options from which we choose in all decision contexts. The second argument considers the significance of the widely held principle that *ought implies can* (and of other principles like it) for the logical priority of the epistemic. I argue that, on the assumption that some principle like *ought implies can* is true and practically useful as a guide to action, then the word "can" in such principles must mean *deliberately can*. Other candidate meanings for the word "can" render such principles practically useless. Thus, by *reductio*, "can" in *ought implies can* (and related principles) means *deliberately can*. But, by definition, *deliberately can* just means *knows enough to*. Therefore, *ought implies knows enough to*: nothing that we cannot know enough to deliberately realize can be an obligation.[1] The nature and extent of our ignorance place brackets around our potential obligations. Epistemic burdens are logically prior to other normative considerations. Since this is a general fact about human decision-making in all contexts, it follows that ignorance is logically prior to incentives in specifically political contexts.

In presenting these arguments, I introduce the central concept of Hayekian political epistemology, that of an *epistemic burden*, i.e., the nature and extent of the ignorance that an actor in a particular context must overcome in order to use some means to deliberately realize some end. I also differentiate between policymakers' *first-order* ignorance of some policy end or of the means to realize it and their *second-order* ignorance of their first-order epistemic circumstances. This distinction allows for more sophisticated judgments to be made about policymakers' epistemic circumstances and their consequences.

Beyond this, I argue in the first chapter that the logical priority of the problem of policymaker ignorance to that of policymaker incentives, much less an analysis of its significance, has been almost entirely ignored throughout the long history of political thought, to the detriment of the usefulness of political thought, much of which the problem of policymaker ignorance shows to be only so much impracticable utopian wankery.[2]

In Chapter 2, I argue that economists of the Austrian School, Mises and Hayek in particular, have come closer than any other political thinkers to recognizing the logical priority of the problem of policymaker ignorance to that of policymaker incentives without, however, fully appreciating its complete generality. If one takes to its logical extreme the political-epistemological reasoning that underlies the arguments that Mises and Hayek directed against multiple forms of government intervention in the economy, one eventually arrives at the problem of policymaker ignorance that is relevant in all political decision contexts; indeed, if one extends the reasoning even further, one eventually arrives at an even more general problem of ignorance that is relevant in all decision contexts, full stop.

The historical development of the Austrians' criticisms of central planning and other forms of economic policy intervention exhibited a gradual generalizing over time of the contexts and policy goals to which political-epistemological reasoning was applied. Mises' ([1920] 1935) original socialist calculation argument was directed at the possibility of effective planning in a fully collectivized socialist oasis completely isolated from all market-generated prices. Hayek's contributions to the English-language socialist calculation debate of the 1930s assumed less extreme political-economic circumstances but arrived at a similar conclusion. Hayek argued that central planners would face insurmountable epistemic burdens even in contexts where factor prices were observable. By 1974, Hayek ([1975] 2014) was arguing that economic policymakers in liberal market economies would, for reasons of their epistemic deficiencies, struggle to contribute anything positive to the comparatively simple policy goal of deliberately managing economic fluctuations. Hayek's arguments pointed to a general epistemic problem for policymakers engaged in top-down economic policymaking, even in the presence of market institutions.

However, though he extended political-epistemological reasoning far beyond the narrow context to which Mises applied it, Hayek did not extend it as far as it can go. The effectiveness of what can be deliberately achieved with regard to economic policymaking is constrained by the nature and extent of the knowledge that relevant policymakers possess, but so too is policymaking with respect to other, non-economic, matters. Policymakers can never get beyond the limits of their epistemic capacities to deliberately realize goals with regard to which they are in some respect and to some degree ignorant. This is a general fact about political action. Indeed, this is ultimately a general fact about *human* action, which can never deliberately realize goals beyond the actor's epistemic purview. What cannot be realized deliberately, moreover, whether within or outside politics, can only be realized if spontaneous forces intervene.

There is a basic schema underlying the Austrians' political-epistemological arguments. They presuppose a *policy goal*, in particular, the goal esteemed by the policy's promoters. They also presuppose the *means* suggested by these promoters for the realization of the goal. They then argue that both *general* (or *theoretical*) *knowledge* of a certain kind and extent, and *particular* (or *empirical*) *knowledge* of a certain kind and extent, is necessary for the deliberate realization of the policy goal via the proposed means. Finally, they argue that relevant policymakers are not in a position to acquire these kinds of knowledge to an adequate degree to deliberately realize the policy goal. If the argument so far is sound in some particular instance, it follows as a corollary that, if the relevant goal is to be realized despite policymakers' impoverished epistemic circumstances, spontaneous forces, that is, forces beyond policymakers' ken and capacities, must intervene.

The success of an attempt to deliberately realize a (policy) goal hinges on such epistemic considerations, that is, whether the actor possesses the necessary kinds of knowledge to an adequate degree, and requires the intervention of non-deliberative forces to the extent that the actor is ignorant of necessary knowledge. What's more, every actor (policymaker) is epistemically limited in some way and to some extent. No one is omniscient and omnipotent. Thus, only some goals can be deliberately realized via (political) action, and it is always an open question whether an actor's (policymaker's) knowledge is adequate to a particular goal's epistemic requirements. Hayekian political epistemology is primarily concerned with attempting to answer such open questions about policymakers, both in particular contexts and in general, and analyzing the consequences of negative answers. Hayekian political epistemology investigates the consequences of policy action in the absence of all or part of the knowledge required to realize some policy goal and, especially, the potential for spontaneous forces to intervene to realize policy goals where policymaker knowledge is inadequate.

In the third chapter, I argue that the full generality of the problem of policymaker ignorance represents both an opportunity and a problem for Austrian School economists. It is an opportunity to extend their epistemological approach to political contexts that they have so far neglected. However, it is a problem in that Austrians have heretofore ignored the question of whether policymakers possess the knowledge necessary to deliberately realize the goal – seemingly universally shared among Austrian economists – of effectively liberalizing relatively illiberal societies. Hayek did not extend political-epistemological reasoning to liberalization policies or to the problems of political liberalism more generally. He apparently assumed, without argument or evidence, and subsequent Austrian economists have made the same unjustified assumption, that only *illiberal* policymaking confronts the problem of policymaker ignorance and that liberalization measures are somehow immune from the problem and its consequences. However, I argue that there are two kinds of epistemic burdens that liberal politicians must overcome in order to make liberalism effective and that Austrians (and other liberals) have failed to show that these burdens are surmountable.

First, there are epistemic burdens involved in transitioning to a more liberal context starting from a relatively illiberal one. If we make the reasonable assumption that policymaking is less epistemically burdensome in liberal than in illiberal environments, because liberalism implies that policymakers are charged with fewer and typically less burdensome policy tasks, it follows that would-be liberalizing policymakers may not be able to surmount the relatively heavy burdens that they confront in illiberal contexts. Policymaking may be relatively epistemically simple in more liberal than in less liberal environments, but this does not mean ·that it is epistemically simple to deliberately realize a liberal system. A proper appeal for liberalism requires showing that either the would-be liberalizing policymaker possesses the knowledge required to deliberately realize an effective transition from a relatively illiberal society to a more liberal one or that extant spontaneous forces are such that a more liberal society can be realized, despite the ignorance of the would-be liberalizing policymaker. The Austrians have no such argument and thus need a theory of *liberal transitions*. Without such a theory of the knowledge requirements of a deliberate transition to a more liberal society and of how either policymakers might acquire the knowledge necessary or spontaneous forces might intervene to realize an effective liberal order, the Austrian case for liberalism is left floating in the air. In effect, Austrians are left in the same position in which their calculation arguments place advocates of centrally planned socialism, that is, with few reasons for believing their preferred political system is a realistic possibility.

Second, there are those epistemic burdens that a policymaker in a liberal context must surmount in order to preserve existing liberal institutions. I argue that sustaining a liberal society requires that policymakers possess the know-how necessary to prevent the deterioration of these institutions, especially the rule of law. One of the constant complaints about life in liberal democracies concerns the tendency for those who succeed in acquiring wealth and power to abrogate the rule of law in their own favor, while the less successful and powerful remain subject to it, a circumstance that leads to the rejection of liberal institutions and to appeals for their replacement with less liberal ones. In order to sustain an effective liberal order, policymakers must surmount the epistemic burden involved in learning how to avoid the public rejection of liberalism.

Part I of the book thus concludes that the problem of policymaker ignorance is the fundamental problem of politics, Austrian economists have come closer than anyone else to recognizing the logical priority of the epistemic in political decision-making, without recognizing its generality, including its significance for their own policy preferences. In short, the problem of policymaker ignorance is fundamental and fully general, and as relevant to liberal as to illiberal policymaking. The second part of the book turns to possible methods of analyzing the problem of policymaker ignorance and even, perhaps, mitigating its effects in the real world. I argue, in particular, that elements of the Austrian School's intellectual apparatus are relevant to an analysis of the problem of policymaker ignorance and to the potential mitigation of its consequences. The second part of the book is primarily concerned with providing a positive, if necessarily tentative, sketch of how Hayekian political epistemology might proceed.

In Chapter 4, I argue that political epistemology requires a general epistemology, which is to say a general theory of what knowledge is and of how it is acquired. I argue further that this must be an empiricist epistemology that leaves no place for the possibility of knowledge acquired via pure reason, without reference to experience. If reason is permitted as a possible source of knowledge, then political-epistemological arguments will be interminable *in principle*, as every party to such a debate can then assert privileged rationalistic access to whatever knowledge might be required to surmount the epistemic burdens associated with their preferred policies. An empiricist epistemology, according to which knowledge is acquired only in virtue of contact with the world of experience, makes such debates resolvable, at least in principle (if perhaps nevertheless practically difficult to resolve).

Hayek's empiricist epistemology fits the required bill quite nicely. On Hayek's theory of knowledge, an organism's (and its species') engagements with the environment are its only source of news. Mises, on the other hand, insisted on the possibility of rationalistic *a priori* knowledge, that is, knowledge that the organism somehow possesses in advance of its first encounters with the environment, prior to its first experiences, and can discover via reflection on its own nature. Mises' rationalist epistemology must be counted among the worst and most incoherent ideas in the history of economic thought and has led subsequent generations of Austrian economists otherwise inclined to defend different aspects of Mises' canon into ceaseless unsolvable difficulties.[3] The proper solution to this quandary is to reject Mises' untenable rationalism altogether in favor of Hayek's naturalized empiricism or something quite like it.

Unfortunately, Hayek never wrote a comprehensive epistemological work, so his theory of knowledge can only be cobbled together in something of a mosaic fashion from his many writings of epistemological significance. I spend a considerable amount of space in Chapter 4 filling in several of the details of Hayek's epistemology required to make it a tenable foundation for political-epistemological analysis.[4] Hayek's epistemology treats knowledge as the ingredients of an effective plan of action: one knows to the extent that one can make, implement, and realize the goals of a plan of action *via* the plan (Scheall 2016). Thus, policymakers are epistemically equipped to realize a policy objective inasmuch as they can plan and realize the objective on the basis of the plan, without need for the intervention of spontaneous forces; to the extent that policymakers cannot deliberately realize the relevant goal on the basis of a self-made plan, they are ignorant of some of the requisite knowledge. Perhaps ironically, Mises' socialist-calculation argument actually rests more securely on a Hayekian epistemological foundation, which makes the possibility of deliberately planning successful action the very definition of knowledge.

More to the pertinent point, there is a considerable difference in the capacities of Hayekian empiricism and Misesian rationalism to explain policymaker ignorance. If policymakers possess the knowledge required to deliberately realize some goal, according to Hayek's epistemology, it must be that prior experience has adapted them to the goal's epistemic requirements. Thus, policymaker ignorance can be established by arguing for the inadequacy of the individual policymaker's experiential history (broadly construed) relative to the knowledge required to deliberately realize the relevant policy end. However, this is impossible on Mises' rationalism, which leaves open the possibility that a policymaker's otherwise inadequate experiential history might be supplemented somehow by knowledge acquired from a non-experiential source of some kind. In order to establish policymaker ignorance on Mises' epistemology, it is necessary to do the impossible and prove a negative; that is, it is necessary to show that there is no non-experiential source of knowledge that might serve to surmount policymakers' epistemic burdens without the need of experience. Hayek's epistemology facilitates empirical inquiry into policymakers' epistemic burdens, while Mises' rationalism undermines the possibility of such inquiry.

In the fifth chapter, I apply the Hayekian theory of social order (Scheall, Butos, and McQuade 2019) to the problem of political order. Social order in some domain is a condition in which the knowledge of actors in the domain is coordinated with relevant environmental circumstances such that everyone can make and successfully implement action plans on the basis of their extant knowledge and learning capacities. In a world where relevant data are constantly changing and individuals are epistemically limited, various mechanisms that tell people *what to do* in response to new circumstances are required to coordinate peoples' plans. Prices serve this purpose, for example, in market economies (Hayek [1945] 2014). Signals indicated by publications and citations in relevant scholarly outlets, which positively or negatively affect a scientist's reputation, play a similar knowledge-coordinating role in scientific domains (McQuade and Butos 2003; Butos and McQuade 2012). A well-ordered political domain would be one in which mechanisms existed that effectively communicated relevant knowledge between policymakers and constituents. We need epistemic mechanisms that convey to both individual policymakers and constituents what to do in response to relevant changes in environmental circumstances, including changes in the knowledge of other individuals in the political domain. Unfortunately, existing democratic institutions serve this epistemic function quite poorly.[5] Standard voting mechanisms convey neither the knowledge that policymakers need to effectively realize policy goals associated with their constituents' interests nor the knowledge that constituents' need concerning policymakers' epistemic capacities to ensure that their policy demands are epistemically feasible.

What I call the "epistemic-mechanistic" approach to the problem of policymaker ignorance would investigate various mechanisms that might serve to convey to both constituents and policymakers the knowledge that members of each group require to adapt their plans to relevant environmental conditions. In Chapter 5, I discuss the sort of epistemic mechanisms that political order requires. The further development of Hayekian political epistemology might necessitate the development of models of various epistemic mechanisms that could serve to coordinate political knowledge, the theoretical investigation of such models, and, perhaps, eventually, their testing in real-world natural experiments.

Inasmuch as we value the ideals typically associated with democracy, especially popular sovereignty, such investigations are quite pressing. It is important to recognize just how poorly existing democratic mechanisms serve these lofty ideals. There is not much popular sovereignty in a system where policymakers cannot effectively acquire knowledge of their constituents' policy demands or of the means to realize them and where constituents have little understanding of the brackets that policymaker ignorance places around the possibilities for successful political action. Without effective epistemic mechanisms, constituents will demand the pursuit of epistemically burdensome policies that policymakers, even if they know *of* them, may not know *how* to deliberately realize. Unless something like Hayekian political epistemology is developed, the problem of policymaker ignorance will continue to engender constituent disappointment, as it has forever, and, more to the point, will contribute to a subtle and silent abrogation of the principle of popular sovereignty.

The epistemic-mechanistic approach aims to mitigate the problem of policymaker ignorance by, in effect, improving the knowledge of both policymakers and constituents in ways conducive to the making of effective plans and thus to political order. On the other hand, the "constitutional" approach to the problem of policymaker ignorance that is the main subject of Chapter 6 takes the knowledge of policymakers and constituents as given and seeks to mitigate the effects of policymaker ignorance from the opposite direction, that is, by limiting political action to goals that political action can positively contribute to realizing, given the nature and extent of policymaker ignorance, and leaving all other goals to spontaneous forces.[6] We can use Hayek's epistemological system to empirically investigate the knowledge capacities of policymakers and the epistemic requirements of various policy objectives. We can ask about the general/theoretical and the particular/empirical knowledge required to realize some policy goal, and we can inquire into the theories and data actually available for policymaking purposes. We can use Hayek's epistemology, in other words, to get some grasp on the epistemic burdens that policymakers confront with respect to various policy objectives and thus on the extent to which spontaneous forces are required to realize particular policy goals.

We might then constitutionally prohibit political action with regard to objectives that existing policymaker knowledge is too impoverished to help realize. Such a constitution would limit political action to areas in which it can be effective and leave all other objectives to spontaneous forces to realize (or not). We cannot make policymakers omniscient and omnipotent. But, by constraining the range of legitimate political motion to pursuits with respect to which their knowledge is adequate, we might make policymakers, in effect, *functionally* omniscient and omnipotent with respect to their specifically political decisions. At the same time, such a constitution would go a long way toward mitigating the problem of policymaker incentives because, in a world of functionally omniscient and omnipotent policymakers, ignorance of the means to realize objectives associated with constituents' interests could not distort policymakers' incentives to pursue constituent-minded objectives. A political system in which policymakers could act only when and where their knowledge was adequate for a positive contribution to success would be one that assigned policy objectives to the public or private realms depending on where the evidence indicated they were most effectively realized and would ensure that our individual and collective goals were realizable as far as humanly possible.

In the concluding chapter, in order to head off potential confusions and concomitant criticisms, I clarify various aspects of the arguments presented in the book. I also draw out a series of important implications of the analysis. The need to finally consider the problem of policymaker ignorance and its consequences is quite serious.

Notes

1 As I show in the subsequent text, the logical priority of the epistemic does not hinge on *logical implication* being the relation that connects ought and can. One might accept a principle weaker than *ought implies can* and still be committed to the logical priority of the epistemic. Indeed, even an extremely weak principle such as *ought makes plausible can* implies the logical priority of the epistemic. See Scheall and Crutchfield (Forthcoming).

2 Political epistemology is a new and something of a burgeoning field (see the essays collected in Friedman 2014). Yet what is called political epistemology in the contemporary literature in fact misses the central insight of this book, namely the logical priority of the epistemic in political (really, all) decision-making. Indeed, this literature considers issues that I set aside here as only of secondary or tertiary importance, for example, whether voters are "wise" or "rational" (Brennan 2016) and the purported epistemic superiority of collective decision-making (Landemore 2012). Even if voters were perfectly rational, even if democratic decision-making were epistemically superior to the alternatives, nothing would ensure that policymakers can acquire the knowledge necessary to deliberately effect whatever policy objectives might be implied by the relevant decision.

3 On the incoherence of Mises' epistemological thought and some of the difficulties into which it has led his admirers, see Scheall (2017a and 2017b).

4 One exception to my claim not to intend to establish new historical theses in the present work can be found in Chapter 4. I argue that our understanding of Hayek's theoretical psychology and the evolutionary epistemology that falls out of it has been hampered by an excessive focus on the significance of Ernst Mach's influence on Hayek's theoretical psychology at the expense of the perhaps no-less-significant influence of Hermann von Helmholtz's physiological psychology. In later work, I hope to expand this argument to investigate the influence of other thinkers not named Mach or Helmholtz on Hayek's work in psychology and naturalized epistemology.

5 See DeCanio (2014).

6 Of course, the epistemic-mechanistic and constitutional approaches might be combined. The effects of the problem of policymaker ignorance might be mitigated by simultaneously both improving the mechanisms that communicate relevant knowledge between policymakers and constituents and limiting political action to policy objectives realizable on the basis of policymakers' existing (or newly improved) knowledge.

Part I

The problem of policymaker ignorance

1 Policymaker ignorance

The first problem of politics and political inquiry[1]

> The assumption which underlies almost all discussion of social topics is that we men need only to make up our minds what kind of a society we want to have, and that then we can devise means for calling that society into existence. It is assumed that we can decide to live on one spot of the earth's surface or another, and to pursue there one industry or another, and then that we can, by our devices, make that industry as productive as any other could be in that place. People believe that we have only to choose whether we will have aristocratic institutions or democratic institutions. It is believed that statesmen can, if they will, put a people in the way of material prosperity. It is believed that rent on land can be abolished if it is not thought expedient to have it. It is assumed that peasant proprietors can be brought into existence anywhere where it is thought that it would be an advantage to have them. These illustrations might be multiplied indefinitely.
>
> – William Graham Sumner, "Sociology" ([1881] 1992, 186)

> To act on the belief that we possess the knowledge and the power which enable us to shape the processes of society entirely to our liking, knowledge which in fact we do *not* possess, is likely to make us do much harm.
>
> – F. A. Hayek, "The Pretence of Knowledge" ([1975] 2014)

When they engaged their socialist rivals in a debate about the possibility of effective centrally planned socialism, the Austrian economists, in particular Ludwig von Mises and Friedrich August (F. A.) Hayek, did not base their main attack on ethical grounds but argued instead that, for epistemic reasons, central planning could not achieve the ambitions promised for it by its defenders. Unlike many other authors who have argued against socialism, before and since, the Austrians did not assume that the primary problem of central planning was that of securing the moral prerequisites of effective socialism.[2] The principal issue was neither that economic actors might be insufficiently motivated to pursue the common good in an institutional environment without private property or the prospect of personal profit, nor that socialist policymakers placed in control of the productive apparatus of the economy might be inclined to use these powers for other than promotion of the general welfare. The main problem, according to Mises and Hayek, was that *even if the ethical requirements of effective socialism could be secured* – even if all political actors could be motivated to pursue only the common good – policymakers could never acquire the knowledge necessary to deliberately realize the goals of socialism. Even if everyone in such a society, policymakers and public citizens alike, were unwaveringly intent on realizing the agreed-upon goals of the central plan, centrally planned socialism would fail to realize the relevant goals for *epistemic* reasons.[3]

A number of historical explanations have been offered for the Austrians' unique epistemic approach to the problems of central planning. According to Leeson and Subrick (2006, 109; italics added), "[a]lthough both argued elsewhere why there is good reason to suspect that those who come to power under socialist political economic organization are likely to have less than pure motives, *for rhetorical purposes, to highlight the importance of the information issue, and to make clear the value-freedom of their own argument*, in making their critique, Mises and Hayek assumed that the socialist directors were angels." Boettke (2018, 122; italics added) suggested the additional reason that "at the time of [Mises'] original challenge, *it was considered illegitimate to invoke incentive-based arguments against socialism* because advocates of socialism had assumed that man's nature would be transformed by the move to socialist production."

Whatever their historical accuracy, which I do not mean to challenge, these explanations fail to express why the Austrians' political-epistemological approach is *important*. Arguing on epistemic grounds against the possibility of effective central planning may have served their rhetorical purposes, or it might have been a charitable sop to their opponents' pretensions of the power of socialism to change human nature for the better, but whether Mises and Hayek recognized it – and the evidence suggests that they did not fully appreciate the significance of their approach – their political-epistemological arguments imply an absolutely fundamental fact about political decision-making that has rarely been noticed by others. This is the *problem of policymaker ignorance*: "the simple and, once it is first recognized, obvious fact that what can be deliberately achieved through political action is necessarily constrained by the nature and extent of policymakers' ignorance, and their capabilities for learning" (Scheall 2019a, 39).

Whether policymakers are angels or devils, what they can deliberately achieve through policy action is constrained by their ignorance. Whether a particular policy goal can be deliberately achieved through political action depends entirely on epistemic circumstances and not at all on ethical ones. Whether a policy goal can be deliberately realized depends on whether the relevant policymakers *know or can learn enough*; the moral quality of their convictions and intentions matters not a whit to whether a policy objective can be realized. In arguing on epistemic grounds against socialism, the Austrians may have meant merely to adopt a rhetorical stance or one especially generous to socialists, but they in fact described the most fundamental problem of politics and political inquiry.

Some terminological clarifications

For my purposes, a *policymaker* is anyone directly involved in the processes of policy design, determination, implementation, and administration. A *constituent* is a person in whose interests the policymaker is, on most modern conceptions of proper political behavior, supposed to make policy, and who, in turn, is expected to behave in conformance with the content of the policies made. A *policy* is any set of rules or directives designed, determined, implemented, and administered by policymakers to which constituents are expected to conform, ostensibly in their own interests. A policy thus can be anything from an ordinance intended to regulate the relevant activities of the members of a local homeowners' association to a constitution meant to govern the political actions and interactions of a nation of diverse citizens.

I will further refine my use of the word *knowledge* (as well as my use of its negation, *ignorance*) in later chapters, but suffice it to say for immediate purposes that the word is used throughout the book in a very broad sense that includes what traditional epistemologists call both *propositional knowledge-that* and *non-propositional knowledge-how*. Expressed more colloquially, I use the word to encompass knowledge of facts and theories, as well as skills, capacities, abilities, talents, powers, and so on.[4] Moreover, not all knowledge need be *explicit*, that is, knowledge that knowers know they possess. Some knowledge might be merely *tacit*, knowledge of which knowers may not be "explicitly aware," but "merely manifest . . . in the discriminations that [they] perform" (Hayek 1952 [2017], 152).

The logically ancillary nature of the problem of policymaker incentives

The problem of policymaker ignorance is the *first* problem of politics; it is logically prior to the other problems of politics. More carefully, I should say the problem of policymaker ignorance is logically prior to the problem that has traditionally, but erroneously, been conceived as the first problem of politics. This latter problem, which we might call the *problem of policymaker incentives*, was clearly expressed by David Hume in his essay "Of the Independency of Parliament." According to Hume ([1741, 1777, 1889] 1987, 44), "[p]olitical writers have established it as a maxim, that, in contriving any system of government, and fixing the several checks and controuls of the constitution, every man ought to be supposed a knave, and to have no other end, in all his actions, than private interest." According to this maxim, political inquiry should start from an assumption about the policymaker's motives and, indeed, about the ethical quality of these motives. The problem of policymaker incentives is that policymakers may not be properly motivated to pursue the goals demanded by those on whose behalf they ostensibly make policy. In order to write an effective constitution, according to Hume's maxim, it is necessary to assume that policymakers have only their own private interests in mind and are inadequately incented to pursue the public's interests.

But notice that a constitution that effectively binds policymakers to the pursuit of their constituents' interests cannot by itself ensure that policymakers either *know what these interests are* or *know how to pursue them effectively*. Like most other writers on these subjects, Hume neglected the significance of policymakers' ignorance and limited learning capacities and failed to recognize the brackets that these epistemic constraints place around what can be deliberately achieved via policy action.

It is rather ironic that Hume, surely history's most famous and perhaps its utmost skeptic about human knowledge, failed to extend his skepticism to policymakers or appreciate the implications of policymaker ignorance. As the greatest historian of his time of Britain and its people, Hume was familiar with phenomena attributable to policymaker ignorance. However, it was instead Hume's close friend, Adam Smith, who, among early-modern thinkers, came nearest to identifying the problem of policymaker ignorance, without, it must be said, fully recognizing its generality or explicating its consequences. Smith's ([1759] 1853, 347–348) infamous "man of system . . . is apt to be very wise in his own conceit, and is often so enamoured with the supposed beauty of his own ideal plan of government, that he cannot suffer the smallest deviation from any part of it." The man of system

> seems to imagine that he can arrange the different members of a great society with as much ease as the hand arranges the different pieces upon a chess-board; he does not consider that the pieces upon the chess-board have no other principle of motion besides that which the hand impresses upon them; but that, in the great chess-board of human society, every single piece has a principle of motion of its own, altogether different from that which the legislature might chuse to impress upon it.

Provided that the principles that guide the man of system's system conform to the "principles of motion" that guide the individual members of society, "the game of human society will go on easily and harmoniously, and is very likely to be happy and successful. If they are opposite or different, the game will go on miserably, and the society must be at all times in the highest degree of disorder."

Implicit in this famous passage is the notion that to ensure a happy, successful, and harmonious society, the man of system must *know* the principles according to which the individual members of society move. Even if he is properly motivated to pursue his constituents' interests, even if he wants nothing more than to conform his system to the principles that move his constituents, such motivations do not bear upon the ultimate success or failure of the system; unless he acquires knowledge of these principles, society will "be at all times in the highest degree of disorder." Social happiness and harmony ultimately depend on the man of system's knowledge, and not on whether he is properly oriented with regard to the motivations of the public. More exactly, in order for the man of system to make policy so as to deliberately ensure a state of harmonious social order, a prerequisite is that he know the principles that motivate his constituents. Whatever his motivations, he cannot conform his system to these principles if he does not know what they are. Thus, the matter of his motivations is subordinate to the issue of his ignorance.

It is important to emphasize, however, that Smith's requirements for social order are incomplete: it is not enough that the man of system know (and so be able to conform to) the principles that motivate his constituents; he must also know or be able to learn *means* adequate to realize the policy objectives associated with these principles. A happy, successful, and harmonious society will not emerge if, despite the fact that the man of system and his constituents are motivationally *sympatico*, the man of system is ignorant of the means to realize the goals associated with his constituents' interests (interests that, *ex hypothesi*, he shares with his constituents). Sympathy of motivations, agreement with regard to relevant interests and related goals, is not sufficient for social harmony; the man of system must also possess knowledge of means adequate to the realization of a harmony-engendering system. Policymaker ignorance leads to social misery and disorder.

Hume and his modern descendants in the public-choice tradition of political economy, who make the assumed knavery of policymakers the *sine qua non* of their analyses, place the normative cart before the epistemic horse that must drive political decision-making if the policy decisions taken are to be effective.[5] They consider how policymakers *ought* to behave without first asking what policymakers *know (or can learn) enough* to do. But, surely, answers to the epistemic question constitute data relevant to a rational answer to the normative question. That is, what policymakers can learn enough to do is significant for how they should behave. If they are not to embark on disastrous or wasteful political projects, the question of what policymakers know enough to do must be addressed first if the question of what they ought to do is to be answered rationally.

It is simply false that policymakers should be assumed knaves and to have only private interest in view. Part of what it means for policymaker ignorance to be the first problem of politics is that it affects the other problems of politics, including the problem of policymaker incentives, while the opposite is not true. Ignorance can distort policymakers' incentive structures, but the arrow of influence does not turn in the opposite direction: incentives cannot affect the nature and extent of policymaker ignorance. Policymakers are relatively less incented to pursue policy objectives that they take themselves to be too ignorant to realize. If policymakers take themselves to be ignorant with respect to the policy objectives demanded by the public, so much the worse for the public. In other words, whether policymakers pursue their own private or the public's interests depends in part on the nature and extent of their ignorance with respect to related courses of action. As I have put the point elsewhere:

> We should assume not that all men are knaves, but that all men are igno-ramuses and that the extent of their knavery is in part a function of the extent of their ignorance. Perhaps unfortunately, "All men are ignoramuses and, because of this, sometimes knaves too" falls from neither tongue nor pen as mellifluously as Hume's famous phrase.
>
> (Scheall 2019a, 43)

Hume's maxim gives bad methodological advice. If we somehow managed to solve the problem of policymaker incentives, we would still have to address the problem of policymaker ignorance. Again, on the assumption that poli-cymakers are perfectly motivated to pursue the policy objectives that their constituents want them to pursue, no mechanism exists to ensure that they know of or know how to realize these objectives, so solving or mitigating the incentives problem would leave the ignorance problem untouched. However, if the nature and extent of their ignorance serves to determine policymakers' incentives – in particular, if ignorance serves to determine the degree to which policymakers pursue their constituents' interests – then mitigating the problem of policymaker ignorance would *ipso facto* contribute to mitigating the problem of policymaker incentives.[6]

As a methodological principle, Hume's maxim prejudicially limits the kinds of explanations that can be offered of particular policy decisions. Given a case in which policymakers actually pursue their constituents' interests, the only explanation that Hume's maxim permits is that constituents must have shared the interests of a bunch of selfish knaves. If policymakers are always to be treated as knaves for the purposes of analysis, then we cannot invoke any altru-istic, non- or anti-knavish, motives that might actually figure in their policy decisions. Thus, Hume's maxim artificially limits the explanations that can be given for political decisions and leaves a (presumably non-empty) class of such decisions, that is, acts of true constituent-mindedness, without a satisfying explanation. On the other hand, what we might call, for lack of a better locu-tion, "Scheall's maxim" – "All persons are ignoramuses; the nature and extent of their ignorance serves to determine the extent of their knavery" – places no such unjustified restriction on explanations of policymakers' pursuit of the public's interests. On a political-epistemological approach to the analysis of political decision-making, provided that policymakers possess the knowledge required to pursue the public's interests, it is possible to explain their pursuit of related policy goals without implying that constituents must share the sympa-thies of a coterie of venal knaves.

The ultimate significance of the Austrians' political-epistemological approach lies less in the fact that it allowed them to score particular rhetorical points against, while adopting a position maximally charitable to, their socialist opponents, than in the fact that the political knowledge (really, ignorance) problem they emphasized is, as a simple logical matter, more fundamental than – logically prior to – the political incentive problem they mostly ignored.[7]

The logical priority of the epistemic

There are a number of ways to establish the priority of the problem of policymaker ignorance to that of policymaker incentives. I might proceed directly to an analysis of the relationship between ignorance and incentives in political contexts, establish the dependence of incentives on ignorance in these contexts, show that no such dependence exists in the opposite direction – ignorance does not depend on incentives – and draw the appropriate conclusion. I offer an argument like this in my "Ignorance and the Incentive Structure confronting Policymakers" (Scheall 2019a). Such a direct approach has the benefits of brevity and of keeping the discussion concentrated on the epistemology of politics. However, for reasons related to arguments developed in later chapters, I approach the priority of the problem of policymaker ignorance in a roundabout way.[8] I argue that, in *all* decision contexts, epistemic considerations are logically prior to incentives. The nature and extent of the ignorance (-that and -how) that the actor must overcome if a course of action is to be effectively pursued – which I call the *epistemic burden* of a course of action – serves to determine whether the course of action is included and, if so, where it is initially ranked, in the actor's incentive structure.[9] In *all* decision contexts, epistemic burdens are logically prior to the moral/ethical, prudential, pecuniary (etc.) considerations that constitute or give rise to incentives. My co-author Parker Crutchfield and I advance an argument like this in another place (Scheall and Crutchfield Forthcoming). If ignorance is logically prior to incentive considerations in *all* contexts, then, naturally, the problem of ignorance is logically prior to the problem of incentives in specifically political contexts.

I offer two arguments in the present chapter for the logical priority of the epistemic as a general feature of human decision-making.[10] The first argument is introspective: internal reflection on our own thinking processes shows that the options from which we choose in any given decision context have been pre-sorted, if only at an un- or sub-conscious level, for our epistemic burdens. Courses of action about which we take ourselves to be irremediably ignorant do not enter our incentive structures. Introspection shows, more generally, that courses of action with regard to which we take ourselves to be relatively ignorant rarely, if ever, rank in our initial incentive structures above options with regard to which we take ourselves to be relatively knowledgeable. Some epistemic work must occur, if only at a less-than-fully conscious level, before incentives can be considered, that is, before other normative (e.g., moral/ ethical, prudential, pecuniary) considerations are applied to a menu of options and a decision is ultimately made. Ignorance brackets the options from which we choose in all decision contexts.

My second argument considers the significance of the widely accepted principle that *ought implies can* (and of other principles like it) for the logical priority of the epistemic. I argue that, on the assumption that some principle like this is true and practically useful as a guide to action, then the word "can" in such principles must mean *deliberately can*. Other candidate meanings for the word "can" render such principles practically useless. Thus, by *reductio*, "can" in *ought implies can* (and related principles) means *deliberately can*. By definition, however, "deliberately can" just means *knows enough to*. Therefore, nothing that we cannot know enough to deliberately realize can be an obligation. The nature and extent of our ignorance places brackets around our potential obligations. Epistemic burdens are logically prior to other (moral/ethical, prudential, pecuniary, etc.) normative considerations.

If either of these arguments is sound, then the logical priority of the epistemic is a general fact about human decision-making – and, therefore, assuming policymakers are human beings, about political decision-making as well.[11]

More about epistemic burdens

The epistemic burden of a course of action is everything that a decision-maker must know (-that and -how), which they do not already know, in order to pursue the course of action effectively, that is, in order to *deliberately* realize the goals(s) relevant to the course of action *via* the course of action. To realize a goal deliberately is to do so entirely on the basis of one's own knowledge (-that and -how) and learning capacity – it is, in other words, to realize the goal without need for the intervention of luck, fortune, or any other spontaneous forces.

Epistemic burdens are subjective to particular actors in specific circumstances and relative to their respective ends and various means. There is decision-maker D's epistemic burden EB with respect to goal G and means M in context C – that is, there is the knowledge missing in C that D must acquire in order to deliberately realize G *via* M – but there is no such thing as the epistemic burden of G *simpliciter*. Different actors in different contexts, with the same ends and the same means to pursue them, might confront different epistemic burdens. Different actors operating in the same (or similar) circumstances, with the same ends and the same means to pursue them, might confront different epistemic burdens. The same actor might confront different epistemic burdens in different contexts with respect to the same means and the same end – indeed, this is trivially true whenever a person *learns* over time to apply some particular means more effectively to the same end.

Actors are typically able to evaluate their epistemic burdens with some facility, but not infallibly. Decision-makers are usually not entirely ignorant of the things about which they are ignorant. I know, for example, that I do not know who will win the next American presidential election or the Major League Baseball World Series in the year 2030. There are "known unknowns," in other words. However, decision-makers can also be ignorant about some of their ignorance. Famously, the phrase "unknown unknowns" entered the lexicon in 2002 when Donald Rumsfeld, at the time U.S. Secretary of Defense, used it to describe the epistemic circumstances of members of the George W. Bush administration who, he claimed, *did not know that they did not know* that there were no caches of weapons of mass destruction to be discovered in Iraq.

The introspective argument for the logical priority of the epistemic

Consider an interesting and important fact about human decision-making that, somewhat surprisingly, is rarely noticed or commented upon: the options that one considers in any given decision context seem to arrive in consciousness already pre-filtered, and roughly pre-sorted, for the nature and extent of our ignorance, which is to say for our epistemic burdens. When one confronts a decision – whether a decision about whom to marry, whether to have children, where to go to college, where to vacation for the summer, where to have dinner, or what movie to see this weekend – it rarely, if ever, happens that courses of action appear in decision-makers' incentive structures that they take themselves to be too ignorant and too incapable of learning enough to achieve. No one seriously considers as an option marrying an extraterrestrial alien spouse, or both having and, at the same time, not having children, or attending college on the moon, or vacationing on Jupiter, or eating dinner in the Marianas Trench, or seeing a film starring both Rudolph Valentino and Scarlett Johansson. Decision-makers do not consider as options potential courses of action that they think (if only pre-consciously) cannot be realized on the basis of their extant knowledge and learning capacity. Such courses of action are typically excluded altogether from the menus of options from which actors ultimately choose. Indeed, other possible, but especially epistemically burdensome, courses of action are typically discounted in an actor's menu of options, seemingly according to the relative weights of the epistemic burdens that must be surmounted in order to realize relevant goals *via* the various courses of action. *Ceteris paribus*, epistemically weightier families, films, and modes of travel are ranked in a decision-maker's initial incentive structure below epistemically lighter ones. The epistemic burden of a course of action relative to other courses of action appears to determine whether it is included and, if so, where it is initially ranked, in an actor's menu of options.

A person's ignorance, then, is an important factor in determining whether a course of action appears to them as an option and, if so, to what extent they are incented to pursue it. However, incentives are completely irrelevant to epistemic burdens. That is, the nature and extent of a person's ignorance with respect to some course of action can affect their incentive to pursue it, but the nature and extent of the incentives they face to pursue a course of action cannot affect the epistemic burden to be overcome if it is to be deliberately realized. In plainer language, you might want something for one reason or another, and it might appear to you to be in your interest that you get it, but this cannot change the way that and the degree to which you are ignorant of its epistemic requirements. I really want a safe and fully functional hovercraft, and I imagine that I would be happier with it than I am without it, but, alas, the considerable desire I have to get such a vehicle cannot alter the fact that I am, and will probably remain, ignorant of how to get it. So, courses of action that involve hovercrafting do not appear to me as options when I consider various modes of travel. The incentives one confronts to pursue a course of action cannot moderate or facilitate overcoming its epistemic burden.

Many different kinds of considerations – *inter alia*, moral/ethical, prudential, and pecuniary considerations – figure in making a decision. However, epistemic burdens seem to be primary in the sense that, before appearing to us as options, the courses of action to which these other considerations are applied have been pre-sorted for the nature and extent of our ignorance. We might consider whether it is moral, prudential, or financially wise to have zero, one, or several children, but the options to which we apply such considerations have already been pre-sorted for the nature and extent of our ignorance: the epistemically impossible option of both having and, at the same time, not having children has been filtered out from, and the epistemically difficult options of having a hundred or a thousand children have been deeply discounted in, the decision-maker's incentive structure before the moral, prudential, and pecuniary aspects of these options are considered.[12]

Ignorance is logically prior to incentives. Some epistemic work must be done, if only at a less-than-fully conscious level, in order to have a menu of options from which a decision can ultimately be made in light of moral, prudential, pecuniary (etc.) incentives.

The argument for the logical priority of the epistemic from **ought implies can** *and similar principles*

It is widely accepted that some sort of relation obtains between the actions that persons *ought* to perform and the actions that they *can* perform. Few believe that people can be obligated to do things that are completely impossible for them to do. Of course, as might be expected, there is some disagreement in the philosophical literature about the logical strength of the relation that obtains between ought and can. The most commonly encountered principle of this sort ascribes an especially strong relation – *logical implication* – to ought and can. If *ought implies can*, then everything that a person can do is, under appropriate circumstances, something that they ought to do – every can is a potential ought. However, some philosophers argue that the relation between ought and can is weaker than logical implication. Stuart Hampshire (1951) and R. M. Hare (1951, 1963), for example, accept that *ought presupposes can*.[13] If this is the right principle, then anything that a person can do is a presupposition of a potential obligation; an action that presupposes an impossibility cannot be an obligation under any circumstances. Walter Sinnott-Armstrong (1984) argues that *ought conversationally implicates can*.[14] If this is right, then the relation between ought and can is not one of pure logic but of conversational pragmatics; anything that a person can do is a conversational implication, according to prevailing standards of discourse, of a potential obligation. A potential obligation cannot be taken to imply, on the basis of conversational conventions, something that the actor cannot do. Indeed, one can imagine other, even weaker, principles such as *ought makes plausible can*. According to this principle, an action is a potential obligation for an actor inasmuch as it is plausible that they can perform it.

It is not my business to pronounce on the correctness of any one of these principles. Nothing in the argument that follows hinges on *implication* rather than, say, *making plausible*, being the particular relation that binds ought and can. My argument hinges instead on the assumption that some such principle (whether among the aforesaid or not) is true and practically useful. Anyone who knew both the true principle and the members of their class of "cans" could use this knowledge to determine the class of their potential obligations, the class of actions that they "ought" to perform under appropriate circumstances and, concomitantly, the class of actions that they cannot be obligated to perform under any circumstances.

My argument via this route to the conclusion of the priority of the epistemic proceeds from the meaning of the word "can" in such principles. If the true principle, whatever it might be, is practically useful – if it is to assist decision-makers in determining their potential obligations – then the meaning of "can" in such principles must be something like *deliberately can* and cannot be anything like *can, with luck* or *possibly can*. If "can" means either *can, with luck* or *possibly can*, then such principles are practically worthless.

For example, if the relevant meaning of "can" is *can, with luck*, then, since virtually anything can happen if luck or fortune intervenes, anything that you can do, even if it requires the intervention of luck or fortune, is a potential obligation. This implies, however, that one's obligations are to some extent determined by lottery, a rather implausible result.

Whatever the case may be in this regard, there is another (for my purposes, intriguingly epistemic) reason to reject the notion that the word "can" in such principles could mean *can, with luck*. To say that a person was "(un)lucky" or "(un)fortunate" with respect to some event means, at least in part, that the event occurred for reasons beyond the person's (perhaps *any* person's) ken or control. We do not know in advance when luck or fortune might intervene to either facilitate or foil our designs. If we cannot distinguish the things that we might be able to do, if luck intervenes, from the things that we cannot do, regardless of luck, then *ought implies* (or *presupposes* or *makes plausible*, etc.) *can, with luck* is worthless as a guide to successful decision-making.

On the other hand, *ought implies* (etc.) *possibly can* makes every possible action (on some conception of *possibility*) a potential obligation; only impossibilities can never be obligations. Without a specification of the relevant meaning of possibility, such a principle is obviously of little practical value. But, more to the point, it seems like the class of potential obligations cannot simply be the class of all possible actions, whatever the relevant meaning of "possibly."

Imagine that the relevant sense of the word is *metaphysical* possibility. Any metaphysically possible action would then, under appropriate circumstances, be a potential obligation. But the class of actions that are metaphysically possible for a person to perform is obviously much larger than the class of potential obligations. It is, for example, metaphysically possible for a person to single-handedly create world peace – there is, at least, no metaphysical impossibility involved in the notion of a single person creating world peace. Yet no one can be obligated to single-handedly create world peace, because, regardless of its metaphysical possibility, it is not possible for a single person to acquire the propositional knowledge (-that), and the powers, talents, skills, abilities, and capacities (the know-how) that creating world peace requires. In short, despite its metaphysical possibility, there is no meaningful sense in which this *can* be done. Similarly, there are *physically* possible actions that would seem not to be potential obligations. One might volunteer to be flayed alive, a physical possibility to be sure, but it is not plausible that one ever *ought* to do this. Conversely, there are actions that are impossible on other conceptions of *possibility* that, nevertheless, would seem to be obligations under certain conditions. One cannot commit a crime without offending against the *legal* sense of possibility. Yet some crimes might be obligations under appropriate circumstances, for example, stealing milk to feed a starving infant. Thus, whatever the sense of possibility, it seems that *possibly can* cannot possibly be the relevant sense of "can" in principles like *ought implies can*.

If these arguments are sound, then the meaning of "can" in the principles under investigation must be more like *deliberately can* than any of the possibilities considered so far. But, of course, to deliberately do something, to deliberately realize some end, is to do so entirely on the basis of one's own knowledge and learning capacity. It is to do the thing, realize the goal, as it were, non-spontaneously, without the intervention of luck, fortune, or any other spontaneous forces. To the extent that one *deliberately can*, one *knows (or can learn) enough to*. Thus, if *ought implies* (or whatever) *can*, then *ought implies deliberately can* or, what is the same thing, *ought implies knows (or can learn) enough to*.

An action can be a potential obligation only to the extent that actors deliberately can – only to the extent that they know enough to – do it. If this is right, then it is sufficient to establish the logical priority of the epistemic in human decision-making. If some principle like *ought implies can* is both true and useful as a guide to practical action, then epistemic burdens are logically prior to incentives.[15] Anyone committed to a principle like *ought implies can* is also committed to the logical priority of epistemic burdens over the moral, prudential, etc., considerations that constitute or give rise to incentives.

The problematic nature of political decision-making in light of the priority of the epistemic

Policymakers are a kind of surrogate decision-maker. They decide on behalf of and ostensibly in the interests of other people, their constituents. However, in cases of surrogate decision-making, there is no guarantee that the option that the person surrogated would choose or, more generally, the options that rank in the surrogated person's own personal incentive structure, figure among the options from which the surrogate decision-maker chooses.[16] There is no guarantee that constituents' preferred polices figure among the options from which policymakers choose. When persons decide, the options from which they choose are all courses of action that they both know *of* and take themselves to know (or take themselves to be capable of learning) *enough to deliberately realize*. This is no less true in cases of surrogate than in cases of personal decision-making. The relevant difference is that, in cases of surrogate decision-making, there is no mechanism, as there is in cases of individual decision-making, that ensures that the courses of action that the surrogate knows of and can learn enough to realize include the courses of action that are in the interests of the person surrogated.

> A sane person will never permit a seemingly impossible option to enter her menu and will discount epistemically burdensome options accordingly. However, no such guarantee exists where one person must decide on behalf and in the interests of some other. Simply put, there is no guarantee in such cases that the surrogate knows the options in the interests of the other party or how to achieve them. You will never leave yourself an option that you cannot know enough to achieve, but a person on whose behalf you must decide might assign such an option to you.
>
> (Scheall and Crutchfield Forthcoming)

Constituents might demand action of policymakers that the latter neither know of nor can learn enough to make effective. Surrogate decision-makers, such as policymakers, can be ignorant of either the courses of action associated with the interests of the people, such as constituents, on whose behalf they decide or, if they know of the relevant courses of action, may be ignorant of means to pursue them effectively. The courses of action associated with the interests of the people on whose behalf surrogates decide may not even appear as options to the surrogates and so will not be chosen, or they may appear as options, but only so deeply discounted in the surrogates' incentive structures that they are unlikely to be chosen.

The priority of the epistemic complicates effective surrogate decision-making. Even if surrogates have nothing but the interests of the surrogated in mind, their ignorance can prevent them from acting in ways that promote those interests. Epistemic burdens serve to determine whether surrogates act in the way that surrogates "ought" to act, that is, in the interests of the surrogated. Epistemic burdens serve to determine whether surrogates, including policymakers, act on the interests of the people surrogated. Epistemic burdens are logically prior to incentives.

Policymaker ignorance and constituent disappointment

Policymaker ignorance leads to constituent disappointment in two ways.[17] First, policymakers might be ignorant of the policy objectives most extensively and most intensely preferred by their constituents. Of course, at least in democratic societies, various mechanisms exist ostensibly to deal with this problem. How-ever, their effectiveness is dubious. Elections, polls, and opinion surveys pro-vide limited evidence of constituents' preferences, but this evidence is time specific, ambiguous, and defeasible. Policymakers acquire anecdotal evidence from direct contact with individual constituents, but inferences from these sam-ples to the entire constituent population are treacherous. Similarly, policymak-ers might learn of constituent preferences by observing historical trends, but these frequently change in ways that can be understood only after the fact. Even if some miracle ensured a harmony of interests between political officials and constituents, it would not ensure that officials *know* of this harmony or that they can take it for granted in seeking to realize their constituent's policy preferences. The problem may be even more profound: the famous "impos-sibility theorem" associated with Nobel Prize–winning economist Kenneth Arrow (1950) shows that, given a few fairly plausible assumptions, no voting system can translate individual preferences into a univocal preference ranking for the entire community. Simply put, in the majority of relevant political con-texts, there is *no such thing* as "the policy objectives most extensively and most intensely preferred by" constituents. Politicians will often struggle to know the policy ends that their constituents most want them to pursue.

Second, even if some ideal democratic mechanism could be devised that perfectly summarized and communicated to politicians the policy preferences of their constituents, nothing would ensure that policymakers know how to realize ends associated with these preferences. Naturally, if policymakers do not know how to realize some policy end, it can be realized only if luck, fortune, or some other spontaneous forces intervene to mitigate the effects of policy-maker ignorance and secure its realization. Policymakers can *deliberately* realize only those policy objectives that they know enough to achieve.

The policymaker-constituent relationship is such that constituents might want policy objectives to be pursued that policymakers either do not know that constituents want pursued or do not know enough to realize. This means that the goals constituents want policymakers to pursue may not appear as options or may appear only as deeply discounted relative to other options in policymakers' incentive structures. Stated another way, given the nature and extent of their ignorance, policymakers may not be adequately incented to pur-sue the objectives most demanded by their constituents. This is especially true where epistemically simpler options are available, such as engaging in political corruption or embarking upon a public charade of constituent-mindedness. Other things equal – for example, if the policymaker expects the same benefits either way – if it is epistemically easier, if the policymaker knows better how to *pretend* to pursue constituents' interests than how to earnestly pursue the dis-covery and realization of goals associated with these interests, the policymaker will likely pursue the epistemically simpler option of a public, media-enabled, charade of pretended constituent-mindedness.

I have argued elsewhere that, other factors held constant, the epistemic bur-den of selfish policymaking, pursuing policy goals that are in policymakers' own selfish interests, is typically (though not necessarily) lower than that of constituent-minded policymaking, that is, pursuing objectives that the policy-maker believes to be in the interests of her constituents. "Other things equal, the relative epistemic complications of satisfying the wishes of the public should incent more [narrowly] self-interested policymaking. We should expect to find more self-interested political behavior where (*ceteris paribus*) the epistemic bur-den of making effective public-minded policy is comparatively heavy" (Scheall, Butos, and McQuade 2019, 435, fn. 8).

This point can be generalized.[18] *Other factors held constant, the relative weights of the epistemic burdens of competing policy objectives serve to determine the objectives that policymakers pursue.* If this is right, then, *ceteris paribus*, policymakers are incented to pursue policy objectives that bear the lowest epistemic burdens relative to other possible pursuits, that is, those goals that they know best or have the best prospects of learning how to realize. Other factors held constant, the policy objectives that constituents demand will be pursued only if they impose a lighter epistemic burden on policymakers than alternative policy objectives. Otherwise, the policy objectives that constituents demand will be ignored in favor of other policy pursuits (perhaps accompanied by a public pretense of the pursuit of constituents' demands). The nature and extent of their igno-rance serve to determine the extent to which policymakers pursue constituent-minded rather than other policy objectives. The relative epistemic burden of constituent-minded policymaking is a factor that contributes to determining how much of it we get.

The problem of policymaker ignorance is logically prior to the problem of policymaker incentives. The more fundamental problem is that of policymakers' ignorance, not whether they are adequately incented to pursue their constituents' interests. Indeed, the extent to which they are incented to pursue constituents' interests is determined, at least in part, by the nature and extent of their ignorance con-cerning these interests and the means available to realize goals associated with them. But the arrow of influence does not point in the opposite direction: the nature and extent of a person's ignorance can distort their incentive structure, but their incentives cannot affect their ignorance.

A taxonomy of ignorant policymakers

I have silently and deliberately ignored various important distinctions to this point in the argument, but it is high time to differentiate between policymak-ers' *first-order* knowledge or ignorance of some policy end, or of the means to realize it, and their *second-order* knowledge or ignorance of their first-order epistemic condition. Donald Rumsfeld was onto something when he lamented the impact of what he claimed were "unknown unknowns" on recent political history. Ignorance of either the first- or second-order varieties can distort the incentives that policymakers confront to pursue their constituents' policy prefer-ences, and thus ignorance can affect whether they pursue constituent-minded objectives rather than other potential ends. The problem of policymaker ignorance serves to determine the extent and precise problematic nature of the problem of policymaker incentives.

In the present chapter, I have focused primarily on policymakers who know that they do not know how to realize some objective, that is, policymakers who are second-order knowledgeable of their first-order ignorance with respect to some policy goal. Such policymakers know that they do not know how to realize the relevant objective and, consequently, that pursuing the objective will end in failure, unless luck, fortune, or other spontaneous forces intervene to realize it. According to the previous analysis, policymakers who know that they are ignorant of how to achieve some objective will either ignore it altogether or – relative to other options about which they take themselves to be less ignorant – systematically discount it in their incentive structures. If, relative to other possible pursuits, policymakers know that the knowledge they can acquire with respect to the objectives their constituents most prefer is inadequate, these objectives are unlikely to be pursued. For example, if policymakers know that they do not know how to realize the objectives their constituents most want realized, but know that they know how to engage in a public relations campaign to convince constituents that they have their constituents' interests at heart, the first option will be systematically discounted relative to the second in their menus of options; other things equal, they will be more likely to flatter to deceive their constituents than to earnestly pursue their interests.

On the other hand, consider policymakers who mistakenly believe that they are ignorant with respect to some policy objective. Such policymakers know enough to realize the policy objective but erroneously believe that they are ignorant of its requirements and so mistakenly believe that acting on the objective is likely to end in failure. Such politicians will be less inclined, other factors held constant, to pursue this objective than they would be if they correctly assessed their first-order epistemic circumstances. Other things equal, policymakers who mistakenly believe they are ignorant with respect to some objective will either ignore it altogether or systematically discount it in their incentive structure relative to other objectives that they believe they know better how to realize. Again, if policymakers believe, if only mistakenly, that they know better how to pretend to pursue constituents' interests than how to deliberately realize goals associated with these interests, they will be more likely to flatter to deceive their constituents. Of course, the overly humble politician who unduly deflates rather than exaggerates their self-conception is a rare creature.

Policymakers who are ignorant of their ignorance with respect to some policy objective are potentially quite dangerous. Such policymakers can easily convince themselves that they know enough to deliberately realize ends that they do not in fact know enough to realize. They face an epistemically distorted incentive to pursue particular policy objectives that they would not face if their second-order knowledge improved enough to permit them to recognize their first-order ignorance. Policymakers who are ignorant of their ignorance mistakenly believe that pursuit of relevant policy objectives will end in success and thus will not discount related courses of action as deeply as the epistemic facts would otherwise dictate. As I will discuss at greater length in the next chapter, in his 1974 Nobel Prize lecture, Hayek diagnosed such policymakers as suffering from a "Pretence of Knowledge."

Finally, consider the privileged epistemic status of policymakers who know that they know how to realize a policy objective. Such policymakers are like the wise captain of the ship of state that Plato (1991) discussed in Book IV of *The Republic*, who knows that he possesses all of the knowledge required to steer the ship to safe harbor. The wise captain of the ship of state can proceed confidently in the pursuit of his constituents' policy demands; ignorance cannot dissuade him from their pursuit. Of course, whether the wise captain of the ship of state is *motivated* to pursue the policy objectives demanded by his constituents is a separate – and, logically speaking, ancillary – question from whether he is capable of deliberately realizing the objectives on the basis of his knowledge and learning capacity.

It is *only* in a political world populated with only wise captains of the ship of state – it is only in a world of omniscient and omnipotent policymakers – that we should be uniquely concerned with policymakers' motives. But this is just a way of saying that we should worry first about policymakers' knowledge before we concern ourselves with their ethics. The nature and extent of policymakers' ignorance serves to determine their incentive structures. In other words, the problem of policymaker ignorance is, in every political context, logically prior to the problem of policymaker incentives.

Reflection and foreshadow

Policymakers are not gods. They are neither omniscient nor omnipotent. Their knowledge of relevant facts and theories is limited, as are their powers, talents, skills, abilities, and capacities, including the capacity to learn new knowledge, acquire new powers, improve existing skills, and so on. To state what is obvious, if sometimes seemingly forgotten: policymakers are mere human beings. True, they are often especially well-educated human beings. However, an advanced degree does not impart the propositional knowledge(-that) that policymakers require to deliberately realize the goals demanded by their constituents. It is also true that policymakers occupy positions of enormous power, influence, and control, but constituents are not marionettes and society has no buttons, levers, or pulleys, so political power does not make the policymaker a puppet-master or the pilot of the airplane of society. Neither omniscient nor omnipotent, policymakers may not even possess the knowledge they need to be effective policymakers, much less gods.

Given policymakers' epistemic limitations, achieving some degree of clarity with respect to the nature and extent of their ignorance, which marks the limits of what they can deliberately achieve via policy action, would seem to be an important thing for political scientists, political philosophers, and political economists to investigate. If we wish to make rational political decisions – if we wish to avoid either political disaster or even just political waste – it would help to better understand what can be deliberately achieved via policy and what can be achieved, if at all, only if non-deliberative spontaneous forces intervene to an adequate degree. Yet, outside of the Austrians' political-epistemological arguments, one rarely encounters analyses of the nature, extent, and consequences of policymaker ignorance.

This neglect is all the more unfortunate given that, unlike the question of whether policymakers are properly motivated to pursue their constituents' interests, the problem of policymaker ignorance is amenable to empirical analysis, at least to some degree. As will be discussed in the second part of the book, we can investigate the epistemic requirements of different policy objectives, the knowledge required to deliberately realize them, and we can inquire into the knowledge that policymakers actually possess; their knowledge of facts and theories; and their skills, capacities, abilities, talents, and powers. We can get some empirical grasp on the likelihood that various objectives can be deliberately realized through political action. We can make a start toward mitigating the problem of policymaker ignorance and thus, if the argument of the present chapter is sound, the problem of policymaker incentives as well.

As we will see, the problem of policymaker ignorance that is implied by the Austrians' political-epistemological approach to the analysis of economic policymaking obtains in other and, indeed, far beyond, political contexts. It is ultimately a fully general fact about human decision-making that ignorance both constrains what can be deliberately achieved via human action and affects the incentives that decision-makers face to pursue various courses of action. What we can – and cannot – deliberately achieve is always and everywhere constrained by our ignorance: we cannot deliberately achieve things that we do not know enough to deliberately achieve; such things can be achieved only if spontaneous forces intervene. The complement of the set of things that we can deliberately achieve on the basis of our knowledge and learning capacity is the set of things that can be achieved, if at all, only if spontaneous forces of some kind intervene to some extent.

My purpose in the present chapter has been to argue for the logical priority of the problem of policymaker ignorance to that of policymaker incentives. In the next chapter, I argue that the Austrians' political-epistemological approach, if further extended and generalized beyond the specific contexts to which Mises and Hayek originally applied it, leads to the problem of policymaker ignorance.

Notes

1 The argument of the present chapter elaborates upon ideas developed in a series of papers that I have published alone and with various co-authors. See Scheall, Butos, and McQuade (2019), Scheall (2019a), Crutchfield and Scheall (2019), and Scheall and Crutchfield (Forthcoming).

2 This is not to say that Austrian economists have ignored the problem of incentives under socialism entirely; see, for example, the section "Responsibility and Initiative in Communal Concerns" in Mises ([1920] 1935, 116–122).

3 The Austrian argument is that "even with the best [people] on top they will not know about what is going on 'at the bottom' in sufficient detail to be able to plan an economy effectively. The problem is not that people will be insufficiently motivated to do the right things but, more fundamentally, that they will not know what the right things are, even if they passionately wanted to do them" (Lavoie [2016] 1985b, 21). Note that Lavoie runs together two knowledge problems in this passage that I will distinguish throughout the book, that is, the problem of knowledge of the "right things" to do and the problem of the knowledge required to do the "right things" effectively. One might possess either kind of knowledge but be ignorant of the other, so these two knowledge problems should be kept distinct.

4 Thus, on this conception of knowledge, to be omniscient and omnipotent is simply to possess all of the knowledge-that and knowledge-how.

5 A policy is effective, on my way of thinking, to the extent that it meets its stated goals at or below its proposed cost. Thus, a policy is ineffective to the extent that either it fails to meet its stated goals or its actual cost exceeds its proposed cost. This notion of policy effectiveness is comparatively modest. For example, Schuck (2014, 41) defines an effective policy as one whose "benefits exceed its costs and . . . is cost-effective." My conception does not require an effective policy to benefit (on net) society or anyone in particular, a requirement distinct and more onerous than that of realizing its specified goals.

6 Methods whereby the problem of policymaker ignorance might be both scientifically analyzed and, ultimately, practically mitigated are considered in the second part of the book.

7 Don Lavoie ([2015] 1985a, 102, fn. 22) came closer than any other Austrian economist to explicating the specifically logical priority of the epistemic in economic policymaking. Perhaps unfortunately, Lavoie did not develop or follow up his note that James Buchanan, the father of public-choice economics,

> in his excellent study of subjectivism entitled *Cost and Choice* (Buchanan 1969, 96–97), contends that the Austrians in the [socialist-calculation] debate overemphasized the "information problems" of central planning instead of the problem of subjective choice, which he considers "relatively . . . more significant". Thus, [Buchanan] argues, "Even if the socialist state should somehow discover an oracle that would allow all calculation to be made perfectly . . . efficiency in allocation will emerge only if . . . men can be motivated" or "trained" to "make choices that do not embody the opportunity costs that they, individually and personally, confront."

Lavoie correctly noted that Buchanan got the logical priority here exactly reversed:

> Although I would agree that even if the problem of knowledge were overcome the problem of motivation would remain, it seems to me that it is the former that is the more fundamental. One could reverse Buchanan's argument and say that even if socialist managers could somehow, as he puts it, be "converted into economic eunuchs . . . to make decisions in accordance with cost criteria that are different from their own", *the central difficulty of obtaining the relevant information would still remain. Even fully motivated planners would not know how to plan rationally* (italics added).

Lavoie might also have noted that, from the perspective of policymakers, the problem of properly motivating people to behave in the relatively selfless ways that central planning requires to succeed is just another aspect of the problem of policymaker ignorance. Figuring out how to train or otherwise convince people to "make decisions in accordance with cost criteria that are different from their own" is just one more thing that policymakers might not know how to do and thus provides just one more example of how ignorance can hinder the effectiveness of central planning. If policymakers were knowledgeable about how to create a selfless society, Buchanan's point would lose all its force. Thus, it is the ignorance problem, not the incentive problem, *contra* Buchanan, that is logically fundamental. It seems that Buchanan (and perhaps Lavoie as well) was too focused on the specific *calculation* problem that Mises raised to notice that knowledge of prices is just one sort of knowledge that policymakers might need to make effective policies.

8 I argue in later chapters that the Austrians' political-epistemological approach, if further extended and generalized beyond the policymaking contexts to which Mises and Hayek originally applied it, leads to the recognition of a fully general *problem of ignorance*. What can be deliberately achieved through human action, in any context, is necessarily constrained by the nature and extent of the decision-maker's ignorance and capabilities for learning. It is ignorance, not incentives, that limits the possibilities for effective action. It will serve the purpose of this argument to have the logical priority of the epistemic already established as a general fact about human decision-making.

9 Epistemic burdens should not be confused with *epistemic costs*. The latter are incurred in the process of trying to surmount epistemic burdens, but there is no necessary relation between the two. A given epistemic burden might be overcome in a more or less costly manner.

10 The arguments offered in this section are based on those advanced in Scheall and Crutchfield (Forthcoming)

11 Samuel DeCanio (2014) comes close to recognizing the priority of the epistemic in political decision-making. He recognizes that (what I'm calling) epistemic burdens do not depend on incentive structures, but he does not see that incentive structures in fact depend on epistemic burdens. David Hebert (2019, 137) thinks that Austrian and public-choice economics are best conceived as "orthogonal . . . akin to the twin parabolas of x^2 and $-x^2$ in that they would share a common origin but point in different directions," and thus, like most other scholars of these subjects, Hebert misses the dependence of the problem of policymaker incentives, the domain of public-choice economics, on the problem of policymaker ignorance, the province of the Austrians. Public-choice and Austrian economics are not orthogonal. The political-epistemological concerns of the Austrians are logically prior to the concerns of public-choice economics. The epistemic horse always drives the cart of incentives.

12 It is important to note that I am merely pointing out a *fact* and not positing a *mechanism* here. It seems apparent that it does, but I have no idea how or by what apparatus the human cognitive system pre-consciously sorts courses of action for the actor's ignorance.

13 Cooper (1966), Martin (2009), Besch (2011), and Driver (2011) also defend *ought presupposes can*, while Mizrahi (2015) denies it, but argues it is "the best candidate for a relation between 'ought' and 'can'."

14 Oppenheim (1987), Vallentyne (1989), Saka (2000), Littlejohn (2009), and Vogelstein (2012) also defend *ought conversationally implicates can*.

15 See Pennington (2011, 247):

> [S]uppose an individual has no intention of "free-riding" but is motivated as a concerned "citizen" to reduce his or her water consumption to "socially responsible" levels. In the absence of property rights and the resultant market prices for water there may be no way for the individual concerned to know what their "socially responsible" level of consumption is. They may, of course, choose to arrive by "guesswork" at some level of consumption below their "normal" rate, but in the absence of prices indicating the most important margins for conservation they would have no idea whether such actions were actually worthwhile. In these circumstances even the most altruistically inclined person is likely to consume

as much water as she potentially requires, because at least she knows what the amount is, whereas the "socially responsible" level of consumption is shrouded in a fog of ignorance.

16 See Crutchfield and Scheall (2019).
17 "Public policy is being conducted in abysmal ignorance of its likely consequences, and this inadequate knowledge of how to achieve goals rationally does explain the policy failures that surround us" (Lavoie [2016] 1985b, 55).
18 The present section includes material drawn from Scheall (2019a).

2　Beyond the socialist oasis

Hayek's extensions of Mises' calculation argument

> Capitalism has so enormously simplified the methods of control and registration that they present no difficulties to those who can read and write. The ability to observe and to make out receipts – this, with a knowledge of the four rules of arithmetic, is all that is required.
>
> – Lenin, *The State and Revolution* (1917, Chapter Five, Section Four)[1]

The present chapter explores the historical development of the Austrians' political-epistemological approach. My goal here is less to retell the history of the Austrian School in the 20th century, a history that has been retold many times by several talented historians of economic thought (see, e.g., Hayek [1968] 1992; Lavoie [1985] 2015; Vaughn 1994; Caldwell 2004; Boettke 2018), than to argue that a particular logic or line of reasoning runs through the Austrians' many engagements with socialists, Keynesians, and other defenders of political intervention in the economy. Over the course of these engagements, the Austrians gradually generalized political-epistemological reasoning by applying it to an ever-broader range of political contexts and policy goals far beyond the fully collectivized socialist oasis to which Mises applied his original calculation argument. Indeed, by the time of "The Pretence of Knowledge," his 1974 Nobel Prize Lecture, Hayek ([1975] 2014) was arguing that economic policymakers in otherwise liberal market economies could not possess the knowledge required to meet the relatively simple (as compared to full-blown central planning) goal of managing the business cycle.

This process of generalizing political-epistemological reasoning is not yet complete. It is not only in the realm of economic policymaking that the nature and extent of their ignorance determines which goals policymakers can deliberately realize and which goals can only be realized if spontaneous forces intervene; neither is it only in the economic arena that ignorance can distort the incentives that policymakers confront to pursue various objectives. These are general facts about political action. Indeed, as we will see, these are general facts about human action, which, in all contexts, can deliberately realize its goals, whatever they might be, only to the extent that the knowledge upon which action is based is adequate. In arguing that the policymaker's ability to realize the goals of central planning was knowledge dependent, the Austrians pointed to a notion of far broader – indeed, ultimately, fully general – significance.

The insurmountable epistemic burden of the administrator of a pure and isolated socialist oasis[2]

The late-1917 revolution that eventually ended with Lenin's Bolsheviks in the Moscow Kremlin, together with the post-World War I rise of socialist parties to positions of power in various governments on the European continent, catalyzed a burgeoning discussion of the problems of the socialist mode of economic organization. Many argued at the time that the purported success of programs to administer food and raw materials during World War I had established the potential superiority of centralized economic administration over market competition (Caldwell 1997, 1). The contributions of Otto Neurath, whom Mises had known and profoundly abhorred since their time together in Eugen Böhm-Bawerk's famous Vienna economics seminar, are perhaps most characteristic of this literature (Caldwell 1997, 6).[3] Neurath (1919) argued that the lessons of economic administration during the war had established the possibility of effective central planning on the basis of "*in natura*" calculations. Socialist economies could do without money and prices expressed in monetary terms, Neurath argued. Comparisons of value in socialist economies could proceed in kind and required no common unit of account, such as money prices provided in competitive economies.[4] A similar proposal was put forward by Otto Bauer (1919), an influential member of the Social Democratic Party of Austria and, unlike Neurath, a friend of Ludwig von Mises, who also participated in Böhm-Bawerk's seminar.

What all socialist proposals, going back to Marx, have in common, is the notion that "[r]ational human production consists in the construction of a plan in the mind in advance, before the steps of the plan are implemented in the material world . . . central planning entails the unification of social planning into one consistent, conscious plan, one complex structure that is coherently raised in the minds of socialist 'architects' before being systematically implemented" (Lavoie [1985] 2015, 39). Whether the terms of the central plan are determined dictatorially or democratically, the fundamental socialist assertion is that conscious and deliberate social planning conducted for the collective from the top down is, or can be made, superior (in respects important to both socialists and non-socialists alike) to economic planning conducted by individuals in a context of private property and spontaneously adjusting prices. Ambitious claims were put forward for the possibilities of central planning in the early days of socialist thought.[5] Central planning promised to be more productive and less wasteful than the market and more rational in what it produced.[6] Income would be distributed entirely according to considerations of need and justice, independently of the capricious whims of vacillating prices. The hated system of wage labor would be eliminated and the sickening swings of the business cycle eradicated. All of this could be achieved, it was alleged (at least at first), with little negative effect on the free choices of consumers and workers, who would remain at leisure to buy what they wanted and work where, and in whatever field, they preferred.

However, as a matter of simple logic, these grander aims could not be achieved unless a preliminary end was first secured. Central planning could not surpass the performance of markets in the relevant respects without first achieving the same level of success. In order to better the competitive system, socialism first had to equal its accomplishments, such as they were. In particular, if the administrators of a centrally planned socialist economy hoped to both maintain their positions of authority and permit a degree of consumer freedom, one of their chief objectives would have to be to deliberately promote equilibrium between the supply of and demand for consumer goods.[7] This is to say that their decisions with respect to the production of such goods would have to cohere with the ever-shifting preferences of consumers, an outcome regularly realized spontaneously in market economies, where shortages and surpluses of consumer goods are relatively rare. Otherwise, the administrators of a centrally planned economy would likely eventually find themselves fighting to maintain their positions in the face of a consumer revolt.

However, according to Mises' ([1920] 1935) argument in "Economic Calculation in the Socialist Commonwealth," the administrators of a pure and isolated socialist oasis, in which private property in the factors of production had been prohibited and the factors collectivized by the state, could never acquire the knowledge necessary to deliberately realize this objective.[8] Under such circumstances, central planners would lack guidance concerning the effectiveness of their production decisions and, therefore, could not deliberately facilitate equilibrium between the supply of and demand for consumer goods. In market economies, producers learn about the economic effectiveness of their decisions through changes in the prices of production goods or, more exactly, through the carrot-and-stick system of profit and loss (Mises [1920] 1935, 97–98, 107–109). Profits are carrots to the producer; they indicate that consumers approve of the producers' decisions. Losses are, of course, sticks (or, perhaps better, cudgels) to the producer; they signal consumer dissatisfaction with the producer's decisions.

Mises' socialist calculation argument does little more than draw out the implications for the effectiveness of central planning of the central planners' impoverished epistemic circumstances: without private property in the factors of production, there would be no markets for these factors; without markets, there would be no prices for the factors of production (Mises [1920] 1935, 92); without prices – without profit and loss – central planners would be ignorant of the economic consequences of their production decisions; without this knowledge, central planners could not deliberately promote equilibrium between supply and demand (Mises [1920] 1935, 103–105; also see Brutzkus 1935, 106–107). Ignorant of changes in market prices for different production goods that reflect vacillations in the demand for the various consumption goods to which the former are inputs, the socialist administrator could not deliberately realize even this minimal goal, a comparatively trifling prerequisite of the more ambitious goals of socialism's defenders. In order to avoid shortages of certain consumption goods and surpluses of others, central planners would have to organize production so as to satisfy consumer demands. Yet without prices for production goods that reflected the ever-shifting demands of capricious consumers, this would be impossible. As a consequence, the goal of promoting equilibrium between supply and demand conditions with regard to consumption goods could be achieved only if spontaneous forces intervened: in order to realize this objective, socialist administrators would either have to get incredibly lucky or otherwise leave economic equilibration to forces beyond their control, that is, to an unconscious system of spontaneously adjusting prices.[9]

Mises' argument presupposed that the ends of central planning were those advanced by its defenders. Indeed, Mises actually worried about a much humbler prerequisite to the realization of the socialists' grander ambitions. Moreover, Mises' argument presupposed the means (originally) believed by its defenders to be essential to socialism – full collectivization of the factors of production and centralized, top-down planning of production on the basis of in-kind calculations – for the deliberate realization of these ends.[10] Mises then asked what knowledge socialist central planners would need in order to make these means effective for the deliberate realization of the preliminary goal of socialism. He argued that, in order to ensure that the goods demanded by consumers were produced in sufficient quality and quantity, central planners would, at a minimum, need knowledge of the relative supply conditions of the various factors of production. In market contexts, factor prices provide this knowledge. However, since there would be no markets after full collectivization, there would be no one with whom the state could engage in exchange and so there would be no factor prices.[11] The source of the relevant knowledge in market environments would not exist in a socialist context, and, just as importantly, there would be no obvious alternative source of the necessary knowledge. As a consequence, spontaneous forces of some kind – even if just preternatural luck – would have to intervene if socialism was to at least match the level of success regularly achieved by the market as a mechanism for the coordination of production and consumption decisions. Since the minimum required knowledge of the relative supply conditions of the various factors of production would not be available to planners, Mises concluded that efficient central planning was impossible, that central planning could lead only to economic waste and not to the goal of supplying consumers with the objects of their demands, much less to the goals revered by all socialists, that is, the eradication of unemployment and the business cycle, more leisure time coupled with improved economic efficiency, and a more just society.[12]

Hayek's epistemology – a first pass[13]

Although much of his work was of epistemological significance, Hayek never wrote a comprehensive epistemological treatise. His theory of knowledge, such as it is, can only be cobbled together from those of his many writings that bear epistemological implications.[14] Hayek first considered epistemology in an essay that he wrote while still a student on the nature of human consciousness (Hayek [1920] 2017). He developed his epistemological ideas more systematically in 1952's *The Sensory Order: An Inquiry into the Foundations of Theoretical Psychology* (Hayek [1952] 2017) and drew further implications from his psychological theory in 1969's "The Primacy of the Abstract" (Hayek [1969] 2014). It is also possible to infer aspects of Hayek's epistemology from his work on the epistemic functions of competitive markets, spontaneously adjusting prices, and systems of largely unwritten rules of social conduct.[15] There are also several arguments and concepts of epistemological significance in his later methodological writings on those scientific disciplines concerned with fundamentally *complex phenomena*.[16]

Explanation, prediction, and control of complex phenomena[17]

For Hayek ([1955] 2014, 201n), explanations and predictions were two opposite sides of the same coin – a prediction explains phenomena yet to be observed, while an explanation predicts (or, more often, retrodicts) phenomena already observed. Our capacity to explain and predict some phenomena is intimately connected with our ability to control them: "While it is evidently possible to predict precisely without being able to control, we shall clearly not be able to control developments further than we can predict the results of our action. A limitation of prediction thus implies a limitation of control, but not vice versa" (Hayek [1955] 2014, 210n). Thus, we should expect to control economic and other social phenomena no further than we can predict them, which is to say, no further than our knowledge permits.

The *degree* of a prediction depends on the extent of relevant knowledge that enters into it. The possibility of either a "full explanation" or a "precise prediction of particular events" requires sufficient knowledge:

> [s]uch prediction will be possible if we can ascertain . . . all the circumstances which influence those events. We need for this both a theory which tells us on what circumstances the events in question will depend, and information on the particular circumstances which may influence the event in which we are interested.
>
> (Hayek [1961] 2014, 376–377)[18]

The higher the degree of an explanation or a prediction, the more relevant knowledge figures in it, the more closely it approximates a "full explanation" or a "precise prediction of particular events," and the more useful it is, other things equal, as a tool of social control.

The various disciplines that Hayek counted as sciences of *complex phenomena* included cognitive psychology (Hayek [1952] 2017), "cybernetics, the theory of automata or machines, general systems theory, and perhaps also

communications theory" ([1955] 2014, 211), as well as economics, linguistics
([1967a] 2014, 283), geology, evolutionary biology, and the branches of astro-
physics that investigate the formation of stars and galaxies ([1967a] 2014, 287).
In addition to the theory of cognitive psychology that he personally developed,
first rather dimly as a student in 1920 and later more precisely and systematically in 1952's *The Sensory Order*, Hayek explicitly discussed two specific examples of scientific theories of complex phenomena, namely Darwin's theory of
evolution by natural selection – "[p]robably the best illustration of a theory of
complex phenomena which is of great value, although it describes merely a
general pattern whose detail we can never fill in" ([1964b] 2014, 266) – and
Walrasian general equilibrium theory, with respect to which Hayek wrote:

> [E]conomic theory is confined to describing kinds of patterns which will
> appear if certain general conditions are satisfied, but can rarely if ever derive
> from this knowledge any predictions of specific phenomena. This is seen
> most clearly if we consider those systems of simultaneous equations which
> since Léon Walras have been widely used to represent the general relations
> between the prices and the quantities of all commodities bought and sold.
> They are so framed that if we were able to fill in all the blanks . . . we could
> calculate the prices and quantities of all the commodities. But, as at least
> the founders of this theory, clearly understood, its purpose is not [quoting
> Pareto (1927, 223–224)] 'to arrive at a numerical calculation of prices',
> because it would be 'absurd' to assume that we can ascertain all the data.
> ([1964b] 2014, 270–271)

Compared to what we can know about systems of simple phenomena explicable in terms of models consisting of relatively few variables, our knowledge
of systems of complex phenomena is necessarily limited (Hayek [1964b] 2014,
261–262). Indeed, ultimately for Hayek, complex phenomena are simply those
with respect to which our knowledge – and, therefore, our capacity for explanation, prediction, and control – is limited. If we possess the knowledge necessary to fully explain, predict, and control some phenomena, then they are
simple, by definition, not complex. Phenomena are complex to the extent that
we cannot explain, predict, and control them.

The reason that our knowledge is limited with respect to complex phenomena, according to Hayek ([1964b] 2014, 262), is that the number of elements
of models of systems of complex phenomena is typically very large, so large
as to constrain our capacity to populate such models with data sufficient to
generate any but circumscribed explanations (i.e., *explanations of the principle*)
and predictions (i.e., *pattern predictions*). I have referred to this elsewhere as
the "data problem" that Hayek raised for the sciences of complex phenomena
(Scheall 2015a). Assuming an adequate model is at hand of the complex phenomena under investigation, this model will typically consist of a large number
of variables and, naturally, the larger the number of variables, the greater the
epistemic burden involved in discovering the values of all of these variables at

the time and place relevant to prediction (explanation). There is also the issue, another aspect of the data problem, that the required data may not exist in the context in which they are needed (Hayek [1968] 2014). The data problem appears when we cannot populate a model with data for all of the relevant causal variables and thus can generate only less-than-full explanations of the principle and pattern predictions of the relevant phenomena.

Although he did not emphasize it nearly as much as he worried about the data problem, Hayek ([1956] 1967) also noted that sciences of complex phenomena confront what I have called a "theory problem" (Scheall 2015a): it is sometimes the case that, even if the data problem were not a problem, that is, even if data for all relevant causal variables were available, the scientific investigator would nevertheless lack a model sufficient to fully explain or precisely predict particular instances of the phenomena. As a matter of course, there are many cases in which, relative to what would be required to generate a precise prediction of the phenomena, available theoretical knowledge is deficient; that is, there are cases where the relevant "algebraic equation or set of such equations [that] defines . . . a class of patterns" (Hayek [1964b] 2014, 259) is itself underspecified – contains gaps or lacunae with regard to the parameters that would be required for a full explanation – so that a precise prediction of particular events could not be generated *even if* all of the relevant data were available.

That Hayek took this theory problem (as distinct from the data problem he explicated at greater length) to be common in sciences of complex phenomena is implicit in the argument of "The Dilemma of Specialization" ([1956] 1967, 124; italics added), an essay in which explicit methodological considerations take a backseat to concerns of best pedagogical practices in the social sciences.[19] "For almost any application of our knowledge to concrete instances," Hayek wrote,

> the knowledge of one discipline, and even of all the scientific knowledge we can bring to bear on the topic will be only a small part of the foundations of our opinions. Let me speak first of the need of using the results of scientific disciplines other than our own, though this is far from all that is required. That concrete reality is not divisible into distinct objects corresponding to the various scientific disciplines is a commonplace, yet a commonplace which severely limits our competence to pronounce as scientists on any particular event. There is scarcely a phenomenon or event in society with which we can deal adequately without knowing a great deal of several disciplines, *not to speak of the knowledge of particular facts that will be required.*

In other words, a theory capable of generating a full explanation of some phenomena may well be a *composite system of theories*, spanning multiple disciplines, each of which might investigate phenomena of greater or lesser complexity.[20] What's more, given that "concrete reality is not divisible into distinct objects corresponding to the various scientific disciplines," there may be causal factors that must be accounted for if an explanation is to be "full," which fall under the heading of no extant scientific discipline. The relevant scientific knowledge may not have been discovered (indeed, it may not even be discover*able*).[21]

Hayek's concern for the theory problem was also implicit in his well-known criticisms of Keynes' ([1930] 1971) *Treatise on Money* in the early 1930s. The main point that Hayek ([1931a] 1995, [1931b] 1995, [1932] 1995) persistently pushed in his multi-part review of the *Treatise* was the absence of any theoretical account of capital in the book (Caldwell 2004, 178). Economic fluctuations were complex phenomena, for Hayek. They could not be satisfactorily dealt with by a theory that ignored and thus implicitly denied the possibility that capital phenomena could figure among the causes of such fluctuations. From Hayek's perspective, this failure to consider the complexities of capital phenomena – a lacuna that was not rectified in Keynes' later *General Theory of Unemployment, Interest, and Money* ([1936] 1973) – was terminal for Keynes' theory, at least as a tool of countercyclical policymaking. To the extent that cyclical phenomena emerged out of capital considerations, Keynes' theory would systematically fail to express their ultimate causes and thus could not be an effective tool to deliberately counter the cycle.[22] But I get slightly ahead of myself. I will return to the question of the epistemic burdens of Keynesian policymakers later in this chapter and yet again later in the book.

The epistemic burdens of socialist administrators in other contexts

Mises' socialist-calculation argument (and related arguments offered by others) provoked various responses from socialist writers. There were those who accepted the criticism with few reservations but who judged the necessary loss of economic efficiency that Mises argued was inherent to central planning a reasonable price to pay for what they considered a more just distribution of society's wealth (Hayek [1935a] 1997, 77). As Hayek noted (also see Mises [1920] 1935, 130), little could be said against such a response, which, assuming it was made in cognizance of the fact that the enforcement of a more just (by some standard) distribution of wealth would reduce society's total wealth, indicated nothing more than a particular value judgment that the economist might reject on ethical grounds but was powerless to counter for scientific reasons. On the other hand, there were those writers who accepted Mises' argument only with respect to the pure and isolated socialist oasis against which it was explicitly directed and who argued that the calculation problem could be solved if either market institutions were introduced to the socialist economy or the freedom of consumers abrogated (Hayek [1935a] 1997, 77–78). Thus, the terms of the debate had shifted by the time Hayek entered the fray in 1935 with his editorial contributions to the *Collectivist Economic Planning* anthology (Hayek [1935a] 1997), in which an English translation of Mises' original contribution to the earlier German-language debate appeared for the first time. Hayek extended and adapted the same basic political–epistemological reasoning that supported Mises' calculation argument to these shifts in the terms of the socialist calculation debate.

The "mathematical solution": not a solution

According to the so-called "mathematical solution" put forward by American economists Fred Taylor (1929) and W. C. Roper (1929) and the Englishman H. D. Dickinson (1933), the calculation problem could be solved by applying to central planning the same theory of general equilibrium that describes the conditions for the existence of equilibrium in a competitive economy.[23] The requirements of rational centrally planned production might be inferred from knowledge of general equilibrium theory plus knowledge of the relevant data (Hayek [1935b] 1997, 93). Given these data, defenders of the mathematical solution argued, solving the calculation problem would be as simple as plugging them into Walrasian general equilibrium theory and solving the resulting simultaneous equations. Unlike Neurath's system of price-less "*in natura*" economic reckoning, the mathematical solution would allow for prices, albeit not as spontaneously determined on markets in an institutional context of private property, but as deliberately decided by economic administrators from the central-planning board.[24] "The supreme economic council gathers statistics from which it constructs a Walrasian system of simultaneous equations, which it then solves" (Lavoie [1985] 2015, 89). *Voila!* In this way, according to defenders of the mathematical solution, equilibrium could be deliberately set and continually maintained in perpetuity across the planned economy.

Of course, the relevant goal of the socialist administrator who would apply general equilibrium theory to solve the calculation problem in the real world need not be perfect economic equilibrium but merely a "result at least comparable with that which the competitive system provides" (Hayek [1935b] 1997, 94). Like Mises, Hayek did not ask more from central planning than its defenders promised as a minimum ambition. However, the socialist administrator who would try to approach economic equilibrium via the mathematical solution would confront an insurmountable epistemic burden, Hayek argued, in the form of a massive data problem. Equilibrium theory starts from the assumption that the data are *given*, but as a practical matter, the socialist administrator would have to *discover* such knowledge. The mathematical solution might reduce the epistemic burden of central planning to that of acquiring knowledge of relevant empirical circumstances, but even this would be beyond the socialist policymaker's ken: "what is practically relevant here is . . . the *nature and amount of concrete information* required if a numerical solution is to be attempted and the magnitude of the task which this numerical solution must involve in any modern community" (Hayek [1935b] 1997, 93–94; italics added).

The mathematical solution would require that, in order to approximate the results of competitive markets, policymakers discover impossibly detailed knowledge concerning each and every good in the economy relevant to their production decisions (Hayek [1935b] 1997, 94–96). For everything to go according to (the central) plan, the instructions given by the socialist administrators to those tasked with implementing production decisions on the ground and in the moment would "have to include and be intimately responsible for details of the most minute description" (Hayek [1935] 1997, 94). A decision to assign certain materials to a particular branch of the socialist economy's productive apparatus would require related decisions about the continued employment, or retirement, of tools and machinery already in use. The success of an enterprise is determined by considerations of this sort, "details of technique, the saving of one material rather than the other[,]" and would have to be considered in any central plan "which is not to be hopelessly wasteful" (Hayek [1935] 1997, 94). In order for the calculations of the planners to approach the minimum degree of economy realized spontaneously by a system of spontaneously adjusting prices, every production good would have to be treated just as it is in such a system, that is, as a unique individual object "determined by its particular state of wear and tear, its location, and so on" (Hayek [1935] 1997, 94). Two different screwdrivers could not figure identically in the production plans of the economic administrators if one were brand new and the other worn or if one were immediately at hand and the other some distance from its intended place of use. The planning authority would require a complete accounting of the properties of each and every one of these individual units with respect to, for example, "costs of movement to any other place where it might possibly be used with greater advantage, cost of eventual repair or changes, etc. etc." (Hayek [1935] 1997, 95).

Hayek argued, in effect, that acquiring these latter data would constitute an epistemic burden that could not be overcome by any human policymaker, and not merely because of the extent of the data required. Much of the necessary data would constitute a kind of know-how, that is, "a technique of thought which enables the individual engineer to find new solutions rapidly as soon as he is confronted with new constellations of circumstances" (Hayek [1935] 1997, 95). However difficult it might be for central planners to acquire data concerning all of the various facts and figures relevant to their task, the ultimate unbreachable constraint would be the impossibility of getting inside the head of "individual engineers" when and where necessary to discover the techniques that facilitate their decision-making. Indeed, much of this knowledge exists only in tacit form in the minds of relevant individuals, who must be situated in a market context in order to access and apply it (Hayek [1968] 2014). Not only knowledge of relevant techniques but knowledge of any improvements in such techniques as would be adopted in a competitive system would have to somehow be brought under the epistemic purview of the socialist administrators if the effects of their conscious decisions were to mirror those of the unconscious adaptations of a system of market prices to ceaseless myriad changes in economic conditions. Policymakers could not acquire even in principle such counterfactual knowledge of techniques as they would exist, and their ongoing modifications as they would occur, under non-existent market conditions.[25]

The epistemic burden of the mathematical solution would extend yet further to the need to acquire data concerning consumers' assessments of the relative importance of the various kinds and quantities of consumption goods to be produced (Hayek [1935] 1997, 95–96). Where both consumers remained free to choose and, in the absence of markets for the factors of production, factor prices failed to reflect consumers' assessments of consumption goods, such data could be conveyed to central planners only via "complete lists of the different quantities of all commodities which would be bought at any possible combination of prices of the different commodities which might be available . . . And as tastes change from moment to moment, the lists would have to be in the process of continuous revision" (Hayek [1935] 1997, 95–96).

Yet, setting aside any worries concerning the difficulty of acquiring all of this knowledge, once it had somehow been gathered, central planners would still confront the epistemic burden of rationally calculating its significance for production, given general equilibrium theory. Indeed, technically, the *calculation* problem as such would not arise until after policymakers had *collected* all of the relevant data. What's more, the collection and calculation of the significance for rational production decisions of all of the required data was not a problem that could be solved once and for all (Hayek [1935] 1997, 96). Every change in relevant data would necessitate ascertainment of the change, *re*-calculation of the entire system of equations, and timely communication of revised instructions to the production managers charged with their actual implementation (Hayek [1935] 1997, 96). One might object that a competitive market system never approaches perfect equilibrium and that Hayek asked too much from central planning, but such an objection would miss the point. The argument is not that competitive markets can, but socialist administration cannot, achieve perfect equilibrium – no system in which economic agents are less than omniscient and omnipotent and relevant circumstances are liable to continuous variation can ever *realize* equilibrium.[26] The argument is that, because competition does, while deliberate economic management does not, permit the spontaneous adjustment to an array of circumstances so massive and so inconstant as to vitiate their comprehensive survey, the former system must afford a nearer approach to equilibrium than the latter:

> [t]he essential thing about [market competition] is that it does react to some extent to all those small changes and differences which would have to be deliberately disregarded under the [centrally planned] system we are discussing if the calculations were to be manageable. In this way rational decision would be impossible in all these questions of detail, which in the aggregate decide the success of productive effort.
>
> (Hayek [1935] 1997, 96)

Given the nature and extent of policymaker ignorance in relevant contexts, attempting to centrally plan the economy using the mathematical solution could not match the results regularly achieved where individuals adjust their economic activity to changes in price signals: "Hayek's conclusion is not that central planning is impossible but that it is likely to result in considerably lower standards of living, since government planners cannot elicit and exploit subjectively held knowledge as effectively as can a competitive market process" (Burczak 2006, 33).

Hayek also considered the possibility that what its defenders really intended by the mathematical solution as a practical recommendation was that a transition from the existing competitive society to a no-less-efficient socialist economy might eventually be realized via deliberate, centrally directed, trial-and-error adjustments to changes in the relevant data. There were two problems with this suggestion, Hayek ([1935] 1997, 96–97) argued. First, its feasibility would require that all changes in economic circumstances be sufficiently "minor" as to be epistemically tractable by the planning authorities – the problem of rationally calculating the implications for production of any "major" changes in the data would remain. But, even if this problem were set aside, Hayek argued, there were few grounds for belief in the capacity of a system of deliberate, centrally directed, trial-and-error price adjustments to match, much less surpass, a system in which such changes occur spontaneously, without deliberate direction from the center and the massive epistemic burdens that must be surmounted for central direction to be minimally effective.

> We need only to remember the difficulties experienced with the fixing of prices, even when applied to a few commodities only, and to contemplate further that, in such a system, price-fixing would have to be applied not to a few but to all commodities, finished or unfinished, and that it would have to bring about as frequent and as varied price-changes as those which occur in a capitalistic society every day and every hour, in order to see that this is not a way in which the solution provided by competition can even be approximately achieved. Almost every change of any single price would make changes of hundreds of other prices necessary and most of these other changes would by no means be proportional but would be affected by the different degrees of elasticity of demand, by the possibilities of substitution and other changes in the method of production. To imagine that all this adjustment could be brought about by successive orders by the central authority when the necessity is noticed, and that then every price is fixed and changed until some degree of equilibrium is obtained is certainly an absurd idea.
>
> (Hayek [1935] 1997, 97)[27]

Like Mises before him, when Hayek argued against central planning, he presupposed both the relevant ends and the means for their realization proposed by his dialectical opponents. He then asked about the nature and extent of the knowledge required to effectively apply the mathematical solution – in either its calculative or trial-and-error versions – as a means to the end of deliberately coordinating consumption and production decisions across the economy.

Making the mathematical solution effective would require general (or theoretical) knowledge, to be supplied by equilibrium theory, and particular knowledge (or empirical data), which, Hayek insisted, central planners would not be able to acquire under the circumstances relevant to their task. The socialist administrator who would seek to implement the mathematical solution in a real-world collectivized setting would confront an insurmountable epistemic burden in the form of 1) acquiring the impossibly detailed knowledge concerning the properties of the manifold of production goods; 2) discovering the relevant non-propositional know-how, the "techniques of thought," of each producer that facilitate the making of rational production decisions; 3) learning consumers' assessments of the relative importance of various kinds and quantities of consumption goods; 4) interpreting and calculating the significance of all of these data for the central plan; 5) conveying appropriate instructions to and exerting adequate control over the managers of production firms; and 6) continuously replicating steps 1) – 5). The epistemic burden of approaching equilibrium via centrally directed trial-and-error adjustments might be rather more surmountable with regard to sufficiently minor changes in the data, but only momentarily, at best. The central planner charged with this task would require a seemingly impossible variety of know-how, that is, the ability to deliberately adapt the prices of all other commodities to every minor change in the economically relevant circumstances of any single commodity with at least the same efficiency as occurs spontaneously under market competition. And, of course, the problem of deliberately adapting the price system to major changes in relevant data would remain.

Hayek's argument against the mathematical solution began the process of broadening the applicability of and generalizing what, in Mises' hands, had been a comparatively simple deductive argument concerning the epistemic circumstances of a central planner in a non-existent and rather unrealistic context, namely one in which central planners could not acquire knowledge of factor prices, even at second hand. Mises' argument was just an elaboration of the epistemic circumstances of the central planner in an imaginary socialist oasis. It explained why central planners would have to refer to prices in order to achieve whatever modicum of success they might be able to achieve, but it did not explain why their success could only be, at best, limited.[28]

This is what Hayek's argument against the mathematical solution achieved. Hayek showed, in effect, that, although knowledge of prices was necessary, it was far from sufficient to make central planning an effective means to the ends of socialism. Hayek's argument emphasized the vast and, for the policymaker, unmanageable *extent* of the knowledge of prices required and that knowledge of prices was not the only *kind* of particular, empirical, or non-theoretical knowledge that the central planner would require in order to deliberately administer equilibrium. The planner would also need to acquire knowledge of the economically relevant know-how and consumption preferences of individual economic agents and possess the ability (a kind of know-how) to calculate and re-calculate the prices of every unit of every good in the economy with every change in relevant data. Even where they possessed knowledge of prices, policymakers' epistemic burdens would remain practically insurmountable. In short, Hayek's argument against the mathematical solution emphasized that the socialist administrator's epistemic burdens would in fact be much heavier than it might have seemed to readers of Mises and (more to my present point) that policymakers in a wider variety of contexts than the pure and isolated socialist oasis would confront similar epistemic burdens in their attempts to deliberately administer economic equilibrium.

Abrogating economic freedom to facilitate solution of the calculation problem

This gradual extending and generalizing of the reasoning underlying Mises' original calculation argument continued when Hayek next considered the proposal by some socialists to abrogate the freedom of choice of consumers and workers as a means of deliberately realizing the preliminary goal of socialism. Given that every shift of the ever-shifting whims of the consumer, as well as every voluntary change of employment, would disturb whatever degree of equilibrium had previously existed and necessitate recalculation of the economic plan, it had been suggested that the calculation problem could be mitigated, if not alleviated, were freedom of choice in consumption and occupation abolished.[29] If the epistemic burden of the socialist administrator would be insurmountable where consumers and workers were free to choose for themselves, because of the need to recalculate the structure of prices with every change in consumption and employment, perhaps it could be surmounted were these freedoms revoked.

Hayek ([1935b] 1997, 98) conceded that the extinction of these liberties would simplify the planners' task to some extent by eliminating the need to factor a number of capricious considerations into their calculations. In order to match the performance of a system of spontaneously adjusting prices, however, the central-planning authority would have to deliberately adapt the plan rapidly and continuously to changing data other than the fickle tastes of consumers and varying employment decisions of wage-earners, for example, to unforeseen changes in "weather . . . the numbers or the state of health of the population, a breakdown of machinery, the discovery or the sudden exhaustion of a mineral deposit, and hundreds of other constant changes" (Hayek [1935b] 1997, 99).

The need to rely on a system of prices that adapts spontaneously to changes in the relevant economic data in order to facilitate the operation of the tendency toward equilibrium would disappear only if production in the socialist state *aimed at no particular result* (Hayek [1935b] 1997, 98–99). Put another way, epistemic burdens would be effectively nil where policymaking aimed at nothing at all. By abolishing the freedoms of the consumer and the worker, the central planner would have

> saved himself the trouble of finding out what people really prefer and avoided the impossible task of combining the individual scales into an agreed common scale which expresses the general ideas of justice. But if he

wants to follow this norm with any degree of rationality or consistency, if he wants to realize what he considers to be the ends of the community, he will have to solve all the problems which we have discussed already.

(Hayek [1935b] 1997, 99)

Note how far this extends the political–epistemological approach beyond the original domain of Mises' argument: so long as economic policymakers aim to deliberately direct the productive apparatus toward *some* goal, whether that of mirroring the success of a spontaneously adjusting price system as an equilibrating mechanism or something decidedly less ambitious, *they need knowledge adequate to the task*. To the extent that existing knowledge is inadequate, there is an epistemic burden to be surmounted in realizing the relevant goals via deliberate political action, whatever they might be.

The epistemic burdens of the central planner under market socialism

Extending political–epistemological reasoning even further, Hayek next considered the possibility of a "competitive solution" to the socialist-calculation problem, that is, the reintroduction of a kind of pseudo-competition to facilitate the setting of rational prices in a socialist environment. Hayek ([1935b] 1997) first considered tentative proposals for "market socialism" that he had heard verbally discussed among colleagues and acquaintances. A few years later, however, Hayek ([1940] 1997) turned in earnest to the specific market-socialist proposals advanced by Oskar Lange and Fred Taylor (1938) and H. D. Dickinson (1939).[30] Like the mathematical solution, which Taylor (1929) and Dickinson (1933) had previously defended, the market-socialist "solution" held that equilibrium theory could be put to work as a means for the deliberate coordination of production and consumption decisions in the socialist state. The market socialists "thought their solution was not just theoretical but a practical guide to an improved 'better' world" (Boettke and Storr 2015, xi). According to these proposals, the equilibrating features of a competitive market economy could be approximated in an otherwise centrally planned economy if firms within particular industries were organized into single monopolies and their managers instructed to produce at prices just sufficient to cover marginal costs. Unlike the mathematical solution, which would place the epistemic burden of collecting and interpreting the required data, and calculating and continuously re-calculating prices, entirely on the central planner, market socialism would take advantage of the plant manager's relative proximity to many of the relevant data. In effect, market socialism would lighten the socialist administrator's epistemic burden by shifting part of it to the managers of the industrial monopolies ultimately responsible for production in such a system.

According to Hayek ([1935b] 1997, 105–106), the notion that such an instruction from the central planner to the production manager might be adequate to the epistemic burdens of deliberately securing equilibrium indicated a naïve belief that the conditions of real, dynamic competition were reflected in the static model of general equilibrium. In my terms, market socialism faced a theory problem that ultimately fed into or manifested as a data problem. The required data, such as general equilibrium theory assumes them to be, would not be accessible – indeed, would not exist – in a context of market socialism. Outside of artificial general equilibrium models, the relevant data, the "costs of production" of each industrial monopoly, could be determined only within a competitive process: "(t)o make a monopolist charge the price that would rule under competition, or a price that is equal to the necessary cost, is impossible, because the competitive or necessary cost *cannot be known* unless there is competition" ([1935b] 1997, 107; italics added). In other words, putting this instruction to work in the service of deliberately coordinating production and consumption decisions across the economy would require that firm managers evaluate an unknowable counter-factual, that is, the firm's marginal costs as they would exist in a non-existent competitive environment.[31] Lange and Dickinson's proposals for market socialism, according to Hayek ([1940] 1997, 130; italics added), "treated . . . the cost curves [as if they] were objectively given facts. What is forgotten is that the method which under given conditions is the cheapest is a thing which *has to be discovered, and to be discovered anew*, sometimes almost from day to day, by the entrepreneur."

As Hayek had earlier argued against the mathematical solution and would later emphasize in "Competition as a Discovery Procedure" ([1968] 2014), the data that deliberate economic administration requires to be effective are created by the very competitive process that deliberate economic administration displaces:

> [*W*]*herever* competition can be rationally justified, it is on the ground that we do *not* know in advance the facts that determine the actions of competitors . . . [C]ompetition is valuable *only* because, and so far as, its results are unpredictable and on the whole different from those anyone has, or could have, deliberately aimed at.
>
> (Hayek [1968] 2014, 304–305; italics in the original)

Market competition is the method by which a firm's costs of production are determined and discovered by its managers. Some of the knowledge required to make market socialism effective would not exist under market socialism or, more generally, outside of an environment in which "anybody who knows a cheaper method" is free "to come in at his own risk and to attract customers by underbidding the other producers" (Hayek [1940] 1997, 130).[32] Without this latter condition, that is, without entrepreneurs risking their own capital, there would be no meaningful "costs of production," and the instruction to produce so that marginal costs equal marginal revenue would not be a practicable directive. In order for such "pseudo-competition" to approach the results of the market system, "it would not really help to get a satisfactory solution to go only half-way. Only if competition exists not only between but also within the different industries can we expect it to serve its purpose" (Hayek [1935b] 1997, 108–109).

Beyond this, even though they could slough off – if ultimately ineffectively – part of their epistemic burden onto plant managers, the administrator of a pseudo-competitive socialist economy would still confront a heavy epistemic burden.[33] The central planners would remain responsible for many decisions with respect to which, if production were not to descend into something resembling chaos, they would have to uncover some new rational basis (Hayek [1935b] 1997, 110). The socialist administrator would, among many other tasks, have to lend capital, hire managers, determine whether and how to use existing capital resources, and decide whether and what new capital goods to produce. Initially, following the transition from a system of private to one of public property, some decisions regarding, for example, the lending of free capital or the hiring of managers, might be made on the basis of past success in the former private economy, but circumstances would continue to change in the new institutional setting with much the same rapidity and unpredictability (Hayek [1935b] 1997, 110). The decisions of the planning authority would have to be based on expectations of the future, but on *whose* expectations? How would investment risk be determined – or, more to the point, how would success or failure *given risk estimates* be determined? Would someone who succeeded at a simple, low-risk, and rather inessential endeavor be afforded more or less freedom in the future than someone who failed at a complex, high-risk, and socially significant project? "There will certainly be a tendency to prefer the safe to the risky enterprise" (Hayek [1935b] 1997, 110). Were it not to engage in only the most mundane of low-risk investments, the pseudo-competitive socialist economy would need an analog of the risk-bearing capitalist speculator – who, it must be remembered, would be permitted to own no capital. Who would be best entrusted with the community's resources to play this important role? Walrasian general equilibrium could provide none of the theoretical knowledge required to answer these questions rationally. The theory problem confronting the central planner under market socialism would be more massive than it might appear at first glance.

Even in the short run, the decision whether one manager or another was making better use of society's resources would require knowledge not available to the relevant authorities. Such decisions could only be made on the basis of an evaluation of the existing resources supporting production, an evaluation that would require an estimation of future returns: "What is to be the decision if another entrepreneur promises to get a higher return out of the plant (or even an individual machine) than that on which the present user bases his valuation? Is the plant or machine to be taken from him and to be given to the other man in his mere promise?" (Hayek [1935b] 1997, 111). Again, none of this is to say that market competition solves these problems without a residue of error, but it is to argue that, in the absence of evidence or an argument that the relevant authorities could overcome their epistemic burdens, there is no reason to suspect that policymakers could acquire the knowledge necessary to deliberately employ market socialism as a means to approximate the results of an unconscious system of spontaneously adjusting prices.

Hayek's argument against market socialism presupposed both the ends and means of the market socialists, namely the imitation of market results using the pseudo-competitive approach of organizing entire industries into single firms and instructing firm managers to produce at prices just sufficient to cover marginal costs. Making these means effective would require that firm managers know their marginal costs. However, according to Hayek, the very concept of *costs* presupposes an institutional context of markets, private property, and real, not pseudo-, competition. Production costs do not exist outside of theoretical models and competitive economies. Managers of industrial-sized firms in a context of collectivized property could not perform the counterfactual evaluation of the costs the firms would incur in a non-existent competitive environment. In order to realize the relevant goal, spontaneous forces would have to intervene: either the central planners and the firm managers onto whom the former slough part of their epistemic burden would have to get preternaturally lucky and somehow conjure counterfactual knowledge of marginal costs as they would exist in a non-existent competitive context, or they could not be content with going only "half way" but would have to go the whole way to market competition and rely primarily upon the price system as an equilibrating device.[34]

Hayek's argument against market socialism extended political-epistemological reasoning to yet another new context. Indeed, for the first time in the development of the Austrians' political-epistemological approach, the problem of policymaker ignorance was raised with regard to a competitive – albeit a merely pseudo-competitive – environment. When Hayek again extended political-epistemological reasoning, it would be to an even broader range of competitive contexts.[35]

The epistemic burden of achieving consensus concerning a central plan

So far, we have considered only the Austrians' political-epistemological arguments concerning policymakers' ignorance of knowledge required to realize a *given* central economic plan. These arguments have all been to the effect that the required knowledge is not available to policymakers who would act to deliberately realize an *agreed-upon* plan. But Hayek ([1944] 2007) also argued that policymaker ignorance would undermine the preliminary goal of *agreeing upon an economic plan*. Policymakers lack the know-how required to secure a sufficient degree of consensus across society with respect to an economic plan *without resort to coercion*. This is why a society that insists on driving the socialist road to its terminus – that drives past the many off-ramps and roundabouts on the road – inevitably ends up in serfdom.

Vague references to the "general welfare" or "public interest" are not criteria upon which the required agreement might be reached. Taken literally, the public interest must encompass the *public's interests*; it "cannot be adequately expressed as a single end, but only as a hierarchy of ends, a comprehensive scale of values in which every need of every person is given its place." The direction of economic activity according to a specific plan assumes "the existence of a complete ethical code in which all the different human values are allotted their due place" (Hayek [1944] 2007, 101).[36] But no sufficiently comprehensive moral code exists to permit the assignment of the particular ends of unique individuals to specific places in the grand scale of values that, if it is to truly serve the welfare of society in *general*, rather than the welfare of only some parts of society, must determine the economic plan. Neither could "any mind comprehend the infinite variety of different needs of different people which compete for the available resources and . . . attach a definite weight to each" (Hayek [1944] 2007, 102).[37]

The uniform moral code presupposed by a comprehensive plan for society's economic activity could only be *enforced*: "this agreement will have to be brought about and a common scale of values will have to be imposed by force and propaganda" (Hayek [1940] 1997, 138). Yet socialism is portrayed by its defenders as a wholly peaceful political philosophy. Hayek's political-epistemological argument, however, is that policymakers are ignorant of peaceful, non-coercive means to deliberately realize the degree of intrasocial consensus required to support a particular economic plan. In particular, policymakers do not know how to convince people to agree with each other on the terms of a central plan; therefore, inasmuch as intrasocial peace is meant to be a concomitant end of socialism, policymakers do not know how to deliberately realize socialism.[38]

To see the point clearly, consider that whether the central plan is decided democratically or dictatorially, there will be resistance to its terms from various quarters – most likely, one imagines, from those classes not favored by the plan, who will have their property re-distributed to those favored by the plan. The question in every such context – whether a majority of eligible voters or a totalitarian dictator decides the central plan – is *what to do about the people who resist*.[39] Recall from the first chapter that, other things equal, the relative weights of the epistemic burdens of competing policy objectives serve to determine the objectives that policymakers pursue. In many, if not most, circumstances, the least epistemically burdensome way to achieve intrasocial consensus concerning a central plan – albeit not a peaceful way – is simply to eliminate the recalcitrant citizens, either via genocide or by otherwise removing their voices from the political arena, or, rather more epistemically burdensome than annihilation of the resisters, if still far less burdensome than somehow realizing intrasocial consensus without coercion, the resisters might be "re-educated" to conform to the central plan via a combination of propaganda, harassment, imprisonment, and torture.[40] Needless to say, the history of centrally planned socialism in practice does not falsify this implication of Hayek's analysis and political-epistemological reasoning.[41]

Of course, this ugly dilemma might be avoided at any time by simply giving up on central planning itself rather than indulging in the coercion required to carry it through, that is, by taking advantage of one of the "many off-ramps and roundabouts on the road" to serfdom. Peaceful socialism requires an adequate degree of consensus, if not unanimity, concerning the central plan; but consensus, much less unanimity, is difficult – perhaps impossible – to achieve in any society of a considerable size that consists of epistemically, ethically, prudentially, and economically diverse individuals.

For Hayek ([1944] 2007, 132–133), economic freedom is a necessary precondition for political freedom. In order to follow one's conscience in political matters – and what else can it mean to be politically free? – this same conscience cannot be co-opted in the interests of others. But this is precisely what is required where individuals are not free to plan their economic activities for themselves. In order to agree upon a centralized plan for the whole economy, a unified scale of values is required, which requires a uniform moral code. Where this uniformity does not exist of its own accord, it must be imposed.[42] Central economic planning means that the moral conscience of any actor who is not content with the central plan must be usurped by that of the planning authority. Thus, the goal of state-socialists everywhere, namely that of thoroughgoing economic planning without diminution of political freedom, cannot be deliberately realized, because we do not know how to achieve adequate agreement on a central plan without assaulting political liberty.

The realization of the typical goals of socialists requires agreement on the terms of a social plan, but no one possesses the know-how required to achieve peaceful consensus with respect to such a plan. In order to deliberately achieve a peaceful socialism effective with respect to the relevant economic plan, before (logically and temporally) policymakers encounter the socialist-calculation problem *per se* – that is, before they confront the epistemic burden of deliberately realizing some agreed-upon plan – they must overcome the epistemic burden of achieving peaceful agreement. In particular, they must know how, that is, they must possess the ability, to mollify those who resist the plan without simply murdering or otherwise coercing them into quiescence. The history of socialism suggests that the required knowledge extends beyond the epistemic capacities of normal human policymakers. The epistemic burden of deliberately realizing peaceful socialism, even of the democratic variety, is heavy, indeed. Perhaps it is impossible to lift.

If, as argued in Chapter 1, their comparative ignorance of the more burdensome knowledge required to deliberately realize relatively ambitious policies incents policymakers into pursuing epistemically simpler policies, then we understand why the history of socialism is littered with instances of policymakers adopting coercive and violent means to secure the required agreement on a central plan. Coercion is comparatively epistemically simple relative to trying to deliberately realize the ends of socialism without resort to coercive means; thus, where these ends are made paramount to peaceful social coexistence, coercion must be the rule.

The epistemic burdens of countercyclical economic policymaking and Keynesian demand management[43]

Hayek also extended political-epistemological reasoning to policymakers in contexts other than the socialistic. Indeed, whether he intended it or not, such reasoning underlies much of Hayek's famous work on the business cycle, including the theory that first made his reputation and informs several of his most powerful arguments against the followers of his great rival, John Maynard Keynes.[44] Hayek ([1975] 2014) directed epistemological arguments against those policymakers who would aim to manage market economies so as to promote continued growth while avoiding both inflation and recession. With this, he extended political-epistemological reasoning to yet another new context and raised the possibility that ignorance might confound economic policymaking even in a (relatively) liberal democracy. Hayek's business cycle arguments emphasized the epistemological difficulties inherent in deliberately realizing via policy means the goal widely believed to be the chief objective of economic policymaking in such an environment, namely that of avoiding extended periods of persistent disequilibrium, that is, episodes of excessive unemployment and/or price inflation.

According to Hayek's (2012a, 2012b) early theory of the cycle, the knowledge required to deliberately maintain economic equilibrium in a money-using economy is not available to the only people – bankers – who could, in principle, act to ensure equilibrium. The subsequent development of Hayek's thought resulted in a theory or, at least, a sketch of one, most clearly articulated in his 1974 Nobel Prize Lecture, "The Pretence of Knowledge" (Hayek [1975] 2014; also see Scheall 2015b) that made political action taken on an inadequate epistemic basis the primary cause of economic disequilibrium. According to this later theory (which I call Hayek's *epistemic theory of industrial fluctuations* [Scheall 2015b]), policymakers cannot acquire the knowledge necessary to improve upon the operations of a spontaneously adjusting price system as an equilibrating mechanism; yet, incented by the conjunction of an appealing, and self-flattering, scientistic methodology and Keynesian-style macroeconomic theory, economic policymakers convince themselves that they can acquire the necessary knowledge. Duped by scientistic methodology into a pretence of knowledge, when they act on this inadequate epistemic basis, their policies actually hinder the operation of the price system as an epistemic mechanism (unless, of course, they are just so preternaturally lucky as to stumble upon an appropriate policy) and tend to interrupt whatever other spontaneous forces might work to facilitate economic coordination.[45]

The role of ignorance in Hayek's early theory of industrial fluctuations

Hayek's early account explains economic disequilibrium in terms of the discombobulating effects that the expansion of unbacked credit has on the delicate links between consumption and production decisions. Credit expansion – a supply of bank loans that exceeds the supply of voluntary savings – or, in Hayek's technical verbiage, a loan rate below the "natural" rate of interest that would equilibrate the demand for loans with the supply of voluntary savings – prevents the re-adjustment of the economy to changes in the economic data.

Hayek's early arguments were directed against the then-popular belief that stabilization of the general price level was both necessary and sufficient to ensure equilibrium, that is, that knowledge of the value of some price index, together with the ability to control its value indirectly via monetary policy, was necessary and sufficient for the purposes of countering cyclical fluctuations.[46] Hayek argued that price-level stabilization was neither necessary nor sufficient for the purposes of countercyclical economic policy.

In effect, Hayek argued that there were both theory and data problems in the study of the complex phenomena of the trade cycle. The prevailing theories were epistemically inadequate and could never be used, even if all of the required data were available, to generate predictions and explanations of sufficient "fullness" to provide policymakers with the degree of social control required to deliberately counter the cycle. But, in any case, the required data were *not* available to economic policymakers. Their know-how, in particular, policymakers' ability to indirectly control economic events via monetary policy, was limited and, moreover, the knowledge of average prices provided by price indices was insufficient. As early as 1925, Hayek ([1925] 1984, 18) wrote that the price-stabilization method "seeks to solve the problem under discussion in what is certainly too simple a fashion." Three years later, Hayek ([1928] 1984, 102) wrote that any attempt to stabilize the general price level as indicated by some index would lead to erroneous signals that would impede the knowledge-coordinating aspects of the price system: such "monetary influences . . . hinder the establishment of the natural price structure."[47] In the last lecture of *Prices and Production*, his early *magnum opus* on business-cycle theory, Hayek ([1931, 1935] 2012a, 266–280) offered further arguments against the belief that price-level stabilization was necessary and sufficient for economic equilibrium.

Instead, Hayek's own positive theory of the cycle led to the conclusion that, in order to neutralize the effects of money on prices, in order to prevent the disequilibrating effects that the injection of new money has on the real economy, the "stream" of circulating currency (i.e., the stock of money multiplied by the velocity of circulation) could not vary, a theoretical conclusion that implied that, in order to counter the cycle, economic policymakers would have to act to deliberately neutralize any change in either the money supply or the velocity of circulation. However, at the same time, Hayek ([1931, 1935] 2012a, 274) emphasized the "enormous" practical difficulties that such a policy would have to overcome to be effective, "difficulties which monetary reformers are always so inclined to underrate." "It is very probable" that strict monetary neutrality "is practically impossible" (Hayek [1931, 1935] 2012a, 282). Not only would policymakers not typically be in an epistemic position to learn about and thus counter changes in the money supply and the velocity of circulation, but securing a constant flow of the money stream would further require complete price and wage flexibility, as well as correct foresight with respect to future price fluctuations. Real-world "frictions" would obstruct the smooth and rapid adaptation of the price system to such changes in the economic data assumed by general equilibrium theory, upon which Hayek's early account of the cycle was based. Such frictions would have to be smoothed in order to achieve monetary neutrality. More exactly, in the real world, policymakers would have to acquire the knowledge necessary to deliberately achieve complete price flexibility and to purposefully ensure that market participants possess correct foresight concerning future price fluctuations. If the conditions required to secure the adaptation of the price system to changed economic circumstances were not first secured, the ideal of monetary neutrality "could not be realized by any kind of monetary policy" (Hayek [1931, 1935] 2012a, 283). In fact, of course, policymakers do not know how to ensure rapid and smooth price adaptations to changes in the data or how to make individuals omniscient with respect to future prices. Monetary neutrality provides no actionable criterion of rational countercyclical policymaking (Hayek [1931, 1935] 2012a, 278–279).[48] Thus, Hayek's early theory of the cycle was driven by his belief in the inadequacy of the knowledge available to economic policymakers in the form of price statistics and the inaccessibility of the relevant knowledge that monetary neutrality requires.

But, more than this, Hayek's own technical-economic explanation attributed industrial fluctuations to a circumstance that he thought common in modern monetary economies, which, in order to facilitate rather than hinder the coordination of production and consumption decisions, would require *knowledge that the relevant actors could not possess*:

> The situation in which the money rate of interest [on loans] is below the natural rate need not . . . originate in a *deliberate lowering* of the rate of interest by the banks. The same effect is obviously produced by an improvement in the expectations of profit or a diminution in the rate of saving, which may drive the "natural rate" (at which the demand for and the supply of savings are equal) above its previous level; while the banks refrain from raising their rate of interest to a proportionate extent, but continue to lend at the previous rate, and thus enable a greater demand for loans to be satisfied than would be possible by the exclusive use of the available supply of savings.
>
> (Hayek [1933] 2012a, 123; italics in the original)

The latter case is important, according to Hayek ([1933] 2012a, 123; italics in the original), not because it is the only way the cycle can manifest on his early theory, but because it is "probably the commonest in practice [and . . .] *must inevitably recur* under the existing credit organization."

The purportedly inevitable recurrence of this case is a consequence of bankers' ignorance of the data necessary to ensure monetary neutrality.[49] Hayek

([1933] 2012a, 131) argued that bankers could not know whether their lending activities constituted the creation of unbacked credit (as the saying goes, "out of thin air") or lending backed by voluntary savings: "[a]s credit created on the basis of additional deposits does not normally appear in the accounts of the same bank that granted the credit, it is fundamentally impossible to distinguish, in individual cases, between" deposits based on savings and those that result from the granting of credit by other banks.[50] The bank that advances a loan is not necessarily the same financial institution that will receive the loaned funds in the form of a deposit. Incoming deposits do not arrive stamped "backed by savings" or "created out of thin air." It is therefore impossible for bankers at the depository institution to know whether they are receiving and subsequently lending on the basis of savings rather than credit. "[T]his consideration rules out, *a priori*, the possibility of bankers limiting the amount of credit granted by them to the amount of 'real' accumulated deposits" (Hayek [1933] 2012a, 131).

Technically, the allegedly unavoidable recurrence of credit creation is a consequence of ignorance *plus* the profit motive. That is, bankers are incented by profit considerations to push lending at least to the limits of their reserves (Hayek [1933] 2012a, 135). Of course, as epistemic burdens serve to determine incentives, while incentives are irrelevant to the determination of epistemic burdens, bankers' ignorance and not their desire for profit is the more fundamental point: if Hayek's argument is sound, then with or without the profit motive – that is, even in a world in which bankers were entirely selfless – so long as the currency was elastic, so long as the money supply could be expanded beyond the available supply of voluntary savings, it would be impossible for epistemic reasons to realize equilibrium between voluntary savings and the demand for loans (Hayek [1933] 2012a, 132). Ulrich Witt (1997, 48) later argued that, for Hayek, "credit expansion is a matter of competitive necessity." It is closer to the truth to say that Hayek made credit expansion a matter of competitive *convenience* but of *epistemic* necessity. This is just the priority of the epistemic applied to the decisions of bankers in the context of an elastic currency.[51]

Even if one rejects the monetary-neutrality theory and subscribes instead to the view that stabilizing the general level of prices is both necessary and sufficient to ensure equilibrium, Hayek would contend that empirical knowledge of the value of a price index could not suffice for the purposes of political administration of equilibrium. No price index could describe the *structure* of relative prices that would counterfactually obtain in equilibrium, which is (part of) the knowledge that economic policymakers in a money-using economy would need to deliberately promote equilibrium.

What Hayek's early theory of the 1930s lacked was a general explanation for the epistemic deficiencies of policymakers.[52] Hayek also lacked a theoretical conception of economic equilibrium (or "order," as he subsequently preferred to call it) that both made sense of and was, in turn, rationalized by his lifelong interest in the limits of human knowledge and their consequences. The Walrasian general equilibrium framework, with its assumption of fully rational

and omniscient market participants, upon which Hayek built his early theory
of the cycle, always rested uncomfortably beside his fallibilist epistemology
(which I explore in more depth in Chapter 4). However, the price theory that
Hayek developed later in the 1930s and 1940s, which started instead from an
assumption of limited and dispersed knowledge among market participants and
showed how a system of spontaneously adjusting prices serves as an epistemic
device to coordinate the bits of knowledge dispersed across individual minds,
fit far more comfortably alongside his epistemology. The result of these developments was a more general political-epistemological argument against countercyclical policymaking.

Hayek's epistemic theory of industrial fluctuations[53]

Hayek essentially quit economic theory and the phenomena of industrial fluctuations as an explicit object of theoretical investigation following the publication of his last major work in technical economics,1941's *The Pure Theory of
Capital* (Hayek [1941] 2007). However, the conjunction of the price theory
that he developed in the 1940s and his later arguments concerning the methods
appropriate to the investigation of complex economic orders implies a broad,
though by no means universal, explanation of economic-cyclical phenomena. Decisions taken on the basis of knowledge that (typically, political) actors
merely pretend to possess or, what in its practical effects is much the same
thing, have deceived themselves into believing they possess, impede the operation of the price system's belief-coordinating function and thereby contribute
to episodes of economic disequilibrium or, better, *disorder*.

Hayek's later theory of industrial fluctuations is *epistemic* in several interre-
lated respects. First, the theory is built upon a conception of economic equilibrium as a condition of well-coordinated knowledge. As Hayek argued in
"Economics and Knowledge" ([1937] 2014), equilibrium (talk of which Hayek
would soon reject in favor of the language of "order") exists to the extent that
the economically relevant beliefs of individual market participants are internally consistent, mutually (i.e., intersubjectively) consistent, and accurate with
respect to other relevant external circumstances. Though a *state* of equilibrium
is a fiction, a *tendency* for the relevant beliefs of economic agents to become
better harmonized operates under normal circumstances: "Experience shows
us that something of this sort does happen, since the empirical observation that
prices tend to correspond to costs was the beginning of our science" (Hayek
[1937] 2014, 73). Thus, Hayek made economic equilibrium ("order") a social-
epistemological concept, a condition concerning the cross-personal coordination of knowledge with relevant circumstances. Hayek's epistemic conception
of equilibrium is "subversive to conventional economics" (Vaughn 2013, 478).
To solve society's economic problem is to discover the various means whereby
this tendency toward equilibrium may be either facilitated or inhibited (Hayek
[1937] 2014, 72–73).

According to Hayek ([1945] 2014), there is an epistemic device that serves
the function of facilitating the cross-personal coordination of knowledge with

relevant circumstances in competitive economies, where individuals plan their own economic activity: the price system communicates to individual market participants much of the knowledge they need to (non-deliberatively) coordinate their beliefs and plans with those of other individuals.[54] "[T]he chief guidance which prices offer is . . . *what to do*" (Hayek [1968] 2014, 311; italics in the original). The price system provides signals that allow individuals to adapt their plans to changes in the data about which they both need to know nothing more than the changed price and would otherwise remain ignorant. Price signals provide knowledge of data, in highly streamlined and economized form, that is necessary for the coordination of dispersed knowledge (Hayek [1945] 2014). However, this epistemic device communicates to policymakers only such data as they need in their own personal, non-political roles as individual market participants to adapt their own personal economic plans to those of other individuals; it does not provide them with knowledge of the data required to deliberately impose and enforce through political action, in a top-down manner, a tendency toward the coordination of dispersed knowledge.

It is clear from Hayek's conceptions of both equilibrium and the price system that whatever encumbers the adjustments of the latter will, other things equal, retard the tendency toward the former. Hayek makes these concepts relevant to the problem of industrial fluctuations with the claim that the price system is frequently so adversely affected because certain decisions – often, but not necessarily, of an economic-political nature – which affect the structure of prices are made on the basis of pretended knowledge. Hayek's explanation of how this pretended knowledge arises and comes to be acted upon concerns the rarely acknowledged and, indeed, frequently, if implicitly, denied epistemic burden of countercyclical economic policymaking, that is, the divide that separates the knowledge that effective political management of economic equilibrium requires and the knowledge that is actually available to policymakers and, especially, the ignorance of policymakers with respect to their ignorance of this latter cleavage. Economic policymakers are *second-order ignorant of their first-order ignorance* – they *don't know that they don't know* how to effectively administer economic equilibrium. Indeed, quite to the contrary, modern economic policymakers typically believe they can acquire the knowledge both necessary and sufficient for effective political management of economic equilibrium – but they are wrong, according to Hayek ([1975] 2014). In keeping with the analysis in Chapter 1, such pretenders to knowledge too easily convince themselves of the adequacy of their knowledge and, consequently, fail to discount such policy pursuits as deeply as their epistemic circumstances would otherwise dictate. Such policymakers "face an epistemically-distorted incentive to pursue particular policy objectives that they would not face, if their second-order knowledge improved enough to permit them to recognize their first-order ignorance" (Chapter 1).

The theories relevant to economic equilibrium – in particular, the Walrasian theory of general equilibrium and the macroeconomic theory (or theories) associated with the followers of Keynes – are meager policy tools, Hayek ([1975] 2014) argued. The Walrasian explanation of general equilibrium *explains* no such thing. The conditions that, for Hayek ([1975] 2014, 364), *constitute* a state of equilibrium are the *assumptions* from which general equilibrium theory proceeds.[55] The problem that confronts economic policymakers is (*inter alia*) how to engender a condition of "[c]omplete knowledge of the relevant factors on the part of all participants in the market" (Hayek [1946] 2014, 107) – that is, economic policymakers must know how to promote a tendency toward a condition in which market participants know everything that they need to coordinate their respective plans. A theory that assumes this condition to hold from the outset, that assumes market participants already know everything they need, is of little practical value to policymakers.[56] The posit that Hayek attributed to Keynes' followers according to which there is a "simple positive correlation between total employment and the size of the aggregate demand for goods and services [, and which] leads to the belief that we can permanently assure full employment by maintaining total money expenditure at an appropriate level" may at best, "only be approximate, but as it is the *only* one on which we have quantitative data, it is accepted as the only causal connection that counts" (Hayek [1975] 2014, 363; italics in the original).[57] Thus, according to Hayek, the theoretical knowledge that effective deliberate political administration of economic equilibrium requires has not yet been discovered. The available theoretical knowledge is not relevant to the problem that confronts economic policymakers, and the relevant theoretical knowledge is not available. The science of the complex phenomena of economic cycles faces a theory problem: it cannot generate predictions full enough for the extent of social control required of effective Keynesian-style demand management.

Whatever the theoretical understanding of policymakers with respect to the economy, the empirical data required are dispersed across and fragmented within the minds of all of the individual market participants (Hayek [1937] 2014, [1945] 2014). This dispersed and fragmented knowledge cannot be conveyed in an easily digestible form to – much less comprehended and properly interpreted by – policymakers:

> [O]ur modern economic system . . . rests on the use of knowledge (and of skills in obtaining relevant information) which no one possesses in its entirety . . . Certainly, we ought not to succumb to the false belief, or delusion, that we can replace it with a different kind of order, which presupposes that all this knowledge can be concentrated in a central brain, or group of brains of any practicable size.
>
> (Hayek [1970] 2014, 347)

It is not possible to measure the degree of discoordination prevailing with respect to people's beliefs relative both to each other and to external circumstances. This requires more direct knowledge of the contents of other people's minds than human beings can achieve. But it is not merely that the knowledge necessary to consciously administer economic equilibrium cannot be acquired by policymakers. As Hayek ([1968] 2014) emphasized in "Competition as a

Discovery Procedure," much of the required knowledge is created by the very competitive process that deliberate economic administration (to some extent) displaces and thus does not exist where it is needed for policymaking purposes. Effective deliberate political administration of economic equilibrium requires that policymakers correctly evaluate multiple complex counterfactuals about events as they would occur in a world in which they do not make the policies that they do. Thus, in part because such empirical knowledge as does exist and is relevant to the problem cannot be communicated, and in part because much of the relevant data do not exist in the absence of the competitive process, policymakers are ignorant of the empirical knowledge that effective political administration of economic equilibrium requires.

Perhaps more importantly, Hayek ([1975] 2014) argued, policymakers are either ignorant of or in denial about this ignorance. That is, policymakers are mistakenly convinced that they both possess an adequate theory and can acquire the relevant data. Policymakers' ignorance of part of the relevant theoretical and empirical considerations is often denied by those "who have hoped that our increasing power of prediction and control, generally regarded as the characteristic result of scientific advance, applied to the processes of society, would soon enable us to mould society entirely to our liking" (Hayek [1975] 2014, 368). Moreover, the attitude of the public toward these same possibilities exacerbates politicians' penchant for denying their manifest ignorance: "so long as the public expects more there will always be some who will pretend, and perhaps honestly believe, that they can do more to meet popular demands than is really in their power" (Hayek [1975] 2014, 369).

The ultimate source of this misplaced optimism is prevailing opinion regarding scientific method (Hayek [1975] 2014, 368). The *scientistic* methodology that holds sway over many macroeconomists, their political advisees, and a large swath of the latter's public constituency treats "as important [that] which happens to be accessible to measurement" (Hayek [1975] 2014, 363). Scientism reifies the techniques of quantitative measurement of the physical sciences to the level of exemplars for all other fields to follow. Scientism is

> an attitude which is decidedly unscientific in the true sense of the word, since it involves a mechanical and uncritical application of habits of thought to fields different from those in which they have been formed. The scientistic as distinguished from the scientific view is not an unprejudiced but a very prejudiced approach which, before it has considered its subject, claims to know what is the most appropriate way of investigating it.
>
> (Hayek 1952 [2010], 80)

On the scientistic approach, the methods of the physical sciences are to be applied in all areas of scientific inquiry without consideration of their aptness for the investigation of non-physical phenomena. The aforementioned macroeconomic theory of Keynes' followers makes the economically relevant variables those that just happen to be measurable. Like a drunk looking for the keys he misplaced elsewhere, defenders of scientism always and only search under the streetlamp, because that's where the light is brightest, even though the keys cannot be found there. Economic policymakers are convinced by the conjunction of scientism and macroeconomic theory that the theoretical understanding required to make management of equilibrium effective is within their cognitive grasp.

Furthermore, the scientistic attitude persuades policymakers that they can also acquire the necessary empirical knowledge in the form of statistical data. In virtue of both its quantitative nature and its very successful application in sciences of less complex phenomena, the statistical method appears the quintessence of scientific virtue. However, statistical data ignore precisely the information that effective countercyclical policymaking requires:

> [i]nformation about aggregates or statistical collectives is of little use for deciding what particular people should do [i.e., how they should adapt their plans to relevant changes in the data] at particular moments which is what they would have to be told by the central authority. The statistician, in order to arrive at his aggregates, must largely abstract from those very details which will decide what particular individuals ought to do.
>
> (Hayek [1961] 2014, 424)[58]

The empirical data available to policymakers are not relevant to the task of the political administration of economic equilibrium.

Blinded by a false methodology, economic policymakers are led into a pretence of knowledge upon which they act, unaware – indeed, convinced otherwise – of the irrelevance and inadequacy of their epistemic position. Policymakers are misled into the false belief that they can possess both the theoretical and empirical knowledge required of effective macroeconomic management by the combination of a methodology that accords special status to measurable parameters, a theory that claims the relevant parameters are those that just happen to be measurable, and the statistical techniques for the analysis of the aggregative variables in which the latter theory trucks. When policymakers pretend to possess the relevant economic knowledge and make policy on the basis of this pretence, their decisions typically impede, either directly or indirectly, the price system's epistemic (i.e., knowledge-coordinating) function:

> [I]n the social fields the erroneous belief that the exercise of some power would have beneficial consequences is likely to lead to a new power to coerce other men being conferred on some authority. Even if such power is not in itself bad, its exercise is likely to impede the functioning of those spontaneous ordering forces by which . . . man is in fact assisted in the pursuit of his aims.
>
> (Hayek [1975] 2014, 371)

It suffices to hamper the operation of the tendency toward equilibrium for those in a position to do so to intervene in the economy on the false assumption that they possess the knowledge required of effective intervention. In acting on a pretence of knowledge, policymakers override the price system's tendency to adapt to changes in economic circumstances. A price system affected, directly or indirectly, by the decisions of policymakers acting under a false pretence of knowledge does a relatively poor job of guiding individual market participants in what they are to do in response to changes in relevant data. Policymakers cannot acquire the knowledge necessary to either imitate or improve upon the effectiveness of the price system in this last regard. The price system, if not artificially manipulated, communicates to individual market participants knowledge necessary for the spontaneous coordination of their respective bits of knowledge. We cannot deliberately facilitate the tendency toward coordination but must leave this goal to the operation of the spontaneous forces embodied in the price system, even if these occasionally break down for non-political reasons. In the present state of knowledge, this is the best we can do given our epistemic limitations, which may be far from optimal in any ideal moral or political sense. Such is Hayek's epistemic theory of industrial fluctuations.[59]

None of this is to say that policymakers might not possess enough knowledge to momentarily improve economic conditions to some degree in the short run. What Hayek denies is that such improvement can be sustained indefinitely. It is an implication of Hayek's early theory of the cycle that, for example, expanding the money supply can temporarily increase production. However, the theory also implies that such a policy sows its own inevitable long-run failure. In any case, it is a straightforward implication of the priority of epistemic burdens to incentives that, since indefinitely maintaining equilibrium is a far more burdensome goal than a one-time fillip to economic activity, the former goal is less likely to be pursued and less likely to be achieved, if pursued, than the latter.

The generality of the reasoning underlying the Austrians' political-epistemological approach

According to Mises' original calculation argument, the effectiveness of central planning in an isolated socialist oasis where the factors of production have been collectivized hinges on the central planner's access to knowledge of factor prices that do not exist in such a context. Central planning would necessarily fail to achieve the vaunted promises of its defenders due to the socialist policymaker's ignorance of knowledge necessary to make it effective. Hayek's contributions to the socialist-calculation debate assumed less extreme political-economic circumstances. Hayek argued that central planners would face insurmountable epistemic burdens even in contexts where factor prices were observable. Indeed, Hayek ultimately extended political-epistemological reasoning far beyond socialist contexts to economic policymakers in a more or less liberal environment, who aim at the more limited goal of avoiding the worst recessionary downturns and inflationary excesses. Hayek's arguments pointed to a general epistemic problem for those engaged in top-down economic management, even where market institutions are present. Hayek's arguments against the possibility of successful economic intervention were all of the same kind: "we are not intellectually equipped to improve the working of our economic system" (Hayek [1935b] 1997, 115).

The Austrians' political–epistemological arguments share some rather obvious features in common. They presuppose a *policy goal*; in particular, they assume the specific goal valued by the policy's advocates. They also presuppose the *policy means* proposed by the policy's defenders for the realization of the goal. They then argue that both *general* (or *theoretical*) knowledge of a certain kind and extent, and *particular* (or *empirical*) knowledge of a certain kind and extent, are necessary for the deliberate realization of the policy goal via the proposed means. And, finally, they argue that these kinds of knowledge will *not* be available to an adequate degree to the persons tasked with applying the proposed policy means to deliberately realize the policy goal. An important corollary of such arguments is that, where the policymaker's ignorance overwhelms the epistemic requirements of the case, the proposed policy goal can be realized only with the assistance of *spontaneous* forces, that is, forces beyond the individual actor's ken and capacities, which, though they may result from human action and interaction, are not deliberately intended by anyone.

Hayek extended this reasoning far beyond the context of the isolated socialist oasis, but he did not extend it as far as it can go. The process of generalizing the Austrians' political–epistemological reasoning across an increasingly broad range of policymaking contexts and policy goals is not yet complete. However, there are no political contexts in which policymaking is not ultimately constrained by the nature and extent of the ignorance of relevant policymakers. The problem of policymaker ignorance potentially manifests in every policymaking situation. Stripped of the particular dress in which it was clothed in the Austrians' specific applications, this reasoning is fully general. The deliberate realization of *every* potential policy goal – whether the goal is effective central planning, maintenance of economic equilibrium, victory in a large-scale military conflict, the safe and fruitful exploration of outer space, health-care or health-insurance reform, regulation of the banking and finance industries, infrastructure design and construction, the provision of healthful dietary guidelines or other public-health directives, or the avoidance of humanity-threatening environmental consequences – ultimately depends on the knowledge possessed by relevant policymakers. In particular, if policymakers are to predict and control events sufficiently well to deliberately realize some policy goal – *any* policy goal – then they need both an adequate theory and enough data to plug into the theory.

Moreover, policymakers are not gods. All policymakers are limited in the knowledge they possess and can acquire via further learning. Thus, only some goals can be deliberately realized via policymaking, and it is always an open question, with respect to a potential policy goal, whether relevant policymakers' knowledge is adequate to its epistemic requirements. It can always be asked whether policymakers know enough to realize the ends that constituents want pursued. It can always be asked whether they know (or can learn) *of* the ends the pursuit of which constituents demand and, if they know of these ends, whether they know (or can learn) how to realize them deliberately, that is, whether they possess knowledge of means adequate to, and thus also the degree of social control required for, their deliberate realization. Furthermore, it can always be asked what might happen if policymakers are ignorant of either the policy goals demanded by constituents or of means sufficient to realize them. If policymakers do not know of the relevant goals, then these goals will be pursued only, as it were, accidentally, that is, only if either policymakers spontaneously stumble upon the goals demanded by their constituents or the goals happen to be those policymakers would pursue anyway, were their constituents' demands immaterial.[60] If policymakers know of the relevant goals but do not know how to realize them, then these goals will not be realized unless spontaneous forces intervene. If constituents' demands are to be satisfied in the presence of policymaker ignorance, spontaneity is required. Finally, the prospects for spontaneous realization of a policy goal, if it is pursued despite the presence of policymaker ignorance, as well as the consequences of its non-realization, can also be investigated.

The generality of the point that the effectiveness of human action is knowledge dependent is by no means restricted to the political realm. It is a fully general fact about planning for action that such planning can deliberately achieve its goals, whatever they might be, only if based on adequate knowledge. The deliberate realization of *goals*, political or otherwise, is always potentially epistemically burdensome, and, in any particular case, whether the goal is the deliberate realization of world peace via political means or your own realization of a personal ambition via means perhaps closer at hand, it is an open question whether the actor can surmount its epistemic burden. There is a problem of policymaker ignorance, but it is merely a specific instance of a fully general *problem of ignorance*.

Reflection and foreshadow

The Austrians' political-epistemological reasoning came to be applied over time to a broader range of policymaking contexts and thus became more generalized. Indeed, taken to its logical extreme, the Austrians' political-epistemological approach ultimately leads to the recognition of a fully general problem of ignorance, one instance of which is the problem of policymaker ignorance that arises in all political contexts.

However, as it is general, the problem of policymaker ignorance arises in political circumstances other than those explicitly considered by Mises and Hayek. Hayek extended and made more general Mises' original calculation argument, but he did not extend the underlying reasoning as far as it could go or note everywhere that it is applicable.

To close Part I of the book, in the next chapter, I argue that the full generality of policymaker ignorance – the fact that it is always an open question, regardless of the relevant policy objective, whether policymakers' knowledge is adequate to the deliberate realization of the objective – leaves the Austrians with a largely unrecognized problem to solve and thus a previously unexamined research program to develop. Most Austrian economists, like Mises and Hayek, defend some variation of classical liberalism and advocate for social and economic liberalization. Austrian political economy supports the notion that comparatively liberal societies better promote the happiness of citizens than less liberal ones. However, as with any policy objective, it is an open question whether policymakers possess the knowledge required to deliberately liberalize society in such a way that these happiness-promoting properties manifest.

There are examples in political history of attempts to liberalize society that did not contribute to improving the happiness of citizens. There are better and worse, more and less effective, ways of liberalizing society. Are policymakers epistemically equipped to deliberately liberalize in the better, more effective ways and avoid the worse, less effective or plainly ineffective ways of liberalizing? What are the consequences for liberalization policies (and for advocacy of liberalization policies) if policymakers are not so equipped? In particular, to the extent that a more liberal, happiness-promoting social order cannot be deliberately realized through political action because relevant policymakers are ignorant of some of the necessary knowledge, what are the prospects that spontaneous forces will intervene to realize such an order? To what extent are spontaneous forces required to realize a society in which spontaneous forces function most effectively? Might the invisible hand of the free market *itself* require the intervention of invisible-hand forces in order to be effectively realized? Political-epistemological reasoning is applicable even to the question of whether the policymaker's knowledge is adequate to the epistemic requirements of liberalization policies. Where would-be liberalizing policymakers confront an insurmountable epistemic burden, effective liberalization cannot be deliberately realized but requires the intervention of spontaneous forces.

Notes

1   Translated and quoted in Brutzkus (1935, 99–100, fn. 1). Brutzkus cites *Moskovsky Rabocy* (Lenin [1917] 1923, 91). The translation of this passage in the *Collected Works* edition of Lenin's *The State and Revolution* available online at the Marxists Internet Archive (www.marxists.org/archive/lenin/works/1917/staterev/ch05.htm#s4) is slightly different (the quotation appears on page 478 of physical copies of Volume 25 of Lenin's *Collected Works* [see Steele 1992, 69]): "the accounting and control necessary for this have been simplified by capitalism to the utmost and reduced to the extraordinarily simple operations – which any literate person can perform – of supervising and recording, knowledge of the four rules of arithmetic, and issuing appropriate receipts" (Lenin [1917] 1960, 478).

2   Relevant to the Lenin epigraph that opens this chapter, the historian Paul Johnson (1983, 94; quoted in Lavoie [1985b] 2016, 228–229) once quipped, "Thus ended, in total failure, the first major experiment in what it was now fashionable to call social engineering. . . . Lenin believed in planning because it was 'scientific'. But he did not know how to do it."

3   Neurath had been an economist at Vienna's *Neue Wiener Handelsakademie* and Director of the Austrian Department of War Economy during World War I and, immediately thereafter, of the Central Economic Planning board of the short-lived (1918–1919)

Bavarian Soviet Republic. Subsequently, upon his return to Vienna, Neurath was a charter member of the *Kreis* that developed around Moritz Schlick – the newly minted chair of *Naturphilosophie* at the University of Vienna – which later became known to the world as the Vienna Circle of Logical Positivism.

4 On the debate about whether socialists, including Karl Marx, ever seriously contemplated central planning without prices, see Lavoie ([1985a] 2015). Lavoie argues that price-less social planning is implicit in Marx and was commonly, if mostly only implicitly, accepted as a necessary element of socialist economics. Indeed, according to Lavoie ([1985a] 2015, 28), "[i]n an important sense Marx's concept of central planning has never actually been abandoned. In its broad outlines, Marx's idea of bringing social production under 'conscious control', rather than leaving it to the whims of the 'anarchic' forces of capitalism" – which is to say, rather than leaving it to an unconscious system of spontaneously adjusting prices – "is still the primary economic *raison d'être* of socialism."

5 "[W]hile Marx didn't say much about economics after the revolution, he did insistently name the state he promised was coming, at history's happy end. He called it 'consciously arranged society'. Acting together, human beings were going to construct for the world a wealth-producing apparatus that far exceeded in efficiency the apparatus formed *ad hoc*, by default, when everyone chaotically scrabbled for survival" (Spufford 2010, 65). Francis Spufford's (2010) ostensibly fictional *Red Plenty* tells the story of the practice of central planning and its consequences better than many factual accounts.

6 See Brutzkus (1935, 32):

> The unitary plan of the socialist economic system is the leading thought of Marxism. With the help of this plan socialism promises not only to take over the highly developed technique of capitalism intact, but hopes also, by further concentration of production and by selecting the most perfect forms of undertakings to raise it to the highest peak of efficiency; and it seeks to achieve a harmony between production and the needs of society which is beyond the reach of capitalism.

7 "To maintain the equilibrium between supply and demand on the market . . . was regarded by the Gosplan [the Soviet economic planning agency] as the most important task of the economic administration" (Brutzkus 1935, 116; see also 130–131). Indeed, at some point in Soviet history, at least "*from the late 1960s on all that the Soviet regime aspired to do was to provide a pacifying minimum of consumer goods to the inhabitants of the vast shoddy apartment buildings ringing every Soviet city. But once upon a time the story of red plenty had been serious: an attempt to beat capitalism on its own terms, and to make Soviet citizens the richest people in the world*" (Spufford 2010, 5; italics in the original).

8 Similar arguments appeared before Mises' socialist calculation argument. Hayek ([1935a] 1997, 68–70) mentions H. H. Gossen (1854) and Edwin Cannan ([1893] 1917) and indicates other partial portents of the debate in Georg Sulzer (1899), Karl Kautsky ([1902] 1907), Nicolaas Pierson ([1902] 1935), and Enrico Barone ([1908] 1935). The latter two contributions are republished in Hayek (1935). Terence Hutchison (1981, 208) names, but doesn't cite, Erwin Nasse, Lujo Brentano, and Albert Schäffle as predecessors and discusses at some length (see Hutchison 1981, 14–16) Friedrich Engels' (1884) recognition of the problem. Moreover, similar arguments against the possibility of rational calculation in a socialist economy were offered independently of, and more or less simultaneously with, Mises' argument by Max Weber (1921) and Boris Brutzkus (1935). See Appendix B of Hayek (1935) for a more comprehensive list of writings relevant to the socialist calculation debates in both German and English.

9 "It is this equilibrating or coordinating tendency, not any alleged achievement of an equilibrium state, that [Mises] claimed as the indispensable advantage of the price system" (Lavoie [1985a] 2015, 56). What socialists needed to show was that "a socialist process of coordination [could] supplant the competitive economy's entrepreneurial equilibration process" (Lavoie [1985a] 2015, 111).

10 As we will see, in response to the criticisms of Mises and others, socialist writers soon proposed different, less extreme means for the deliberate promotion of economic equilibrium in centrally planned economies.

11 "'Did you know that last year more than half of the hosiery delivered to shops was sub-standard?'

> 'Let's say that I had an anecdotal appreciation of that fact, from trying to put some of it on.'
> 'Kostya really knows how to talk to girls, don't you think?' said Valentin. 'No, no, go on: league after league of malformed stockings . . . '
> 'The point being that it was incredibly hard for the stores to send the bad stuff back to the knitting mills, because it all counted towards their output targets. What we need is a planning system that counts the *value* of production rather than the quantity. But that, in turn, requires prices which express the value of what's produced.'
> 'The value to whom?'
> 'Good question,' said Valentin."

(Spufford 2010, 164; italics in the original)

12 "It is true that milk is produced [in the Soviet Union, circa 1920], bread is baked, rolling-stock is repaired, and coal is transported; but no one is able to know how much these processes cost us. This state of affairs necessarily led the economic system to catastrophe, and the catastrophe has come about" (Brutzkus 1935, 13).

13 The current section addresses various elements of Hayek's epistemology that are important to understanding the discussion that follows in the present chapter. Hayek's general theory of knowledge and its significance for political epistemology are the main subjects of Chapter 4.

14 I agree with psychologist Walter Weimer's (1982, 263) view that Hayek was "at all times an epistemologist, especially when doing technical economics, and even in his historical and popular writings."

15 See esp. Hayek ([1937] 2014, [1945] 2014, [1946] 2014, [1962] 2014, and [1967b] 2014).

16 See esp. Hayek ([1952] 2010, [1955] 2014, [1956] 1967, [1964a] 2014, [1964b] 2014, [1967a] 2014, [1968] 2014, [1970] 2014, and [1975] 2014).

17 The following section reproduces, with minor emendations, parts of the argument of Scheall (2015a).

18 A "full" explanation need not be complete in the sense of encompassing every detail of the phenomena under investigation: an explanation "can never explain everything to be observed on a particular set of events" (Hayek 1952, 182). The concept of explanatory "fullness" should be thought of as sensitive to the would-be explainer's purposes and prevailing context.

19 The question why Hayek emphasized the data problem at the expense of the theory problem seems to be bound up with his political-epistemological strategy against both socialists and advocates of countercyclical economic policy. As we will see, Hayek's arguments against these programs emphasized that the data problem sufficed to undermine their effectiveness. Thus, he was able to argue against these policy measures without getting (too) involved in interminable disputes over theoretical *bona fides*. In effect, Hayek's attitude was that, whatever might be said for or against the relevant economic theories *qua* theories, the absence of the required data sufficed to undermine their usefulness as policy instruments.

20 The case in which a full explanation requires theoretical input from a number of disciplines illustrates the theory problem in all its ignominy, but the problem can just as well manifest in sciences where self-contained explanations are possible. All that is necessary (and sufficient) for the theory problem to arise is that, relative to the requirements of a full explanation of the phenomena under investigation, there be gaps in the specification of the causal elements of the theory (or composite system of theories) meant to generate such an explanation.

21 Brutzkus (1935, 38–44; italics added) noted the theory and data problems that socialist administrators confronted in trying to make central planning effective: "Thus the socialist state is not in a position, *even with the help of all its scientific theory and immense statistical apparatus*, to measure the needs of its citizens or to reduce these needs to one level; *for this reason it is unable to provide production with the guidance which it needs.*"

22 In his rejoinder to Hayek's critical review of the *Treatise*, Keynes ([1931] 1973, 252–253) accepted that a treatment of capital would figure in a perfected theory of a money-using economy, but insisted that the theory presented in the *Treatise* was adequate for his scientific purposes at the time. Hayek and Keynes obviously had different conceptions of the requisite "fullness" of a satisfactory, policy-relevant explanation of a money-using economy (or misconceived each other's scientific purposes).

23 See Appendix B of Hayek (1935) for a more comprehensive list of writings relevant to the socialist calculation debates in both German and English.

24 "'I still don't get it,' said Chekuskin. 'Why should the upgrade cost less?'

> 'We didn't get it either,' said Ryszard. 'We asked for clarification. We said, why is our lovely new machine worth less than our old one? And do you know what they said, the *sovnarkhoz* [Regional Economic Soviet]? No? They pointed out that the new one weighs less. They said, and I'm quoting, "Pricing of equipment in the chemical industry is calculated chiefly by weight."'"

(Spufford 2010, 263)

25 According to Lavoie ([1985a] 2015, 93), this is "Hayek's primary argument against the mathematical solution." The fundamental point is not that collecting, interpreting, and so on all of the relevant empirical data would be difficult for policymakers but that "the relevant detailed knowledge of production processes cannot be considered 'given' to the central planning board but rather resides and is continually regenerated in decentralized form throughout the economy." It is not just difficult, but impossible in principle, for central planners to acquire the knowledge necessary to apply the mathematical solution to the calculation problem. Also see Lavoie ([1985b] 2016, 56–57).

26 "To the Austrians, equilibrium implies the complete compatibility of separately made plans with one another through time, evidently a situation that would be a miraculous coincidence in the real world" (Lavoie [1985a] 2015, 65). "We should not expect equilibrium to exist unless all external change had ceased" (Hayek [1935] 1997, 96).

27 It also remains to be determined "just what is supposed to be happening while the planning board is conducting its trials and somehow identifying its errors" (Lavoie [1985a] 2015, 130).

28 Brutzkus (1935, 48) notes that, during the initial Bolshevik experiment with "natural socialism" or "war communism," that is, central planning without reference to prices, in the years (1920–March 1921) immediately following the October Revolution, "only those enterprises in the Soviet republic have retained their vitality which – in spite of very considerable opposition from the authorities – have retained their contact with the free market and have obtained supplies on their own account without relying on the favour of the governing boards." Otherwise, this experiment contributed to the "appalling famine of 1921–2" (Brutzkus 1935, 109). Brutzkus (1935, 94; also see 109) argues that the "renunciation" of this experiment in March 1921 "under the [market-driven, money-based] New Economic Policy led almost without exception to an improvement of the situation." Finally, Brutzkus (1935, 219–222) discusses how the very limited success, such as it was, of the first five-year plans of the Soviet Union hinged on the planners' ability to refer to what limited price data remained in the wake of the end of the N. E. P. in 1928.

29 Hayek ([1935b] 1997, 98, fn 9) referred to the work of the British Marxian economist Maurice Dobb (1933).

30 See also Durbin ([1936] 1968) and Lerner (1937, 1938, and 1944).

31 Related to this, note Lavoie's ([1985a] 2015, 122, fn. 3) perceptive point that

> [a]lthough all of the market socialists casually employ the terminology of "supply and demand", none of them explicitly offers any explanation of the basis upon which individuals who own no title to the means of production are supposed to express "demand" for [or, for that matter, "offer a supply" of] factors. To simply assert that socialist managers should act so as to equate supplies and demands is to gloss over the underlying legal framework within which supply and demand have meaning.

32 The same criticism applies to the mathematical solution, which assumes that knowledge of the coefficients that would attach to the variables of the Walrasian system of simultaneous equations in equilibrium is given to the central planner. In fact, these parameters would have to be discovered empirically, an impossibility where equilibrium does not already exist. The main problem with the mathematical solution "was *formulating* the equations – not solving them" (Lavoie [1985a] 2015, 91).

33 The market socialists falsely assumed that "all of the information required for general equilibrium except the correct prices" was given to the central planner and that plant managers could easily acquire the missing price knowledge by reading "from known cost curves the optimal quantities . . . to produce to equate . . . marginal costs" with the product's selling price (Lavoie [1985a] 2015, 123; also 160–161).

34 "There is no evidence to show that the socialist economic plan, even when based on a money system, is able to meet the requirements of the masses in a normal way. On the other hand, there is evidence that such a system can, more easily than any other, be misused to achieve non-economic aims while shelving entirely the problem of maintaining the nation's supplies," that is, while ignoring the problem of satisfying consumer demand (Brutzkus 1935, 234).

35 Hayek's arguments against market socialism raise "issues that are far more general than the question of the workability of these particular schemes" (Lavoie [1985a] 2015, 170).

    See Burczak (2006, 5–11) for a discussion of several modern theories of socialism that fail to adequately confront Hayek's epistemic critique. Unlike many socialist writers, Burczak (2006, 138) takes Hayek's epistemological criticism of central planning seriously and aims to develop a socialism immune to it: "[n]ational economic planning, whether authoritarian or democratic, is a dubious ambition for the future of socialism."

> Because the Right has appropriated Hayek's thought in defense of small government capitalism, those of other political persuasions . . . tend to dismiss Hayek's ideas as reactionary. But this dismissal is a mistake. . . . For Hayek, the knowledge of economic actors is beset with error, uncertainty, social prejudice, and subjective perception. So, too, is the knowledge of government officials. And so is the knowledge of the economic theorist. It is precisely Hayek's . . . skepticism about the attainability of objective knowledge and his corresponding rejection of a scientistic understanding of society that place the biggest obstacles in the way of classical forms of socialism based on government planning or government control of the market. Socialists and other advocates of government activism in the economy ignore Hayek's insights at their intellectual peril.
>
> (Burczak 2006, 1–2)

36 "Socialists often talked of a social goal or 'common purpose' around which society is to be organized. However, such talk about the 'common good', 'general welfare', or 'general interest' could not possibly prescribe a *definite meaning*, or indicate a particular course of action. One cannot substitute a single scale of greater or lesser for a definite meaning. Happiness and welfare of people and individuals depends on an infinite variety of combinations" (Francis 1985, 79).

37 "There is . . . no uncontroversial definition of a just distribution of resources. Whenever government officials attempt to alter the distribution of income or wealth, they are imposing their subjective value judgments on others, rather than acting in the common

interest. In other words, Hayek thinks that there is an ethical knowledge problem that stands in the way of a rationally constructed welfare state" (Burczak 2006, 2).

38 Hayek (see esp. 1976) offered in a number of places a similar argument against the possibility of intrasocial consensus on a particular conception of "social justice" (he always put the phrase in scare quotes for a reason) upon which a fairer distribution of society's wealth might be based. In the real world, there are many different and mutually inconsistent conceptions of social justice, so that the pursuit of any one such conception would necessarily mean the disappointment of some others.

39 "If the general plan is to succeed, it is not sufficient that the budget shall be rightly handled; the entire life of the people must be subjugated to the plan . . . no group interests or private interests may be permitted to come into conflict with the all-powerful state" (Brutzkus 1935, 133).

40 *Baggy two-piece suits are not the obvious costume for philosopher kings: but that, in theory, was what the apparatchiks who ruled the Soviet Union in the 1960s were supposed to be. Lenin's state made the same bet that Plato had twenty-five centuries earlier, when he proposed that enlightened intelligence given absolute powers would serve the public good better than the grubby politicking of republics.*

> *But the Soviet experiment had run into exactly the difficulty that Plato's admirers encountered, back in the fifth century BC, when they attempted to mould philosophical monarchies for Syracuse and Macedonia. The recipe called for rule by heavily-armed virtue – or in the Leninist case, not exactly virtue, but a sort of intentionally post-ethical counterpart to it, self-righteously brutal. Wisdom was to be set aside where it could be ruthless. Once such a system existed, though, the qualities required to rise in it had much more to do with ruthlessness than wisdom. Lenin's original core of Bolsheviks, and the socialists like Trotsky who joined them, were many of them highly educated people, literate in multiple European languages, learned in the scholastic traditions of Marxism; and they preserved these attributes even as they murdered and lied and tortured and terrorized. They were social scientists who thought principle required them to behave like gangsters. But their successors – the vydizhentsy who refilled the Central Committee in the thirties – were not the most selfless people in Soviet society, or the most principled, or the most scrupulous. They were the most ambitious, the most domineering, the most manipulative, the most greedy, the most sycophantic; people whose adherence to Bolshevik ideas was inseparable from the power that came with them. Gradually their loyalty to the ideas became more and more instrumental, more and more a matter of what the ideas would let them grip in their two hands.*
>
> (Spufford 2010, 269, 271–272; italics in the original)

41 As is well known, in the first decade or so of the Soviet Union, and especially in the first five-year plan of 1928–1933, it was peasant farmers who most resisted, first attempts to build up heavy industry on their backs and second the collectivization of agriculture (see Brutzkus 1935, Part Two, Chapter Three), and who most suffered as a consequence:

> The most important task remained – that of bringing the middle-class peasants into the collectives. These however would never have given up their own farms voluntarily. Only by force could the government achieve its purpose, and Stalin ventured on this perilous course. On January 6th, 1930, the political bureaus decided to collectivise the Steppe area by spring, and the other areas at a more moderate rate. Twenty-five thousand reliable communists were sent into the country armed with unlimited powers. According to their secret instructions, the well-to-do peasants and all who opposed collectivisation were to be turned out of their farms into the snow; they were to be transported to the marshy forests of North Russia and Siberia to do forced labour (forestry, road-making, canal-building, and so on). Anyone who offered resistance was to be shot at once, without reference to the central authorities. This was called "Dekulakisation" . . . Nevertheless, there was [still] a certain amount of resistance, both passive and active.
>
> (Brutzkus 1935, 155–156)

The "dekulaked" peasants who were not killed, of course, were made forced laborers or, less euphemistically, *slaves*. Unfortunately, despite the brutality of collectivization, "the Steppe regions and the whole of the Ukraine were [in 1932–3] plunged in famine such as had not been experienced in Soviet Russia since 1921–2," an earlier famine itself caused by the disastrous experiment with money-less "natural socialism" that followed the October Revolution. In 1932, "free market trading in agricultural products was once more permitted" (Brutzkus 1935, 184). Also see Figes ([1996] 2017, esp. Chapter 14, Section 3, and Chapter 16, Section 2).

42 "[A] genuine altruism, which is not only conceivable but indeed only possible in a free society, is quite inconsistent with the promotion of a 'social morality' by coercive law" (Barry 1979, 55).

43 The present section reproduces parts of Scheall (2015b), with various modifications.

44 Hayek's early writings on the business cycle are anthologized in Hayek (2012a and 2012b). Vital sources in the extensive secondary literature on Hayek's theory of the trade cycle include O'Driscoll (1977), Haberler (1986), Steele (1992), Cottrell (1994), Colonna and Hagemann (1994), Garrison (2000), and Klausinger (2012a and 2012b).

45 "[S]uch influence as a government can exert within a market will, *except by accident*, be discoordinating" (Lavoie [1985b] 2016, 49, fn. 15; italics added).

46 See White (1999a, 110): "Hayek's early work, up to and including *Prices and Production*, aimed at providing a theoretically well-grounded critique of the dominant monetary policy prescription of the day . . . The error of the price-stabilization program was not just an abstract theoretical issue. Hayek believed that the program was inspiring the Bank of England and the U.S. Federal Reserve System between 1925 and 1929 in a harmful and ultimately futile joint effort at monetary expansion to prevent the fall in prices that should have accompanied the outflow of gold from Britain and the rapid growth of real output in the U.S. economy. Hayek subsequently considered the deep crisis of 1929–32 to have been the inevitable reaction."

47 Hayek ([1976, 1978] 1990) eventually came around to the price-level stabilization argument, albeit with a typically idiosyncratic twist that emphasized the epistemic features of his particular proposal. In particular, he "advocated allowing private firms to issue fiat-type monies chiefly on the grounds that a system of competitive issuers would more effectively achieve price-level stability than would a central bank" (White 1999a, 117). In other words, Hayek came to believe that the price level might be an effective tool for the maintenance of economic equilibrium in the context of competitive issuers of money, where individual users of money would be free to search for the issuers of the most reliable circulating medium, but that the price level remained an inadequate tool when wielded by a central authority with a monopoly on the issuance of money. This said, as White (1999a, 117) points out, Hayek discussed price-level stabilization as perhaps the most *practicable* policy norm as early as 1933 (see Hayek [1933] 1984), though, for the reasons emphasized elsewhere in his early business cycle work, stabilization was neither necessary nor sufficient for equilibrium. In any case, though Hayek modified his view regarding stabilization schemes, it is significant for our purposes to note that he apparently did so for epistemic reasons. His proposal for the issuance of fiat monies by private firms would facilitate "foresight, calculation, and accounting" (Hayek [1976, 1978] 1990, 73).

48 "[N]eutrality of money was a policy goal in a world in which these assumptions did not and could not apply" (O'Driscoll 1977, 55).

49 White (1999b) argues that the alleged inevitability of this case is dubious. Be this as it may, I am less interested here in the correctness of Hayek's early theory than in the causal role that it assigns to action taken on an inadequate epistemic basis in generating fluctuations in economic activity.

50 Also see Hayek ([1929] 1984, 192).

51 The preceding analysis assumes a context without a central bank. Where there is a central bank, in order for central bankers to prevent the cycle, they would have to know

the value of the natural rate of interest. However, the natural rate is a merely theoretical figure, and its value at any given time and place is empirically unknowable. Where the currency is elastic, knowledge of the natural rate would mean evaluating an unknowable counterfactual, that is, in effect, the rate of interest that would obtain were the currency not elastic and, therefore, the supply of loanable funds identical with the extent of voluntary savings.

52 Hayek "began a project on scientific methodology in the early 1940s, and he has moved further in this direction in his interests ever since. His Nobel Laureate lecture [i.e., "The Pretence of Knowledge"] represents the culmination of this intellectual phase. Nowhere else has he more clearly spelled out his disagreement with macroeconomic thinking as fundamental and methodological" (O'Driscoll 1977, 140–141). In my own estimation, Hayek's Nobel lecture is the apotheosis of his thought.

53 The current section explicates a mere sketch of an epistemic theory of industrial fluctuations that can be cobbled together from several of Hayek's writings, some seemingly disparate. It is no part of the argument that Hayek *intended* to construct an epistemic theory of the cycle.

54 Knowledge of relevant prices is necessary but, of course, not sufficient for the adaptation of individual plans to changing circumstances. The operation of the tendency toward equilibrium also requires that market participants possess knowledge of relevant natural phenomena, knowledge of the given social- and legal-institutional context, as well as some knowledge of their fellow market participants and of other external circumstances (Hayek [1961] 2014).

55 "Hayek believed that his contemporaries were not always in touch with the 'fictions' and limitations inherent in general equilibrium theory and were prone to confuse statements about equilibrium with the theory of the approach to equilibrium" (O'Driscoll 1977, 19; also see Zappia 1999).

56 Of course, as we have seen, this same criticism applies equally to Hayek's own early theory of the cycle, which was built on general equilibrium assumptions.

57 Whether this postulate can also be attributed to Keynes himself is at least doubtable. Indeed, there are many respects in which Keynes' conception of economic phenomena as complex is remarkably similar to Hayek's. See Hoover (2006, 92): "Keynes' vision of the economy is that it is complex and our knowledge of it is bound to be incomplete and frequently qualitative only . . . Keynes would have [been skeptical of] the 'Keynesian' efforts to use macroeconometric models to 'fine-tune' the economy."

58 Hayek long argued against the causal import of economic aggregates. In his original review of Keynes' *Treatise of Money*, Hayek ([1931a] 1995, 128) argued that "Mr. Keynes' aggregates conceal the most fundamental mechanisms of change." His view remained unchanged 35 years later: "the artificial simplification necessary for macro-theory . . . tends to conceal nearly all that really matters" (Hayek [1966] 1978, 289, also 285–286). On Hayek's attitude toward aggregation, see Repapis (2011, 706–707).

59 In her excellent chapter on Keynes in a recent anthology of brief biographies of great economists, Victoria Bateman (2018, 149; italics added) beautifully summarizes the problem of policymaker ignorance that confronts true-believing Keynesians:

> [W]hilst Austrian economists in many ways agree with Keynes that the future is unknowable, they argue that it is just as unknowable to the policymaker as it is to the private sector. Trusting in government to guide investment in the economy could therefore very easily take us in the wrong direction. . . . The policymaker cannot tell what the future holds and so may end up ploughing taxpayers' money into a series of white elephant projects. Whilst economists working in the standard free-market tradition questioned the motives of policymakers and politicians, with public choice theory showing that they cannot be assumed to be benevolent, it is policymakers' inability to predict the future that presents just as much of an obstacle to the practical application of Keynesian thinking, according to the Austrian School. *Even if the state*

is *trustworthy and uncorrupt, it cannot be expected to know what the future holds.* Whilst Keynes presented a believable attack on the market, he did not accompany it with a convincing enough case that governments can do much better.

60 Recall from Chapter 1 that, if we adopt Hume's methodological maxim and assume that all policymakers are knaves, then cases in which policymakers actually pursue the goals demanded by their constituents can be explained only in terms of the coincidence of interests of constituents and a bunch of selfish knaves.

3   Liberalism and the problem of policymaker ignorance

Only fools believe that they know all, but there are many.
— F. A. Hayek, *Law, Legislation and Liberty* (1979, 130)

The full generality of the problem of policymaker ignorance represents both opportunity and discomfiture for the Austrian School. It is an opportunity to extend the political-epistemological approach to policy goals and policymaking contexts that have previously escaped their notice as relevant targets of political-epistemological reasoning. It is the main business of the second part of the book to argue for the relevance of Hayekian ideas to a scientific analysis and, perhaps ultimately, even to the practical mitigation of the problem of policymaker ignorance and its consequences. However, it is also a discomfiture for the Austrians that among the policy goals and policymaking contexts to which their political-epistemological approach still must be applied are those associated with the political liberalism that they nearly all defend, seemingly without fully appreciating the epistemic burdens inherent in effective political and economic liberalism. Austrian economists, and indeed Hayek himself, have offered defenses of liberal political systems founded on the relative epistemic simplicity of policymaking *within* liberal contexts.[1] What they have not shown is that policymakers possess the knowledge required to deliberately realize an effective liberal order; neither have they shown that, in the presence of policymaker ignorance, extant spontaneous forces are likely to manifest such an order. Thus, from a political-epistemological perspective, the Austrian argument for liberalism floats in the air, unmoored from any reason to think an effective liberal order is epistemically plausible. The Austrians seem to have a well-grounded political-epistemological argument against socialism, but this is not the same thing as a well-grounded political-epistemological argument for liberalism.

If one of the marks of liberal political systems is that fewer and typically less challenging tasks are assigned to policymakers in liberal political environments, that is, that more and comparatively more difficult tasks are left to spontaneous forces in liberal societies, then it follows as a matter of course that policymaking is less epistemically burdensome – requires less and generally more easily acquired knowledge – in comparatively liberal contexts. There is less that policymakers need to know to deliberately realize the relatively few and less challenging tasks assigned to them. As far as it goes, I have nothing to say against this defense of liberalism, which really just draws out the logical implications of the different scopes and scales of the tasks assigned to policymakers in political contexts of varying degrees of liberality. However, I will argue that this defense does not go very far at all. It is at best an incomplete defense of liberalism, which ultimately neglects much of the significance of the Austrians' own political-epistemological approach.

In the present chapter, I argue that the epistemic burdens of effective liberalism are of two basic kinds.

First, there are those epistemic burdens that, starting from a relatively illiberal context, would-be liberalizing policymakers must overcome in order to realize an effective liberal order. From a political-epistemological standpoint, a complete defense of liberalism (indeed, of any political system) requires more than establishing the relative epistemic simplicity of policymaking *within* such a system; it must be shown that a political system of the relevant kind can be realized through some combination of deliberate policymaking and spontaneous forces. Without such an argument – which Austrian economists and liberals more generally do *not* have – the case for liberalism (or whatever) is left ungrounded. In effect, the Austrians are left in the same position with respect to an effective liberal order as their socialist rivals are with regard to an effective centrally planned economy: with few reasons for thinking such a system a practicable, real-world possibility. That policymaking is less epistemically burdensome in more liberal contexts is immaterial if there is no reason to think such contexts can be realized, because policymakers' epistemic burdens are too heavy for, and extant spontaneous forces inadequate to, their realization. Liberals need a theory of *liberal transitions*, that is, a theory of how more liberal contexts can be realized starting from relatively illiberal circumstances through a combination of deliberate policy action and spontaneous forces.

Second, there are those epistemic burdens that policymakers within liberal orders must overcome in order to maintain the effectiveness of the existing order. I suggest that the long-term effectiveness of a liberal order hinges on policymakers acquiring the know-how necessary to maintain in perpetuity the rule of law, one of the fundamental institutional conditions of an effective liberal order; however, those who succeed in acquiring wealth and power in an institutional environment of the rule of law, private-property rights, and competitive markets are often able to abrogate the rule of law in their own favor, while those less successful and less powerful remain subject to it, a circumstance that quite naturally fosters resentment and undermines belief in such institutions among the latter classes and tends to eventually lead to calls for the replacement of liberal social institutions with less liberal ones. In order to sustain an effective liberal order, policymakers must surmount the epistemic burden of acquiring the know-how necessary to avoid this outcome.

I argue that Austrians have not paid adequate attention to these epistemic burdens. Indeed, it is not clear that Austrian economists have yet recognized just how burdensome policymaking of the liberalizing and liberal order-sustaining varieties can be. However, the fact that the Austrians' political-epistemological approach is applicable to the liberal political systems they themselves prefer and thus suggests a lacuna in their case for liberalism is no argument for *il*liberal government. If the problem of policymaker ignorance is a problem for liberals, it is no less a problem for defenders of other political systems, within which policymakers' epistemic burdens are necessarily much heavier, because of the more extensive and more difficult objectives they are charged with deliberately realizing in less liberal contexts. Methods of analyzing the extent to which policymaker ignorance is a problem and the possibilities for its real-world mitigation in various political contexts are addressed in Part II of the book. Suffice it to say for the present moment that, in advance of the empirical analyses required to determine policymakers' epistemic burdens in particular contexts – that is, in the absence of evidence that policymakers possess the knowledge required to realize some policy objective – neither liberalism nor illiberalism but *skepticism* – in the Humean sense of unbelief/agnosticism rather than positive disbelief/atheism – is the ideological implication of the problem of policymaker ignorance. If you have not been shown that policymakers can realize some goal, why would you believe that they can?

The epistemic burdens of realizing an effective liberal order: the problem of the epistemic requirements of liberal transitions

If I am right that there is a general problem of ignorance that attaches to human action in all contexts, a particular instance of which is the problem of policymaker ignorance that is potentially relevant in every political context, regardless of the policy goal or the policymakers, then it is an open question whether policymakers possess the knowledge required to realize the policy goals that Austrians themselves advocate. Of course, most relevant in this respect is the goal, apparently universally shared by Austrian-School economists, of creating a more liberal society in the classical sense of "liberal," that is, in the sense of limited government under the rule of law, respectful of individual freedom and the congeries of rights associated with the ownership and transfer of private property. Austrians differ among themselves with regard to how far individual freedom should be given free rein – there are small-government classical liberals, minimal-state libertarians, and no-government anarcho-capitalists within their ranks – but it is fair to say that all Austrians desire, at least, and many of them advocate for, a more liberal society than can presently be found anywhere.

Like any other policy goal, if it is realizable, a more liberal society can be realized either via political action, spontaneous forces, or a combination of purposeful policymaking and spontaneity. Like any other policy goal, the deliberate realization of a more liberal society requires that policymakers who would aim to bring it about possess knowledge adequate to its realization. If would-be liberalizing policymakers' epistemic capacities are inadequate to the deliberate realization of a more liberal society, then, if such a society can be realized at all, spontaneous forces must intervene. That is, spontaneous forces of some kind and to some extent may be required to realize a liberal order in which spontaneous forces function most effectively; in order to achieve a well-functioning invisible hand that effectively channels private interest into the public's welfare, invisible-hand forces may need to already be present in society to some degree.

There are reasons to think that deliberately creating an effective liberal order is more epistemically burdensome than many liberals recognize. *Effective* liberalization – that is, liberalizing policies that manifest the happiness-promoting properties that Austrians and other liberals commonly ascribe to well-ordered liberal societies – is not necessarily as simple as instituting the rule of law, assigning property rights, and removing barriers to free exchange. More exactly, such institutions might be created where they have not previously existed, but whether they ultimately promote the happiness of the people involved or contribute instead to social disorder seems to depend crucially on various cultural prerequisites, on a certain historical preparedness to receive liberal institutions so that their prosperity- and happiness-generating properties fruitfully emerge.

There are several examples in recent political history of attempts to liberalize society that have not been conducive to the satisfaction of relevant constituents. There would seem to be better and worse, more and less effective – indeed, plainly *ineffective* – ways of liberalizing society.[2] Foremost among ineffective liberalizing strategies seems to be the long- and oft-practiced one of forcing the social institutions of liberalism upon societies ill conditioned to receive them. As the 21st-century American experience in countries like Afghanistan (and the 19th-century British experience in Afghanistan) and Iraq seems to indicate, making an effective liberal order is not a simple matter where these prerequisites do not exist. The liberalization, such as it was, of many former Soviet bloc countries left much for the committed liberal to desire. The social institutions that underlie an effective liberal order seem to manifest their happiness-promoting properties only where certain kinds of historical experiences precede them.

I do not mean to suggest that Austrian economists are unaware of this problem. Indeed, their frequent scientific allies and collaborators in economic history, and the experimental and New Institutionalist schools of economics – Deirdre McCloskey (2007, 2011, 2017), William Easterly (2002, 2006, 2015), and the Nobel Prize winners Vernon Smith (2008) and Douglass North (1982, 1990, 2010) come to mind, in particular – have probably done more than even anti-liberals to highlight the sensitivity of the effectiveness of liberalism to institutional context. Whatever might be said about Austrians of earlier generations prior to the fall of communism and the liberalizations, such as they were, of the 1990s, most of today's Austrian economists acknowledge that liberal government cannot just be dropped down from on high into any institutional context, come what may, and be expected to function effectively.

What Austrians have not recognized, however, is that their political-epistemological approach is relevant to this problem and that such an analysis complicates their own case for liberalism. Indeed, it is not obvious that would-be liberalizing policymakers are any better epistemically equipped to deliberately realize an effective liberal order than socialist central planners are epistemically equipped to deliberately coordinate supply and demand. In both cases, policymakers require knowledge that they may not be able to access in the circumstances in which they need it. In both cases, the relevant goal may be realizable only if the appropriate kind of spontaneous forces intervene to an adequate degree.

Policymaking always occurs *in medias res*, in a *given* context that policymakers must take as they find it. It may be that life is wonderful for everyone, policymakers included, in the centrally planned utopia of socialists' dreams, but this fact is of no use to the policymaker who would try to create such a world starting from decidedly non-utopian conditions. Likewise, it may well be that policymaking is less epistemically burdensome *inside* liberal contexts than outside them, but this fact is not of much use to the policymaker who, starting from outside a liberal environment, would seek to create one.

Many liberals, some even within Austrian circles (most famously Murray Rothbard [1982]), though not Hayek himself, have seemed to think that, regardless of the existing cultural context, creating an effective liberal order is as simple as instituting certain principles of social interaction, which they call "natural rights," without a hint of irony or recognition of the historical fact that such rights have actually proven capable of manifesting an effective liberal order only under unique cultural circumstances. The non-aggression principle is all well and good given circumstances conducive to mutual respect between persons conceived as autonomous individuals. It is less "natural" under circumstances the inhabitants of which have never known such a conception. A system of natural rights (for certain classes of persons) might have manifested something like an effective liberal order in 18th-century America; it is less obvious what might have followed from a system of natural rights instituted in, say, a community in the path of the 13th-century Mongol horde.

Related to this, Hayek (1961 [2014], 412–413) was early to note many of the problems with the transfer of technologies from more to less developed countries (see McGinn 1990, 200–201). He argued that the advanced technologies of modern industrial societies could not simply be successfully imitated in less developed countries, if the technologies were ill adapted to the epistemic, economic, and other cultural circumstances of the importing country. If this is right, then inasmuch as systems of political rights or political systems more generally can be assimilated to technologies – tools to facilitate human interaction with the environment – it follows that the effectiveness of different political systems is likewise sensitive to such cultural-contextual circumstances.

Where liberalization is the relevant goal of policy action, unless they are to rely on spontaneous forces, policymakers must possess knowledge of means adequate to deliberately realize an effective liberal order. However, the adequacy of the means by which it is typically supposed such an order might be created, namely by instituting the appropriate array of social institutions, the rule of law, private-property rights, markets, and so on, depends on the appropriate cultural prerequisites being in place. Thus, to deliberately realize an effective liberal order, the policymaker needs to know that these cultural prerequisites obtain. More carefully, on the assumption that policymakers possess the general or theoretical knowledge provided by traditional liberal political theory, according to which these are the appropriate social institutions for effective liberalism, policymakers still need the required particular or empirical knowledge that the cultural circumstances of their time and place are apt for these institutions to manifest the prosperity- and happiness-generating properties liberals claim for them. Where would-be liberalizing policymakers do not know how far the cultural prerequisites of an effective liberal order obtain in the given context, attempts to liberalize are potentially quite hazardous, as much recent history shows. Unless policymakers know that the given context to which the cultural history of a society has led is such that introducing or expanding the institutions of liberalism will manifest their happiness-promoting qualities, they will not be able to deliberately realize such a liberal order. Just like socialist central planners, would-be liberalizing policymakers need data adequate to their task – in particular, they need knowledge of the prevailing cultural circumstances of their time and place – and, without these data, they cannot reasonably be expected to deliberately realize the relevant goal. In the absence of the required knowledge, an effective liberal order could be realized only if either policymakers got lucky and the necessary cultural prerequisites obtained, or emerged spontaneously, despite their ignorance.

Would-be liberalizing policymakers might instead know that the prerequisites of an effective liberal order do *not* obtain in the given context, that is, that the prevailing cultural circumstances are not conducive to the realization of an effective liberal order via the standard institutional means. If they know *this*, then, insofar as they also possess the theoretical knowledge provided by traditional liberal political theory and are committed to pursuing liberalization come what may, they also know that the required cultural pre-conditions will first have to be realized, a potentially quite epistemically burdensome goal, before they might, from this future more fruitful context, create an effective liberal order via the normal institutional means. Under such circumstances, policymakers already possess much of the required knowledge concerning the inaptness of their given circumstances for effective liberalization policies. That is, they have a theory that describes what appropriate circumstances would look like and can observe that such circumstances do not obtain. What they would appear to lack is a theory of how the required cultural pre-conditions can be realized that conduce to the eventual deliberate realization of liberalism via the standard institutional means, beginning from cultural circumstances that are not so conducive. They need a theory adequate to create conditions in which the rule of law, private-property rights, and so on might be instituted such that social harmony and economic prosperity will follow. If policymakers lack the knowledge required to deliberately create the cultural prerequisites of effective liberalization policies, these pre-conditions will manifest only if spontaneous forces intervene.

In short, would-be liberalizing policymakers always confront the same problem: they occupy an epistemic environment more burdensome than the one they aim to realize; thus, though their epistemic circumstances might be improved if they could bring about a more liberal order, they may not be able to acquire the necessary knowledge. Defenders of liberalism need to do more than merely extol the virtues of life inside a liberal order; they also need to show that such an order might be realized in actual fact. Ultimately, this is no more than an application to their preferred liberalism of what Austrians themselves demand from socialists: do not tell us how wonderful life will be in the perfected socialist (liberal) commonwealth, show us how to get there from here – or shut up!

There are many unanswered questions that those inclined to accept the happiness- and prosperity-generating properties of effective liberalism must address. How to create a more liberal order starting from a relatively illiberal environment? How to realize a world in which spontaneous forces operate most effectively, beginning from a world in which obstacles may exist to the effective operation of spontaneous forces? How to create and enforce a rule-of-law system, starting from circumstances where the rule of law either has not previously existed or has existed but been routinely abrogated? How to create a political system in which rent seeking is minimized, beginning from a system in which rent seeking is widespread? How to create a "robust" political system, when the existing system is not robust, but "fragile"? Colloquially expressed, the would-be liberalizer always confronts the problem of *the knowledge required to get there (a more liberal environment) from here (a less liberal context)*. It is not difficult to imagine a free-market society without (or with minimal) government intervention, but unless one is just going to leave it to luck, fortune, and any other extant spontaneous forces, such a society cannot be realized without deliberate action on the part of policymakers, and this means that policymaker ignorance is a potential problem to be overcome if such a society is to be realized.

There is a problem of the epistemic requirements of liberal transitions, that is, of social transformations from less liberal to more liberal contexts. More to the point, Austrian-School economists do not seem to fully appreciate this problem, much less have they developed a theoretical analysis of or a practical solution to it, though I will argue in the second part of the book that they possess many of the tools necessary to make a start on such a project.

The artificiality of the assumption of the committed liberalizer

For present purposes, I have assumed policymakers committed to pursuing liberalization policies, come what may. Of course, this is an artificial assumption, because – as we know by now – first- and second-order ignorance with respect to effective liberalization policies will distort would-be liberalizing policymakers' incentives to pursue them. If policymakers recognize their ignorance – if they are second-order knowledgeable about their first-order ignorance – with respect to creating an effective liberal order, and if they thus recognize that attempts to create such an order are likely to end in failure, they will be less incented to pursue this goal, other things equal, relative to other policy pursuits with respect to which they take themselves to be less ignorant. This explains the frequently observed tendency for policymakers who promise liberalizing, government-limiting, freedom-enhancing policies during their election campaigns to pursue other policies once in office. Indeed, it contributes to an explanation of the general tendency for elected officials to ignore their campaign promises, whatever they might be, once in office. To the extent that earnestly attempting to follow through on their promises is epistemically burdensome for policymakers relative to other potential policy pursuits, for example, engaging in a bit of political window-dressing to make it appear that they are trying realize their promises, we are likely to observe more theatrical political playacting than earnest political promise-keeping.

On the other hand, if would-be liberalizing policymakers are ignorant of their ignorance with respect to effective liberalization policies – if they merely pretend to the required knowledge – they will fail to discount the pursuit of a liberal order as deeply as their impoverished first-order epistemic circumstances would otherwise dictate and may well rush headlong into liberalization policies destined to fail to manifest an effective, happiness-promoting, liberal order. It seems fair to say that this describes the epistemic circumstances of the unreflective gung-ho liberalizers of the post-Soviet 1990s, who did not know that they did not know that there were cultural prerequisites to effective liberalization which did not obtain in the relevant cases.[3]

Conversely, if policymakers are ignorant of their knowledge, if they mistakenly believe that they do not know how to realize an effective liberal order, they will discount the pursuit of this goal more than their fertile first-order epistemic circumstances would otherwise dictate and may well resist liberalization policies that would prove effective if pursued.

It is only those policymakers who know that they know enough to deliberately realize an effective liberal order – the wise captains of the ship of state – whose incentives to pursue liberalization policies cannot be distorted by ignorance.

Hayek's failure to see the problem of the epistemic requirements of liberal transitions

On Hayek's (1976, 2) conception, social order (née "equilibrium") is a product of social evolution, an emergent product of individuals following *general* and *impersonal* rules of conduct that aim not "at some aggregate of known particular results[, but] merely at creating conditions likely to improve the chances of all in the pursuit of their different aims."[4] Such impersonal rules play a crucial epistemic function in society. They are an adaptive response to our ignorance of the various ends of different individuals and the concomitant impossibility of universal agreement on social ends; in effect, they economize on the knowledge that would otherwise be required to survive in human society:

> Among the members of a Great Society who mostly do not know each other, there will exist no agreement on the relative importance of their respective ends. There would exist not harmony but open conflict of interests if agreement were necessary as to which particular interests should be given preference over others. What makes agreement and peace in such a society possible is that individuals are not required to agree on ends but only on means [i.e., general and impersonal rules of social conduct] which are capable of serving a great variety of purposes and which each hopes will assist him in the pursuit of his own purposes.
>
> (Hayek 1976, 3)

The various systems of rules of conduct from which different social orders emerge exist not because individuals consciously recognize and agree upon their utility, either for themselves as individuals or for their respective communities, but simply because the relevant social orders survive – they are naturally selected – while other societies, based on systems of rules less well adapted to environmental circumstances, perish (Hayek 1976, 4–5). In order to persist, a social order must fit prevailing environmental circumstances, including the presence of a population of partially ignorant actors, and this means that resort must be made to general and impersonal rules in order to mitigate the consequences of this ignorance.

This account of the emergence of social order, Hayek was quick to point out, does not mean that we have to content ourselves with the systems of rules of conduct inherited from our biological and cultural ancestors – we are not necessarily impotent to improve upon the existing social order by modifying the underlying rules.[5] We might either add rules to, remove rules from, or otherwise alter the content of rules in the existing system of rules. The goal of any such reform of the existing system of rules of social conduct is to "increase the likelihood that the expectations of others will not be disappointed" (Hayek 1976, 25–26). What the policymaker wants to avoid at all costs are modifications of the prevailing system of rules that contribute to breakdowns of the existing order, such as it may be, that is, that contribute to *disorder* or, more exactly, which increase the likelihood that individual expectations will be disappointed and thus decrease the probability of any given organism's survival in the post-reform environment.

However, contrary to what Hayek seemed to believe, policymaker ignorance is not a potential problem only for policies aimed at deliberately realizing *particular* states of affairs. It can also be a problem for the goal of instituting or modifying *general* rules. More exactly, to aim at changing a system of general rules *is* to aim at a particular state of affairs: it is to aim to bring about circumstances in which the revised system of rules is instituted and followed. From a political–epistemological perspective, to aim at supplementing, rescinding, or modifying the general rules from which a social order emerges is not a different *kind* of thing from aiming at a particular state of affairs, say, at a specific distribution of society's resources. Both require knowledge that may not be easily acquired by human policymakers; both may require surmounting insurmountable epistemic burdens.

Assuming that policymakers possess adequate theoretical knowledge in the form of Hayek's account of social order as an emergent product of a well-adapted system of rules of social conduct, the question remains whether they possess empirical knowledge of relevant data sufficient to deliberately modify the existing system of rules to promote greater order. Much of the empirical knowledge required to fruitfully modify the existing system of rules concerns these rules, their mutual interrelations, and the relationship of individual rules and of the entire system of rules to circumstances in the prevailing environment. That is, in order to intervene effectively upon the existing system of rules, policymakers need adequate knowledge concerning these rules and their appropriateness in prevailing environmental conditions, and they need to be able to identify the particular modifications to the existing system of rules that will promote or hinder social order. Given the existing social order and prevailing environmental circumstances, including the underlying system of rules of conduct, only certain modifications of the rules will tend to promote rather than impede social order. So, if policymakers are to deliberately modify the existing system of rules so as to realize greater social order, they need to know quite a bit about their existing circumstances.

However, when he came to consider the features of an ideal liberal order, Hayek (1979) provided no argument or evidence that policymakers could overcome their epistemic burdens to promote greater social order via deliberate modification of the existing system of rules of social conduct; neither did he provide grounds to think that extant spontaneous forces were adequate to realize such an order non-deliberately.

Consider Hayek's mature thought concerning industrial fluctuations and their amelioration. At the height of global stagflation in the mid-1970s, Hayek suggested that market discipline was the best way to avoid the price-distorting over-issuances of currency that, on his theory of the cycle, were the proximate cause – ignorance being the ultimate cause – of economic disorder. In particular, Hayek ([1976, 1978] 1990) argued that over-issuance would be less likely were the traditional government monopoly on money creation rescinded in favor of market competition among private issuers of a variety of currencies. Hayek ([1976, 1978] 1990, 73) defended his proposal in part on political-epistemological grounds: by removing discretion over money creation from policymakers, the pretence of knowledge could be nullified (Hayek [1976, 1978] 1990, 23). Monetary policymaking would be less epistemically burdensome and thus less likely to wreak havoc on the economy were currencies denationalized. More generally, it would facilitate "foresight, calculation, and accounting" (Hayek [1976, 1978] 1990, 73), and thus episodes of misdirected investment would be less common and perhaps less severe where money was denationalized as compared to a context where effective countercyclical poli-cymaking required the surmounting of weighty epistemic burdens.

This is at best an incomplete argument. It is predicated on an assumption that is not supported by any evidence or argument in Hayek's system, that either policymakers know how to get to a world of denationalized currencies from here or extant spontaneous forces suffice for the realization of denational-ized monetary institutions. Whatever the supposed epistemic and economic benefits of denationalization, what is missing is any reason to suppose that poli-cymakers can acquire the combination of theoretical and empirical knowledge necessary to deliberately realize an effective system of denationalized currencies or that extant spontaneous forces are adequate to its realization.

It is not obvious that policymakers can acquire the knowledge required to denationalize existing monetary institutions. What is obvious is that there is no extant theory of how currencies might be denationalized. Hayek's theory con-siders the effects of denationalization but does not provide general principles for denationalizing existing monetary arrangements. It is also obvious, moreover, that denationalization would manifest the consequences Hayek claimed for it, if at all, only under particular conditions of time and place. It is not clear what it would even *mean* to denationalize the currency of, say, North Korea, or of the modern European Union, or of those countries that employ some national-ized currency other than their own (such as the American dollar) in domestic and international transactions. More to the point, the deliberate realization of effective denationalization would be possible only under special epistemic con-ditions: policymakers would need to know that they occupy a context in which denationalization of the currency will manifest the trade cycle–moderating properties Hayek claimed for it. If policymakers' knowledge in this regard is deficient, effective currency denationalization, like any other goal, could be realized only if spontaneous forces intervened to an adequate degree.

Hayek ([1976, 1978] 1990, 84) readily admitted that realizing denationaliza-tion may be possible only in a context more liberal than the existing one: "the sort of monetary system I propose may be possible only under a limited gov-ernment such as we do not have, and a limitation of government may require that it be deprived of the monopoly of issuing money. Indeed the latter should necessarily follow from the former." The epistemic feasibility of deliberately realizing free competition in currency would require that policymakers know that they are situated in an appropriately liberal context. Hayek's positive argu-ment for denationalization of the currency was only as good as his positive argument for limited government. Indeed, they were meant to be aspects of the same proposal (Hayek 1979, 148).

Hayek's three-volume opus *Law, Legislation and Liberty* (1973, 1976, 1979) aimed to explain why the ideals upon which liberal constitutionalism has tra-ditionally been based – and which Hayek's earlier *Constitution of Liberty* ([1960] 2011) merely described – have, in practice, always proven inadequate to prevent political encroachment on individual liberty (Hayek 1973, 1). Hayek's goal was to uncover principles for delineating the realm of deliberate policymaking from that of spontaneous-ordering forces adequate to check any intrusion of the former upon the latter.[6]

Hayek (1979, 104) argued that such encroachment could be avoided "by dividing the supreme power between two distinct democratically elected assemblies, i.e., by applying the principle of the separation of powers on the highest level." There should be two assemblies, Hayek (1979, 104; italics in the original) argued, organized along different lines and charged with distinct duties (lawmakers in the two chambers would thus confront different kinds of epistemic burdens), namely a *legislature* that would "represent the *opinion* of the people about which sorts of government actions are just and which are not," and a *governmental* cameral that would "be guided by the *will* of the people on the particular measures to be taken within the frame of rules laid down by the" legislature. We need one legislative chamber to decide general rules of just conduct on the basis of a democratic expression of the opinions of the individual members of the community "about what *kind* of [governmental] action is right or wrong" (Hayek 1979, 112; italics in the original). These rules would determine the contours of policymaking in the governmental chamber but not the specific policy actions to be taken within these boundaries (Hayek 1979, 109–110). These would ultimately be decided by the willingness of the individual members of the community to be subjected to the relevant policy measures. In short, the legislative assembly would write the constitution that would determine the rules by which the governmental body would operate in accordance with the will of the people.

In order to do their respective jobs effectively, the members of the governmental chamber would need some knowledge of the will of the people with respect to the policies proposed within the framework of general rules determined by the legislature, and the members of the legislature would need some knowledge of the opinions of the people concerning the justness of different kinds of potential governmental actions. It is not clear what sort of epistemic mechanisms might convey to the members of the different chambers the specific kind of knowledge they would require to perform their respective tasks effectively. Although Hayek attempted to describe various epistemic mechanisms – in effect, different voting procedures – that he thought appropriate to this proposal, he provided few reasons to think these mechanisms practically capable of conveying the necessary knowledge to relevant policymakers.

With respect to the governmental assembly, Hayek (1979, 112–113) merely indicated that "[t]he system of periodic election of the whole body of representatives is well designed not only to make them responsive to the fluctuating wishes of the electorate, but also to make them organize into parties and to render them dependent on the agreed aims of parties committed to support particular interests and particular programmes of actions." One might dispute the efficacy of political parties as a means of accurately expressing the public will, especially where choices are limited to a few uniquely powerful parties that can effectively collude to quash the interests of smaller factions – it is dubious that, say, the platforms of the American Democratic and Republican parties are accurate and epistemically adequate representations of the will of their respective members, much less that they express the will of the vast numbers of party-independent voters in the United States.

Hayek provided even fewer reasons to suppose that members of the legislative assembly could acquire the knowledge of their constituents' opinions necessary to write an effective constitution. Hayek (1979, 113) recommended a legislative chamber composed of what might be described as "elites." From a political-epistemological perspective, what is problematic about this recommendation is not *per se* the notion that elites should legislate but the fact that Hayek offered no reason to suspect that his elites could acquire the knowledge of the opinions of the community about the justice of different kinds of political action required for effective legislation.[7] "What would . . . appear to be needed for the purposes of legislation proper," Hayek (1979, 113) wrote,

> is an assembly of men and women elected at a relatively mature age for fairly long periods, such as fifteen years, so that they would not have to be concerned about being re-elected, after which period, to make them wholly independent of party discipline, they should not be re-eligible nor forced to return to earning a living in the market but be assured of continued public employment in such honorific but neutral positions as lay judges, so that during their tenure as legislators they would be neither dependent on party support nor concerned about their personal future. To assure that only people who have already proved themselves in the ordinary business of life should be elected and at the same time to prevent the assembly containing too high a proportion of old persons, it would seem wise to rely on the old experience that a man's contemporaries are his fairest judges and to ask each group of people of the same age once in their lives, say in the calendar year in which they reached the age of 45, to select from their midst representatives to serve for fifteen years.
>
> The result would be a legislative assembly of men and women between their 45th and 60th years, one-fifteenth of whom would be replaced every year. The whole would thus mirror that part of the population which had already gained experience and had had an opportunity to make their reputation, but who would still be in their best years.

Hayek failed to explain how a yearly election that turned over one-fifteenth of the legislators might convey to the newly elected and incumbent members of the legislative assembly the knowledge of public opinion regarding matters of justice that they would need to legislate effectively. The members of the legislature would be elected for single 15-year terms. A few would be turned over via democratic election every year. But, beyond this occasional turnover – which would affect relatively few legislators every year – how could constituents effectively convey their opinions regarding matters of justice? More exactly, how would legislators acquire this knowledge at sufficiently regular intervals?[8] If no efficient method existed by which this knowledge might be conveyed, then, just like socialist central planners, legislators would lack the empirical knowledge required to do their job effectively.

I am not even considering the epistemic burden involved in effective legislation *given* knowledge of public opinion concerning matters of justice. On the assumption that such opinions could be effectively conveyed to the legislator, the problem would remain of the epistemic burden involved in legislating in conformance with expressed opinion, that is, in discovering means adequate to the realization of the relevant legislative goals thus expressed. As ever, policymakers would need either a theory and data adequate to deliberately modify the existing system of rules effectively or the assistance of spontaneous forces. Suffice it to say that Hayek offered no argument that policymakers could acquire the necessary knowledge and no reason to think extant spontaneous forces might suffice to modify the existing system of rules in a way consistent with constituents' expressed opinion concerning matters of justice.

However, all of these issues are peripheral to my main concern in this section. Granting for the sake of argument the alleged epistemic properties of Hayek's re-designed electoral institutions, in particular, granting the relative epistemic ease of governmental and legislative policymaking in such a context, Hayek offered no reason to suspect either that policymakers could acquire the knowledge necessary to deliberately realize his ideal bi-cameral liberal democracy or that such a political system might evolve spontaneously from existing circumstances. Policymaking might be relatively epistemically simple within such a system. This does not mean it is epistemically simple to realize such a system.

The epistemic burdens of instituting Hayek's preferred liberalism are readily apparent. Hayek was clear that his proposal would work only in certain contexts, but he did not provide much guidance concerning the contexts that would be apt for a deliberate transition to a Hayekian world. He indicated that his proposals were not intended for countries "with a firmly established constitutional tradition" (Hayek 1979, 107) – unless, apparently, "the breakdown of the existing institutions becomes unmistakable" (Hayek 1979, xiii).[9] The effectiveness of his proposals, Hayek argued (1979, 108), presupposed an existing order in which particular conditions obtained, especially a background of "unwritten traditions and beliefs." Naturally, in order to deliberately realize a Hayekian liberal order, policymakers would need an adequate theory and sufficient empirical knowledge about the existing context – that is, about circumstances of time and place relevant to the background of unwritten social traditions and beliefs – to recognize its aptness for the necessary modifications to the existing system of rules of social conduct. Unfortunately, Hayek provided no reason to think policymakers could surmount these epistemic burdens.

The foregoing considerations cast considerable doubt on the epistemic feasibility of Hayek's suggestions for both the de-monopolization of money and a liberal constitutionalism that effectively constrains deliberate political action from unwelcome encroachment on the private realm. Recall that the former depends on the presence of the latter. We can deliberately de-nationalize the currency only if we know that we are in a sufficiently liberal order. However, we can deliberately realize such an order only under even more specialized epistemic conditions, about which Hayek provided little guidance. At a minimum, a deliberate transition to such an order would be feasible only under special epistemic conditions in which the policymaker knew quite a lot about the aptness of the existing order for such a transition. What's more, there are reasons to suspect that were a transition to such an order epistemically feasible, legislating within such an order would not be: there would exist in such a Hayekian liberal order no epistemic mechanism via which the opinions of the public concerning changes to the existing system of rules of conduct could be conveyed to policymakers in an efficient and timely manner.

We have been offered no argument that Hayek's preferred liberalism is markedly more practicable than the less liberal systems he so thoroughly attacked on epistemic grounds. The problem should be familiar by now: just as a socialist economy seems to lack a mechanism whereby the relevant empirical knowledge can be conveyed to the socialist administrator (on the perhaps dubious assumption of the adequacy of the relevant theoretical knowledge), so too is there no apparent mechanism by which would-be liberalizing policymakers' ignorance of the required empirical knowledge might be corrected or quashed.

Hayek did not seem to appreciate the extent to which his proposals for liberal reform committed him to a kind of reasoning that he had often criticized as "constructivist." Constructivist thinking assumes that social institutions can be changed at will in order to realize various social goals (Hayek [1970] 2014, 338). As Milton Friedman and Anna Schwartz (1987, 312) put the relevant point against Hayek:

> The element of paradox arises particularly with respect to the views of Hayek[.] His latest works have been devoted to explaining how gradual cultural evolution – a widespread invisible hand process – produces institutions and social arrangements that are far superior to those that are deliberately constructed by explicit human design. Yet he recommends in his recent publications on competitive currencies replacing the results of such an invisible hand process by a deliberate construct – the introduction of currency competition.[10]

Hayek did not seem to appreciate the significance of this criticism: "It has been said that my suggestion to 'construct' wholly new monetary institutions is in conflict with my general philosophical attitude. But nothing is further from my thoughts than any wish to design new institutions. What I propose is simply to remove the existing obstacles which for ages have prevented the evolution of desirable institutions in money" (Hayek [1976, 1978] 1990, 132fn3). There are at least two problems with this defense. First, Hayek surely did suggest "new institutions" and not merely the removal of obstacles in his positive program for political liberalism. What is the proposal for a unique bicameral political system, not to mention his elaborate scheme for electing legislators, if not designs of new social institutions? Yet, second and perhaps more importantly, even if we accept that his intention was not to design new institutions, Hayek seemed to believe there was a difference in *kind* between "design[ing] new institutions" and "remov[ing . . .] existing obstacles" to the effective functioning of a liberal order. From a political-epistemological perspective, however, there is no such difference: both tasks bear an epistemic burden potentially insurmountable for human policymakers. The only question is the relative weight of these burdens in various cases and political contexts. It might be that there is a necessary difference in *degree* between designing institutions and removing obstacles. It might be that the relative weight of the epistemic burden of designing institutions is always heavier than that of removing obstacles to the proper functioning of liberal society. Yet even this seems unlikely to be true *per se*: we can at least imagine obstacles that would be quite burdensome to remove – the obstacles preventing currency denationalization in certain countries and contexts might be an example – and new institutions that would be quite simple to design.[11] In any case, no argument for this general conclusion is to be found in Hayek. He needed, but did not provide, an argument to the effect that policymakers could acquire knowledge adequate to the removal of existing obstacles but could not acquire knowledge sufficient for the design of new institutions. To say that policymakers can acquire the knowledge required to remove existing obstacles but not the knowledge necessary to design institutions is to assume without argument a proposition that needs to be explicitly defended.

In Hayek's defense, it was not his goal to address the epistemic requirements of effective liberal transitions in the works in question (i.e., *Law, Legislation and Liberty* and *The Denationalization of Money*), works in which he explicitly aimed to theorize about "liberal Utopia" (1973, 62–65), which perhaps were never meant to be attempted in practice. Long before he considered currency denationalization and "applying the principle of the separation of powers on the highest level" (Hayek 1979, 104), Hayek ([1949] 1997, 237) had written that

> we must be able to offer a new liberal programme which appeals to the imagination. . . . What we lack is a liberal Utopia . . . a truly liberal radicalism . . . [T]he main lesson which the true liberal must learn from the success of the socialists is that it was their courage to be Utopian which gained them the support of the intellectuals.

However, whether or not it was their enthusiasm for Utopian fables that won intellectuals over to socialism, it was surely the Austrians' political-epistemological approach that allowed them to diagnose many of the practical problems of socialism. Before spinning his own Utopian myths without regard for their epistemic burdens, Hayek might have carried the political-epistemological approach as far as it could go to see what it implied about Utopia. If he had, he might have resisted the temptation to Utopian theorizing.

From a political-epistemological perspective, the perfect world would be one in which the divide between public and private was determined, in the first instance, by epistemic circumstances, and only in the second, third, and fourth instances, by principles of justice and other normative considerations. A political-epistemological Utopia would respect and reflect the logical priority of the epistemic, in other words. Political epistemology fetishizes policies that are epistemically feasible and thus realizable. A political-epistemological Utopia would therefore be a world that, first and foremost, was realizable on the basis of existing policymakers' knowledge and learning capacities and, second, in which policy objectives were first winnowed down to those realizable on the basis of the knowledge and learning capacities of political actors in the reformed Utopian world and only subsequently considered in the light of normative considerations. A political-epistemological Utopia would be realizable and moreover would permit the pursuit of only realizable policy goals. A political-epistemological Utopia would exalt realizability and thus would not look very Utopian.

Whether a socialist or a liberal draws the line, attempts to delineate the realms of private and public activity that fail to acknowledge the logical priority of the epistemic are liable to fall prey to the problem of policymaker ignorance. Attempts to theorize how the world should be that fail to acknowledge that there only so many ways that it can be deliberately made to be tend toward the impracticable.

The qualification that a political-epistemological Utopia itself be epistemically feasible is of course necessary if political epistemology is not to run headlong into the problem of policymaker ignorance. At first glance, it might seem that the ideal world from a political-epistemological perspective would be one in which the line separating the public and private realms was determined entirely by epistemic circumstances, that is, a world where policymakers were assigned tasks in accordance with and in proportion to their epistemic capacities. In such a world, goals would be assigned to the public realm only to the extent that policymakers could acquire knowledge necessary to contribute to their realization; other goals, that is, those to which policymakers could not contribute to realizing on the basis of their epistemic capacities, would be left to the private realm and the operation of spontaneous forces. In such a world, our ambitions – individual and collective, private and public – would be achievable as far and as well as humanly possible. We could not improve upon a world in which goals were distributed to the public and private realms in proportion to how far they were realizable in each realm on the basis of relevant actors' knowledge and learning capacities. However, deliberately realizing such a world, starting from our present circumstances, may well involve an epistemic burden heavier than present policymakers could carry and thus would be less than ideal on its own terms. Even this seeming political-epistemological Utopia would ignore the logical priority of the epistemic and place the normative cart before the epistemic horse: it would make epistemically feasible policymaking the normative goal without first considering whether epistemically feasible policymaking is itself epistemically feasible; it implies that we *ought* to pursue epistemically feasible policymaking without first considering whether we *know enough* to deliberately realize a world in which policymaking is epistemically feasible. Thus, a true political-epistemological Utopia would be a world in which policymaking was most epistemically feasible subject to the constraint that the world itself be feasible on the basis of policymakers' existing epistemic capacities and available spontaneous forces; it would be the most epistemically feasible policymaking context that could be realized given policymakers' extant knowledge and learning capacities, and existing spontaneous forces.

Utopian theorizing of the sort in which Hayek engaged in the 1970s was incongruous for a man who spent much of his career undermining Utopian proposals on epistemic grounds and who thought that "[t]he curious task of economics" was "to demonstrate to men how little they really know about what they imagine they can design." This proposition seems to imply that our social designs must always be founded on realistic epistemic assumptions and that Utopian thinking is necessarily dubious inasmuch as it requires setting this restriction aside.

Political epistemology > "epistemic institutionalism"

In his recent book on Hayek as an economist and social philosopher, modern-day Austrian economist Peter Boettke (2018, xiv) argues that Hayek's research program is best understood as an exercise in "epistemic institutionalism," according to which "the central question of economics becomes one about the institutional prerequisites required for learning and error correction among individuals in society." I think that this is a fair characterization of Hayek's intellectual project. However, I would point out that there were both *positive* and *negative* aspects to Hayek's epistemic institutionalism, which neither Hayek nor subsequent Austrian economists have reconciled.

The negative aspect of Hayek's epistemic institutionalism is apparent in his arguments against the epistemic appropriateness of the relevant institutions of socialist central planning, countercyclical policymaking, and Keynesian demand management, while the positive aspect of Hayek's epistemic institutionalism is manifest in his writings on monetary denationalization and ideal liberal orders and more successfully, I would think, in his work on the epistemic functions of markets and prices and of systems of largely tacit rules of social conduct. The negative aspect of Hayek's project addressed epistemically inappropriate institutions. The positive side of the project actually had two elements, however, one we might call "realistic," which considered the epistemic properties of existing institutions, such as market prices, and another we might call "idealistic," which imagined perfected epistemic institutions. On pain of inconsistency, such idealistic inquiries cannot neglect the negative and realistic sides of epistemic institutionalism. That epistemic circumstances are not conducive to their realization undermines positive idealistic proposals for institutional reform – if this is not the upshot of the Austrians' political-epistemological approach to economic policymaking, then I do not know what is. Hayek's negative arguments that policymakers could not possess the knowledge required to deliberately promote the tendency toward economic order and that, consequently, if this result were to be secured, policymakers would have to rely to some extent on spontaneous forces rest awkwardly next to his positive arguments for dena-tionalized currencies and bicameral assemblies, institutions that may also be realizable only with the assistance of spontaneous forces, because policymakers cannot acquire the knowledge necessary to realize them deliberately. I would suggest that the minimum criterion to meet for an Austrian economist who offers a positive policy proposal is that it not be liable to a counterargument based on the Austrians' own political-epistemological approach.

It is not enough to investigate the institutions most conducive to the acqui-sition and coordination of individual knowledge. Political epistemology must also investigate the consequences of non-ideal epistemic circumstances, espe-cially our existing circumstances, in which knowledge is neither easily acquired nor especially well coordinated. Given that political-epistemic circumstances are not already conducive, we need to ask about the epistemic requirements of deliberately realizing through policy means various epistemically conducive institutions and the prospects for spontaneous forces to mitigate the effects of any relevant policymaker ignorance. We need a political epistemology that considers not only epistemically conducive institutions in the abstract but the epistemic burdens of realizing such institutions in the here and now and any extant spontaneous forces that might serve to reduce the deleterious conse-quences of policymaker ignorance. Otherwise, a more limited political epis-temology will chronically recommend institutions for their alleged epistemic conduciveness that may well be unrealizable for epistemic reasons.

Robust political economy: not a solution

A further example of the Austrians' predicament with respect to the political-epistemological approach is implicit in the recent literature on so-called *robust political economy* (RPE), which "combines the research program of two related theorists: F. A. Hayek and James Buchanan" (Cowen 2018, 93). RPE "is an approach to comparative institutional analysis that examines the capacity of institutions to cope with worst-case scenarios. These scenarios are premised on the problem of limited altruism and limited knowledge within human interactions. These problems are taken to be the core challenges to social co-operation" (Cowen 2018, 92). Political-economic institutions are said to be *robust* to the extent that they generate positive consequences even under less-than-ideal conditions, especially "worst-case scenarios" with respect to the epistemic capacities and motivations of individual actors, including policymak-ers (Pennington 2011, 2). Of course, as we know by now, epistemic burdens serve to determine motivations, so, in what follows, I will ignore those aspects of RPE specifically addressed to the ancillary problem of "limited altruism" and focus on the primary and determinative problem of "limited knowledge." The manner and extent to which knowledge is limited serve to determine the extent to which altruism is limited.

Robust political-economic institutions do not require that actors be omniscient and omnipotent in order to generate positive social outcomes. Robust institutions can generate positive outcomes even when actors, including policymakers, are ignorant, unlearning, and incompetent.

> It is 'easy' for a political economy populated by perfectly omniscient . . . individuals to perform well. But what if individuals have cognitive limitations? . . . In this case, reasonable political economic performance becomes more difficult. While a robust political economy can handle these imperfections, a fragile political economy cannot and will produce poverty where ideal conditions do not hold.
>
> (Leeson and Subrick 2006, 108)

Leeson and Subrick (2006, 109) argue that, other things equal, liberal political-economic institutions tend to be more robust than socialist institutions (also see Boettke and Leeson 2004, 2006, and Pennington 2011, 6).

From a political-epistemological perspective, there is a sense in which the RPE research program is obviously on the right track. In particular, its methodological aspects are in perfect keeping with the present argument. As Leeson and Subrick (2006, 108) note, "examining the desirability of competing political economic organizations when only 'best-case' assumptions are used may . . . be misleading." However, inasmuch as the RPE research program makes an ideal out of institutional robustness, to the extent that RPE encompasses an appeal based on their supposed robustness for the social institutions of "a minimal state dedicated to protecting private property and voluntary exchange within the framework of the rule of law" (Cowen 2018, 92; also see Pennington 2011, 2), it falls prey to the problem of policymaker ignorance.

Indeed, an appeal for robust institutions implicitly assumes the same best-case epistemic scenario that the argument for robust political-economic institutions denigrates. There is really only one context in which it makes sense to appeal for robust institutions, namely a context in which existing institutions are fragile and actors, including policymakers, are not omniscient. There is no need for robust institutions in any other contexts. For example, if institutions are already robust, there is no need for them to be made robust, whether actors are omniscient or not. Similarly, if institutions are fragile, but actors are omniscient, institutions can be made robust, but there is no need for them to be made so: actors are already omniscient and know everything they need to realize their goals. Thus, it is only in contexts in which institutions are fragile and actors are not omniscient that it makes any sense to appeal for robust institutions. Unfortunately, in such a context, an appeal for the existing fragile institutions to be made robust runs headlong into the problem of policymaker ignorance. Any attempt to make fragile institutions robust in the presence of policymaker ignorance must fail, because policymakers are ignorant and existing institutions are fragile, and, therefore, policymaker ignorance must prevent the realization of more robust institutions (unless spontaneous forces intervene). In short, robust institutions are a reasonable goal of policymaking only in a context where they could not be deliberately realized, because policymakers could not acquire the necessary knowledge.

It is one thing to say that we want robust political-economic institutions – that is, institutions that are resistant to ignorance, institutions the positive consequences of which do not require policymakers to be omniscient and omnipotent – but it is quite another thing to create such robust political-economic institutions where existing institutions are fragile, that is, where institutions are susceptible to ignorance and thus where policymaker ignorance is likely to wreak havoc. If institutional robustness reigns, then policymaking can be effective whatever the epistemic capacities of policymakers. But, if robustness already reigns, there is no need to create it, and the suggestion to create robust institutions is irrelevant. It is only where existing institutions are comparatively fragile that it makes sense to pursue more robust institutions. Unfortunately, to the extent that the existing context is fragile, policymakers must be omniscient and omnipotent in order to deliberately realize relevant policy goals, *including*, one would assume, the goal of a more robust institutional environment. A fragile system cannot "handle the imperfections" of ignorant policymakers, whether they aim to generate economic prosperity or more robustness in their institutional circumstances. If policymakers are omniscient, then they will be able to create robust institutions, even if existing institutions are fragile. But, if policymakers are ignorant, the effectiveness of policies to create robust institutions will depend on the robustness of existing institutions. In the presence of policymaker ignorance, the effects of policies to create robust political-economic institutions will only be as robust as the existing institutional context. Where present institutions are fragile, where the consequences of policymaking are susceptible to ignorance, advocating for robust institutions may be no less utopian than an appeal for centrally planned socialism. A robust political-economic institutional context can be deliberately created only in environments that are already robust, where ignorance cannot confound, but there is no need for policymaking to create, robust institutions or in fragile environments populated with omniscient policymakers.[12] Where policymakers are ignorant and fragility reigns, that is, where the results of policymaking are susceptible to policymaker ignorance – the only context, in other words, where robust institutions are actually needed – it is impossible to create robust institutions.

The fact that they occupy a fragile context constitutes an insurmountable epistemic burden weighing upon ignorant policymakers: they must possess the knowledge necessary to overcome the fragility of their institutional environment. They have to make policies that will manifest the positive consequences at which they aim, despite their ignorance. But, *given* their ignorance, they will not be able to make such policies, and, *given* the fragility of their environment, attempts to make their institutional circumstances more robust will fail. Like would-be central planners in a context of full collectivization, who cannot acquire the knowledge of factor prices required of their goal, policymakers who would aim to make their institutional context more robust cannot acquire the knowledge needed to realize the goal in those contexts where they need it. In order to realize a robust institutional environment starting from an institutional context in which fragility reigns, spontaneous forces *must* intervene.

If it is true that liberal institutions tend to be more robust than socialist ones or, more generally, that relatively liberal institutions tend to be more robust than relatively illiberal ones, then to point out that the combination of policymaker ignorance *plus* institutional fragility confounds the call for more robust political institutions is just to restate the problem of the epistemic requirements of liberal transitions. It is just to note that, like every policy goal, the success of deliberate policy efforts aimed at liberalization depends on the knowledge and learning capacities of relevant policymakers and on the effectiveness of any spontaneous forces that might serve to mitigate policymaker ignorance or its effects. The RPE research program merely describes a policy goal, but what is needed is an analysis that shows how the goal can be achieved in those contexts where it might be desirable, that is, that shows how policymakers in illiberal or fragile contexts might come to acquire the missing knowledge or how, in spite of policymaker ignorance, spontaneous forces might function to bring about more liberal, more robust institutions.

The epistemic burden of policymaking within liberal environments

One of the cultural prerequisites of an effective liberal order seems to be a certain desire or, at least, a modicum of respect for individual liberty among relevant constituents. Where constituents are accustomed to and content with dependency on the state, removing the relevant state supports and entitlements, even if it means greater personal liberty for each constituent, often fosters resentment that can undermine the liberalizing project in the long run. Thus, part of the epistemic burden of the would-be liberalizing policymaker under such circumstances consists of the knowledge required to prepare the psychology of constituents for liberalization. Moreover, if an effective liberal order is to endure once it emerges, this is a problem that the policymaker must solve – and must possess the knowledge necessary to solve – more or less continuously. It is difficult to sustain an effective liberal order when the constituency rejects the institutions of liberalism. Thus, the committed liberal policymaker must possess the knowledge necessary to prevent constituents from rejecting the rule of law, private-property rights, and respect for the individual.

The rule of law is a necessary institutional component of any well-ordered liberal society. However, there is plenty of evidence that it is difficult to maintain a system of truly equal treatment under the law, perhaps *especially* in the presence of private-property rights and free markets. Simply put, those individuals who have been most successful under a system of markets and property rights, those who have attracted wealth and won power, are often able to abrogate the rule of law in their own favor, while the less successful and less powerful remain subject to it, a circumstance that quite naturally fosters resentment among the latter classes and undermines their belief in the happiness-promoting properties of liberal institutions. The rule of law can be, and often is, nullified by precisely those people who most benefit from the liberal free-market system that presupposes the rule of law.[13]

In recent decades, the issue of income inequality, of the gap separating the wealth and incomes of the richest (the "1%") and the rest (the "99%") in Western market economies, has become a topic of much discussion, debate, and ongoing concern. It is probably this issue more than any other that explains the otherwise bizarre reemergence of socialistic schemes as politically popular alternatives to competitive economies. Income inequality threatens the sustainability of liberal democracies. I would venture to suggest, however, that it is less income inequality *per se* that raises the ire of contemporary political progressives than the lamentable power that great wealth provides to the powerful to ensure their own favored treatment under the law and thereby both avoid various consequences to which less powerful people are subject and secure further future benefits for themselves and their progeny. Constituents are right to complain about government bailouts to wealthy bankers and about "crony capitalism," more generally. At a minimum, the wealthy can afford better legal representation than the rest of society and thus can too easily avoid the legal consequences of their actions. Legal justice is not infrequently bought and paid for. The wealthy can afford to not only provide for their children but secure better futures for them. They can send their kids to the best primary schools. When this fails, they can either use their power and influence to secure or, apparently, simply purchase, their kids' admission to better colleges.[14] However, what is regrettable here, I would think, is less the wealth *per se* than the special treatment that wealth can buy, the fact that constitutional safeguards against such negations of the principle of *equality of opportunity* are so feeble and easily undermined. It is more the degree of control over government and politics, the legal system, and the economy that extreme wealth can secure than wealth itself that leads to calls for a socialist future.

Austrian economists and others sympathetic to markets must do more than merely bemoan "crony capitalism." They have to confront head-on the criticism that cronyism is inherent in capitalism, that making profits necessarily implies the ability to garner and use political power to an individual's or a firm's further benefit.[15] It is not enough to simply institute the rule of law. Once instituted, it must be perpetually maintained if the resulting liberal order is to survive and thrive. Otherwise, those citizens not in a position to take advantage of it, unable to nullify the rule in their favor, will eventually come to think the game of society rigged – and they will not be wrong. It is the responsibility of policymakers, if it belongs to anyone, to keep the system from being gamed by the wealthy and powerful. However, this bears an epistemic burden. The effectiveness of the rule of law and, therefore, the effectiveness (*qua* liberal) of a liberal society depends on the know-how of the policymaker to enforce the rule properly, that is, to prevent its abrogation by the powerful. Otherwise, if this epistemic burden cannot be met, but the rules of the game are nevertheless to be properly enforced and the game is to remain fair, spontaneous forces must intervene to prevent the nullification of the rule of law.

The epistemic burden of policy inaction

As noted previously, one of the supposed benefits of liberal government is the comparative epistemic simplicity of policymaking in such environments. This is a straightforward matter of logic: policymakers are assigned fewer and, typically, less challenging tasks in liberal contexts. However, this is not to say to say that policy inaction, "doing nothing" about some supposedly problematic social phenomena, is necessarily less epistemically burdensome than an active, interventionist policy of "doing something." Presumably, there is rarely, if ever, an epistemic burden involved in knowing *how* to do nothing. Policymakers, like the rest of us, typically know how to stand still. However, the propositional knowledge required to do nothing *effectively* may be quite extensive. Inasmuch as doing nothing is adopted as a *means* to a particular end, it might require considerable knowledge *that* doing nothing is an adequate means for the realization of the relevant goal. Doing nothing might have no aim other than "letting the chips fall where they may," in which case the epistemic burden of a do-nothing policy is nil. Inasmuch as a do-nothing policy is aimed at no particular end, it bears no epistemic burden. This is essentially the same as Hayek's point, described in Chapter 2, that the epistemic burdens of the socialist central planner might be manageable if planning "aimed at no particular result, at nothing at all." But to the extent that doing nothing is adopted as a way of realizing some particular end – if the policymaker adopts a do-nothing policy in the belief that the "chips" will fall in a particular way – such a policy bears an epistemic burden that cognitively limited policymakers may not be able to meet.

To the extent that policy inaction is intended as a means to some end, policymakers potentially confront an epistemic burden with regard to it. Seemingly, though not really paradoxically, inasmuch as it is adopted as a means to some end, deliberately refraining from attempting to control society, doing nothing, is a form of social control; that is, it is an instance of the use of policy means, if only policy inaction, to deliberately realize a particular social outcome. For example, when Hayek and his close friend (and London School of Economics faculty chair) Lionel Robbins, together with other members of the LSE economics faculty, came out against public works and state management of investment during the Great Depression (see Gregory, Hayek, Plant, and Robbins 1932), they thought that "doing nothing" under the circumstances was a better means to the end of promoting economic equilibrium and renewed growth; they did not mean to let the chips fall where they may. In order to deliberately realize this end by doing nothing, policymakers would have needed theoretical knowledge of the operation of spontaneous forces and the empirical knowledge that prevailing circumstances were conducive to the operation of spontaneous forces adequate to predict that a do-nothing policy would realize the relevant goal.

Indeed, to the extent that the effective operation of the spontaneous forces upon which the success of a do-nothing policy depends requires the deliberate elimination of particular obstacles, policymakers might, in fact, have to *do* quite a lot to ensure that spontaneous forces operate effectively, and their epistemic burdens would increase commensurably. As noted previously, from a political-epistemological perspective, there is no difference in kind between erecting new institutions and removing obstacles to the effective operation of spontaneous forces: both potentially involve an epistemic burden that policymakers may not be able to surmount. In order to ensure that the invisible hand functions as well as it can, it may be necessary for policymakers to deliberately remove or minimize various restraints on its operation, and this may require overcoming heavy epistemic burdens. Policymakers would need empirical knowledge of existing constraints on the effective operation of spontaneous forces and a theory of how to either remove them or moderate their effects so that any spontaneous forces operating in society might function effectively.[16] Without this knowledge – again, seemingly, though not really paradoxically – the intervention of spontaneous forces may be necessary in order that any obstacles that prevent the most effective operation of spontaneous forces might recede.

Reflection and foreshadow

It may be, as liberals believe, that one of the benefits of liberal political systems is that policymaking is relatively epistemically simple in more liberal environments. There is, in essence, less for policymakers to do and thus less that they must know in order to realize the relatively few policy goals assigned to them under liberal government. It follows as a plain logical matter that policymaking is comparatively epistemically simple in contexts where the realization of fewer and less challenging goals is assigned to political action. Inasmuch as liberal political systems assign relatively few goals to political action, the comparative epistemic simplicity of policymaking in liberal environments follows as a matter of course. However, that policymaking is less epistemically burdensome *within* more liberal contexts is of no use to the would-be liberalizing policymaker in a comparatively illiberal and thus more epistemically burdensome policymaking context. The comparatively simple epistemic circumstances of the context that they want to realize do not exist in the context in which they find themselves, the context in which they must actually make effective liberalizing policies. Realizing a world in which policymakers' epistemic burdens are relatively light might require that policymakers first overcome significant epistemic burdens.

The Austrians and other defenders of liberalism confront a problem of the epistemic requirements of liberal transitions. Such transitions from a less liberal to a more liberal context start from more epistemically burdensome contexts than they are intended to eventually realize. Given that would-be liberalizing policymakers find themselves in relatively epistemically burdensome environments, can they acquire the knowledge necessary to deliberately realize more liberal, less epistemically burdensome circumstances? What are the epistemic requirements of deliberately realizing an effective liberal order starting from relatively illiberal and, therefore, more epistemically challenging policymaking circumstances? What are the epistemic capacities of would-be liberalizing policymakers in such an environment? Are their epistemic burdens surmountable? If not, what are the prospects for the intervention of spontaneous forces to secure a transition to an effective liberal order? The Austrians lack an analysis of the epistemic requirements of liberal transitions.

Ultimately, my argument against the Austrians is that they tend to adopt an unduly simplistic attitude toward the difficulties of creating an effective liberal order. Austrian economists are quick to point out the epistemic difficulties of less liberal political programs, like central planning and macroeconomic demand management, but rarely acknowledge the complexity of their own preferred political program. "Complexity for thee, but not for me" is the implicit attitude of many adherents to Austrian economics. A clear example of this can be found in Don Lavoie's ([1985] 2015 and [1985] 2016) otherwise excellent work on economic planning. "Given the enormity of our ignorance," Lavoie ([1985] 2016, 117) wrote,

> it makes sense for us to adopt a general perspective of "hands off" or laissez-faire unless severe catastrophe . . . is otherwise imminent. And in those rare cases when an interventionist policy *is* recommended, the policy itself, it seems, tends . . . to be more a matter of quickly getting something that has been obstructing the [market process] out of the way, and then getting those hands off again, rather than continually shaping the way these processes work.

Like Hayek, Lavoie seemed to think there was a difference in kind between "continually shaping processes" and either "adopting laissez-faire" or "getting obstructions out of the way." But, from a political-epistemological perspective, there is, at best, a difference in degree between these prospective goals of economic policymaking. To the extent that Lavoie recommended do-nothing or do-nothing-but-remove-obstructions policies as means to the furtherance of some end(s), would-be liberalizing policymakers potentially confront epistemic burdens with regard to these policies, epistemic burdens that Lavoie simply assumed without argument would be surmountable by cognitively limited policymakers, apparently, in every institutional context with few, if any, exceptions. To advocate do-nothing or do-nothing-but policies without showing that the policymakers can acquire the knowledge necessary to make them effective means for the realization of relevant goals, whatever they might be, is, as Lavoie ([1985] 2016) argued about other policy schemes, "to desire an outcome, not to specify any means for its attainment."[17]

Granting the Austrian argument that spontaneous-ordering forces function most effectively in a liberal political-economic environment, this fact is of little use to the policymaker outside such a context who would aim to bring it about. Austrians lack analyses of the epistemic requirements of liberal transitions, of the likelihood that these requirements can be met by epistemically limited policymakers in various institutional contexts, and of the operation of spontaneous forces to bring about, in the presence of policymaker ignorance, the very conditions in which spontaneous forces function most effectively. Where the rule of law, private property rights, and individual freedom are absent, historically ignored, culturally antithetical, or easily nullified, policymakers confront a heavy epistemic burden in instituting and enforcing them.

All of this being said, it would be a mistake to infer from this attack on the Austrians that I mean to defend a more "progressive" political economy. The Austrians are right, without having explicitly recognized it heretofore, that the first problem of politics is epistemic. In emphasizing the complexity of social phenomena and thus our limited ability to understand and control society, the Austrians are on firm ground. My complaint against them is that they have not yet recognized the full generality of this problem and so seem to have ignored its relevance to their own political penchants. The Austrians' political-epistemological approach implies neither liberalism in general nor inaction in particular policymaking contexts, but skepticism in the absence of evidence that policymakers possess the knowledge required to realize some policy objective. Without evidence either that policymakers possess theoretical and empirical knowledge sufficient to produce predictions of a degree great enough to control society in the way required of a particular policy objective or that extant spontaneous forces are adequate to compensate for the effects of policymaker ignorance, no reason has been given to believe the relevant goal is realizable. If *ought implies* (or whatever) *knows enough to*, then related normative political beliefs – beliefs that policymakers ought to pursue related policy objectives – are unsupported. Yet if the Austrians have not confronted the epistemic difficulties of effective liberalism, their progressivist rivals are in a state of denial that approaches the perverse about the complexity and epistemic tractability of many of their preferred policies. Somehow, though no very plausible counter-argument has ever been offered against the Austrians' political-epistemological arguments, though no political-epistemological analysis exists to support their normative political beliefs, progressives have managed to convince themselves that they are epistemically equipped to re-shape and positively reform both the planet's environment and the global economy.

At the time of this writing, the American political scene is roiling over Congresswoman Alexandria Ocasio-Cortez's Green New Deal (among other progressive proposals, such as "Medicare for all" and the forgiveness of student-loan debt). As too often happens, the discussion around Representative Ocasio-Cortez's proposal has centered on its moral properties – that is, on the question whether we are, in some sense, morally obligated to pursue some such program – and not on the obvious fact that several of its ambitions are plainly impossible on anything like a plausible assessment of policymakers' epistemic capacities, a fact that undercuts any moral obligation to pursue the Green New Deal, given that *ought implies* (or whatever) *knows enough to*. The more tasks assigned to policy-makers and the more ambitious these tasks – and what is modern progressivism, if not an attempt to give to policymakers more tasks and more ambitious tasks to deliberately realize? – the greater the scope for the problem of policymaker ignorance to wreak havoc and the greater the need for a positive political-epistemological analysis to establish the epistemic feasibility of particular policy pursuits. Nothing in the present chapter should be interpreted to imply a pref-erence for progressive political or economic philosophy.

My aim in the second part of the book is to sketch the research program required to analyze the problem of policymaker ignorance in particular politi-cal contexts and, ultimately, to mitigate policymaker ignorance and its effects in the real world. I will argue that there are tools in the existing arsenal of Austrian economics relevant to an analysis of the problem.

Notes

1 See Hayek (1973, 1976, [1976, 1978] 1990, 1979); also see Boettke and Leeson (2004, 2006), Leeson and Subrick (2006), Pennington (2011), and Boettke (2018).
2 Ronald Coase ([1991] 2016, 66) saw the point comparatively early: "The value of including . . . institutional factors in the corpus of mainstream economics is made clear by recent events in Eastern Europe. These ex-communist countries are advised to move to a market economy, and their leaders wish to do so, but without the appropriate insti-tutions no market economy of any significance is possible. If we knew more about our own economy, we would be in a better position to advise them."
3 The most gung-ho and unreflective of the 90s-era liberalizers continues to be the main-stream (i.e., non-Austrian) economist Jeffrey Sachs (see, e.g., 2006; against Sachs, see Easterly 2006 and Munk 2014).
4 A rule, for Hayek ([1967a] 2014, 278), is any "statement by which a *regularity* of the conduct of individuals can be described, irrespective of whether such a rule is 'known' to the individuals in any other sense than that they normally act in accordance with it."
5 See Hayek (1973, 88–89) for the conditions in which it might be necessary to deliber-ately revise the existing system of rules of conduct. In general, these are cases in which "the spontaneous process of growth [has led] into an impasse from which it cannot extri-cate itself by its own forces or which it will at least not correct quickly enough" (Hayek 1973, 88).
6 I merely note in passing a potential problem for Hayek and other liberals. Like their socialist (and social democrat) rivals, liberals propose to delineate the realm of private activity from that of deliberate political action according to principles of justice. Liberals tend to draw such lines in terms of principles of *commutative* rather than of *distributive* jus-tice. That is, liberals want to divide private and public so as to ensure just *treatment*, while non-liberals want to guarantee just *outcomes*. However, as with concepts of distributive justice, there are competing notions of commutative justice (see the sub-section "The Epistemic Burden of Achieving Consensus Concerning a Central Plan" in Chapter 2). On the considerable differences just between *libertarians*, with respect to principles of justice, see Nozick ([1974] 2013, 140–142), Barry (1979, 124–150), and Vallentyne (2011). Thus, like the socialist, the liberal requires some non-coercive means of realizing intrasocial consensus concerning appropriate principles of justice. Suffice it to say that it is not obvious why the discovery of such means should necessarily pose more of a problem to the socialist grasping after agreement on principles of distributive justice than to the liberal in search of agreement on principles of commutative justice. A Hayekian might respond that the relevant difference is that distributive, but not commutative,

justice requires agreement on a "complete ethical code in which all the different human values are allotted their due place" (Hayek [1944] 2007, 101). However, the relevant question is whether sufficient ethical agreement exists to support an adequate consensus concerning principles of justice. The mere fact that commutative justice may not require *comprehensive* ethical agreement does not establish that whatever level of ethical agreement it does require (for, surely, it requires some) can be realized non-coercively. If this is right, then liberals confront the same problem as their socialist counterparts, if perhaps to a lesser degree: how to bring about peaceful, non-coercive, intrasocial agreement concerning principles of (commutative) justice.

7 Burczak (2006, 59–66) offers a persuasive argument that Hayek's legal theory (see, e.g., 1973, 115–122) vastly overestimates the epistemic capacities of common law judges to "discover impartial, universally applicable rules to adjudicate economic conflicts" (Burczak 2006, 60) and, moreover, that said overestimation is manifestly inconsistent with Hayek's skeptical epistemology (about which see Chapter 4): Hayek "does not recognize that common law judges may also act according to their subjective theory-laden perceptions of just outcomes . . . [and] that, like economic opportunity and true knowledge, a singular sense of justice – or the common good – is not 'out there' waiting to be found" (Burczak 2006, 79). This is a perceptive criticism, but it is just one instance of a more general inconsistency that runs through Hayek's political philosophy: everyone is ignorant, but some people – common law judges and the elites who are to legislate in Hayek's ideal liberal order – are somehow less ignorant than others.

8 It is hard to see how this problem could be adequately solved by social clubs (Hayek 1979, 117–119) that might provide "an education in, and an incentive for, interest in public institutions as well as training in parliamentary procedures" (Hayek 1979, 118). Effective legislation would seem to require more regular updating regarding public opinions concerning matters of justice than some such system of political "education" could provide.

9 See also Hayek (1979, 152; italics added):

> What I have been trying to sketch in these volumes [i.e., *Law, Legislation and Liberty* and *The Denationalization of Money*] has been a guide out of the process of degeneration of the existing form of government, and to construct an intellectual emergency equipment which will be available when we have no choice but to replace the tottering structure by some better edifice rather than resort in despair to some sort of dictatorial regime. *Government is of necessity the product of intellectual design.* If we can give it a shape in which it provides a beneficial framework for the free growth of society, without giving to any one power to control this growth in the particular, we may well hope to see the growth of civilization continue.

Against this claim that government is necessarily the product of deliberate rational design, see Devins, Koppl, et al (2015, 612–613)

> Hayek spoke of the impossibility of effective centralized economic planning, given the ubiquity of unintended consequences. But he saw legal institutions as different – as "economies" that could be planned and controlled – and argued for the creation and protection of legal institutions, such as respect for the rule of law and private property rights, that would set the preconditions necessary to give rise to normatively desirable spontaneous orders. Similarly, James Buchanan argued that "[i]nstitutions, defined broadly, are variables subject to deliberative evaluation and to explicit choice". Buchanan adhered to a rationality principle that requires "the minimal step of classifying alternatives into goods and bads". And he insisted that if persons are going to live together "they must live by rules that they can also choose." In short, both thinkers agreed that although economic planning would be futile, legal planning would be valuable.

I wholeheartedly endorse the authors' view that this "distinction made by Hayek and Buchanan between spontaneous orders and economies is illusory."

> What appear to be economies are really self-organizing networks or systems akin to spontaneous orders. Legal institutions, designed to be economies, become spontaneous orders as they evolve in response to shifting political and social environments, unforeseen and unforeseeable by the designers of these institutions. All institutions, even the most seemingly fundamental, evolve so as to drift, even dislodge, from their original premises, so that attempts to engineer these institutions will always fall apart in the long run.
>
> (Devins, Koppl, et al. 2015, 613)

10 Norman Barry (1979, 190) offers a similar assessment: "The results of these explorations seem startlingly radical for a writer who has so frequently and effectively stressed the importance of the slow growth of institutions." Also see Andrew Gamble (2006, 128): "*Law, Legislation, and Liberty* contains the outline of a utopian scheme to reform political institutions and remove the defects of democracy. His writings are full of other ideas for redesigning particular institutions and improving the workings of competition, as for example in his proposal for removing the state monopoly on money."

11 A test for the reader: review the laundry list of obstacles that policymakers would have to remove in order to deliberately realize Lavoie's ([1985b] 2016, 238–239) allegedly "workable ideal" of a "Jeffersonian, market-guided society," and consider the epistemic burdens that policymakers would have to surmount in order to remove these obstacles.

12 Pennington (2011, 6) recognizes that "[i]f robust institutions are those that cope best with human imperfections then so too must the process of institutional design," but suggests nothing beyond this for approaching robustness where existing institutions are fragile and policymakers ignorant.

13 See Frank Knight (1935, 296; italics added): "As no one needs to be told, the realities in both business and politics have been very different from these ideals. . . . And the main weakness is the same in both cases, as compared with an ideal system in which 'each should count for one and none for more than one'; it lies in the natural cumulative tendency toward inequality in status, through *the use of power to get more power.*"

14 Of course, this issue famously blew up in 2019, around the time of the writing of the current essay. See https://en.wikipedia.org/wiki/2019_college_admissions_bribery_scandal

15 For the criticism, see Chomsky (2008); for an attempt to deal with it and similar criticisms, see Zingales (2012).

16 In other words, a pure do-nothing policy is necessarily less epistemically burdensome than a *do-nothing-but-remove-obstacles* policy (or, stated another way, it is always – indeed, trivially – less epistemically burdensome to secure necessary conditions than it is to secure necessary *and* sufficient conditions).

17 Or, again, see Lavoie's ([1985b] 2016, 187) even more oblivious comment that:

> [A]ctually to bring about a free-market system would be a far cry from inaction. On the contrary, it would require a drastic reversal of the policy directions of the present century; it would entail the substantial modification of several major components of our economy from our credit and monetary institutions to the scope and dimensions of our property rights system.

Lavoie offers precisely zero reasons to think either that policymakers are adequately equipped epistemically to deliberately realize these ends (or, more exactly, to deliberately realize the prosperity- and happiness-promoting tendencies associated with a liberal order such as Lavoie desires) or that spontaneous forces of the appropriate kind exist to a sufficient extent to realize these goals, despite policymaker ignorance.

Part II

Hayekian political epistemology

4 The epistemological aspects of Hayekian political epistemology

My main goal in this second part of the book is to extend the Austrians' political-epistemological approach in order to show how the problem of policymaker ignorance might be mitigated or, at the very least, effectively analyzed. "Hayekian political epistemology," as I will call the social-scientific and social-philosophical discipline that takes the problem of policymaker ignorance as its main object, aims to analyze the knowledge requirements of effective policymaking and the epistemic capacities of policymakers in various contexts and with respect to particular policy goals.

Hayekian political epistemology requires a general epistemology, a theory of what knowledge is and of how it is acquired. In the present chapter, I argue that Hayek's own epistemology, which conceives of knowledge as the explicit and tacit suppositions of an effective plan of action, provides a natural foundation for political epistemology. On Hayek's theory of knowledge, policymakers know enough to realize some policy objective to the extent that they can make a plan and realize the objective on the basis of this plan, without any need for the intervention of spontaneous forces; to the extent that policymakers cannot make a plan for the realization of the relevant goal and deliberately realize the goal on the basis of this plan, they are ignorant of some of the requisite knowledge, and spontaneous forces must intervene if the goal is to be realized despite this ignorance.

Hayek versus Mises on matters epistemological, part one

Hayek's friendship with Ludwig von Mises began in October 1921 when, near completion of his Doctor of Law degree at the University of Vienna and with a letter of recommendation from (second-generation Austrian economist and Hayek's teacher) Friedrich von Wieser in hand, Hayek appeared in Mises' offices at the Viennese Chamber of Commerce to inquire about a job in the temporary agency (the *Abrechnungsamt* or "Office of Accounts") of which Mises was a director, established after World War I to resolve prewar debts unsettled among the former belligerents.[1] Mises' article on "Economic Calculation in the Socialist Commonwealth" had previously appeared in the *Archiv für Sozialwissenschaften und Sozialpolitik* in April of 1920. Indeed, Mises was probably working on his extended, book-length treatment of socialism around the time that Hayek arrived in Mises' offices at the Chamber of Commerce. *Die Gemeinwirtschaft: Untersuchungen über den Sozialismus* (*Socialism: An Economic and Sociological Analysis*) was published in 1922.

Hayek would work for Mises in the *Abrechnungsamt* until his trip to the United States in early 1923 and again after his return to Vienna the following year. Hayek also joined Mises' famous *Privatseminar* at that time and began collaborating with him to establish the Austrian Institute for Business Cycle Research. Hayek would be the Institute's first director. During these years, prior to Hayek's relocation in 1931 to England and the Tooke Chair of Economic Science and Statistics at the London School of Economics, Mises was, according to Hayek (1994, 68), "unquestionably the personal contact from whom I profited most, not only by way of intellectual stimulation but also for his direct assistance in my career."

There is no reason to doubt Hayek's testimony about Mises' intellectual and professional influence on his early career. However, we should avoid the temptation, too often indulged by some who write about the Austrian School, to amplify Mises' long-term influence on Hayek's thinking.[2] Mises and Hayek's friendship lasted until the end of the former's life. Mises died in 1973, while Hayek lived another 19 years. After Hayek left Vienna for London in 1931, their relationship was never again as close as it was before, being mostly limited to correspondence and the rare personal reunion. Perhaps more importantly, Hayek's scholarly circles expanded considerably after 1931 to include such highbrow luminaries as, among many others, Lionel Robbins, John Maynard Keynes, Ronald Coase, Frank Knight, Ludwig Wittgenstein, and Karl Popper, and later, when he moved to Chicago in 1950, Aaron Director, Milton Friedman, George Stigler, and Enrico Fermi, who were every bit the equals of Mises. It is implausible that Mises' own research program provides an adequate perspective upon the work of the fully formed polymathic genius that Hayek became. In particular, I reject the characterization of Hayek's career, especially popular among American devotees of Austrian economics, as little more than an elaboration of insights to be found originally in Mises.

If you have read this far, you know that I credit Mises with originating a form of political-epistemological reasoning that Hayek subsequently elaborated upon and expanded to a much broader array of policymaking contexts and policy goals. I am happy to acknowledge Mises' priority as founder of the Austrians' political-epistemological approach. However, it is to give more credit to Mises than he is due for ideas that are ultimately, in their impure alloying, more Hayekian than Misesian to claim, as Peter Boettke (2018, 18) does, that

> The best way to understand Hayek's vast contributions to economics and classical liberalism is to view them in light of the study of social cooperation laid out by Mises. Mises, the great system builder, provided Hayek with this research program. Hayek became the great dissector and analyzer. His life's work can best be appreciated as an attempt to make explicit what

Mises had left implicit, to refine what Mises had outlined, and to answer questions Mises had left unanswered.

Presumably, Boettke inherited this position from his teacher, Don Lavoie ([1985] 2015, 26), who argued both that Hayek's "later contributions have altered and indeed immeasurably improved Mises' [socialist calculation] argument" and that "this improvement should be understood as essentially an elaboration of the meaning that Mises originally attached to his own words." Such claims ignore the several respects in which Hayek did more than merely dissect, analyze, explicate, refine, fill in lacunae in, and elaborate on the meaning of, Mises' writings.

The Austrian "study of social cooperation," such as it is, is more commonly identified with Hayek and especially his theory of economic order and the fundamental role this theory assigns to the knowledge-coordinating function of the price system. The Lavoie-Boettke line also ignores the fact that, far from being provided a research program by Mises, before he ever met the latter, Hayek had already developed a sophisticated research program in theoretical cognitive psychology that subsequently influenced and figured in much of his work in the social sciences, including the Austrians' "study of social cooperation."[3] Hayek, not Mises, provided the bulk of the essential material with which this "study" is typically associated. Indeed, *contra* Boettke, it is nearer to the truth to say that Hayek blended aspects of the existing canon of Austrian economics as he inherited it from Carl Menger, Eugen Böhm-Bawerk, Wieser (his teacher), and Mises with his pre-existing research program in theoretical psychology to develop a social-scientific research program that, although built on the shoulders of his predecessors in both economics and psychology, was uniquely Hayek's own.

To the extent that I have made any contribution to the historical literature on Hayek and the Austrians, I have consistently pushed two central theses. First, I have argued that it is incumbent upon Hayek scholars to avoid the temptation to oversimplify his life and career or the individual events that constituted his life and career (Scheall 2015b, 2015c, 2019b). Given the significance to Hayek's methodology of *complexity* and the constraints that complexity imposes on explanations in the social and psychological sciences (among other disciplines), his own personal and intellectual journey must be treated as the complex phenomenon that it was. It is not conducive to clear thinking to try to jam Hayek (or any scholar, for that matter) into some category that he fits only if large swaths of his work are ignored. Claims like "[t]he best way to understand Hayek's vast contributions . . . is to view them" as developments of Mises' research program, claims that are defensible only if large swaths of Hayek's work are ignored, must be avoided. Second, subject to this latter caveat, I have argued that no account of Hayek's career that ignores his work in theoretical psychology and especially the epistemology that follows from it (and other of his writings) can be an adequate explanation (Scheall 2015d, 2016, 2017a).[4] Going back to his very first academic writing in 1920, prior to meeting Mises,

Hayek was interested in the nature of knowledge and the manner in which it is acquired. Though I would resist the claim that Hayek was nothing more than a theoretical psychologist and a naturalistic-evolutionary epistemologist, precisely because it can be defended only if large swaths of his work are ignored, I wholeheartedly endorse Walter Weimer's (1982, 263) view that Hayek was "at all times an epistemologist, especially when doing technical economics, and even in his historical and popular writings."[5] The single problem that most occupied Hayek's thinking for the longest time was *knowledge*, and this concern figured in virtually everything that he wrote.

Furthermore, whatever the case may be with regard to the precise nature and extent of Mises' influence on Hayek's thinking, particularly in the post-1931 long run, it is especially important to not overdraw the similarities between the two in matters epistemological. Hayek's epistemological ideas were first developed in an essay on the nature of human consciousness that he wrote while still a student in 1920, before he ever encountered Mises (see Hayek [1920] 2017). He seemingly maintained the basic elements of this epistemology throughout the course of his long career. Therefore, it can be said with confidence that Mises' influence on Hayek, whatever its exact nature, did not encompass epistemology to any significant degree (Scheall 2015c, fn 21, 42, 2015d, 2017).

Hayek's work in theoretical psychology (and the naturalistic epistemology that follows from it) is the fly in the salve that Lavoie and Boettke would like to place over the intellectual relationship between Mises and Hayek. As Hayek (1978a, 58; 1978b, 137; 1994, 72–73) himself frequently emphasized after Mises' passing (Caldwell 2004, 223), he and his mentor held radically different theories of knowledge. Their epistemological differences undermine claims to the effect that Hayek merely developed Mises' research program or elaborated on the meaning of Mises' words. On Hayek's ([1920] 2017, [1952] 2017) epistemology, there is no source of knowledge other than experience, be it the experience of the individual organism or of the species of which the organism is a member. As an evolutionary epistemologist, Hayek was open to the possibility that some knowledge might be either naturally selected or passed along to future generations as a kind of genetic inheritance, but he argued that, in the last analysis, all knowledge is due to the organism's or its ancestors' encounters with the environment. On the other hand, Mises ([1933] 2003, [1949] 1998, 1962) insisted on the possibility of rationalistic *a priori* knowledge, that is, knowledge that the organism somehow possesses in advance of its first encounters with the environment, prior to its first experiences, and can discover via internal self-reflection, merely in virtue of being the kind of organism that it is. A theory of knowledge-learning and knowledge-coordination that posits the possibility of rationalistic *a priori* knowledge *means* something very different from – supports different implications than – a theory that rejects this posit. A social theory built on Hayek's radical empiricism can be likened to a theory founded on Mises' rationalistic apriorism only if the substantive differences between the two epistemological perspectives are ignored. In short, the

Lavoie-Boettke line ignores the dictate to treat Hayek's and Mises' respective intellectual journeys as the complex phenomena that they were.[6]

The epistemological differences between Mises and Hayek are of some significance in the present context, for they entail distinct possibilities for political epistemology. Hayek (1994, 72–73) argued that Mises' rationalistic apriorism painted him into a corner with respect to the socialist calculation argument. There was a disconnect, according to Hayek, between Mises' argument and the epistemology that supported it: "I believe I can now even explain why what I admit was a masterly critique by Mises of socialism has not been really effective. Because Mises remained in the end himself a rationalist-utilitarian, and with rationalist-utilitarianism, the rejection of socialism is irreconcilable[,]" Hayek (1994, 72–73) argued.

> Mises' postulate – if we are strictly rational and decide all the bases, we can see that socialism is wrong – is a mistake. If we remain strict rationalists, utilitarians, that implies we can arrange everything according to our pleasure. So Mises never could free himself from that fundamental philosophy, in which we have all grown up, that reason can do everything better than mere habit. . . . In this respect, although I accept nearly everything of his criticism of socialism, I now understand why it has not been fully effective, because in his case it's still based on the fundamental mistake of rationalism and socialism, that we have the intellectual power to arrange everything rationally[.]

It is inconsistent for a rationalist, such as Mises, whose rationalism commits him to the thesis that "we can arrange everything according to our pleasure" to insist that we cannot arrange everything to our pleasure in the socialist commonwealth.

There is a significant difference in the resources available respectively to Mises-the-rationalist and Hayek-the-empiricist to explain cases of policymaker ignorance. For Hayek, if policymakers possess the knowledge required to deliberately realize some goal, this can only be because prior experience has adapted them to the epistemic requirements of the circumstances at hand. Consequently, an argument for the policymaker's ignorance of some of the knowledge required to realize some goal can proceed empirically by arguing from evidence of a policymaker's (ontogentic and phylogentic) experience to the conclusion that this is inadequate to the epistemic burdens of the tasks they face. On the other hand, for Mises, if a policymaker possesses the knowledge required to deliberately realize some policy objective, it might be that the policymaker's experience has inculcated knowledge adequate to the objective, or it could be that divine providence, or some other no less mystical force, has provided adequate rationalistic *a priori* knowledge. As a result, an argument for the policymaker's ignorance could *not* proceed entirely empirically but would require proving a negative, that is, that there is no source of *a priori* knowledge that suffices to overcome the epistemic burden of a particular policy objective. If one insists, as Mises did, that there is a source of knowledge – an ill-defined and poorly understood source of knowledge, at that – other than the environment, then one cannot consistently argue that policymakers lack knowledge requisite to their peculiar tasks, because it can always be asserted that decision-makers can discover the missing knowledge *a priori* by inner reflection on the significance of their humanity.

Hayek's empiricism makes policymaker knowledge and ignorance a potential object of empirical inquiry, while Mises' apriorism makes such inquiry practically impossible. There is no arguing with an apriorist, who can always insist that there is some *a priori* knowledge either not empirically accessible or, more generally, accessible only to a select few with the faculty required for its discovery. With regard to political epistemology, an apriorist can always assert, on grounds of their own *a priori* knowledge, that some empirical analysis of the extent of a policy-maker's knowledge fails to include the policymaker's *a priori* knowledge, and that, in virtue of this *a priori* knowledge, the policymaker possesses all of the knowledge required to deliberately realize some policy objective, whatever the deficiencies of their experience. If it does not make political epistemology impossible in principle, an aprioristic epistemological attitude at least confounds it.

Hayek's theory of knowledge provides a more secure foundation for political-epistemological inquiry than does Mises', and it is Hayek's epistemology that will be explicated and defended in the present chapter and assumed throughout the remainder of the book.

Hayek as theoretical psychologist and epistemological naturalist

In another context, I would be prepared to defend the claim that the clarified and re-constructed version of Hayek's theory of knowledge that I offer here is powerful enough to elucidate, if not solve, many problems that have long befuddled traditional epistemologists without raising new problems of similar difficulty in their stead. However, such a defense of Hayek against the leading lights of traditional epistemology – Plato, Descartes, Leibniz, Locke, Berkeley, Hume, Kant, and their more contemporary 20th- and 21st-century descendants – would take us too far afield from the specific problems of political epistemology that are our main concern. What matters for our purposes is not how well Hayek's epistemology stands up against Descartes' or Hume's but its significance for the analysis of political knowledge and ignorance. This being said, however, it is difficult even to state Hayek's epistemology without some consideration of the contexts in which it was developed, the intellectual traditions it was built upon, and various philosophical notions that Hayek considered in the development of his theoretical psychology.

Some historical background

As a student, Hayek was initially more attracted to psychology than to economics. As was common at the time, psychology was ensconced in the philosophy department at the University of Vienna. To modern eyes, the psychology that Hayek absorbed there would seem to have more in common with a kind of naturalistic and evolutionary epistemology grounded in modern cognitive science than with either of the psychological traditions – the psychoanalytical approach of Sigmund Freud and the "empirical psychology" of Franz Brentano – that were closely associated with the city of Vienna at the time of Hayek's matriculation at the University.

The main representative of Viennese philosophical psychology at the time, Adolf Stöhr, had been a significant scholar in his day. He occupied the same chair in the philosophy of inductive sciences at the University of Vienna that had previously been occupied in turn by Ernst Mach and Ludwig Boltzmann and that would be taken over upon Stöhr's own impending death by Moritz Schlick, the lodestar around whom the Vienna Circle of Logical Positivism soon gathered. Stöhr's work was a harbinger of several trends that later dominated Viennese philosophy. His system of logic stressed the role of language in human thought processes (Stöhr 1910). We think and communicate our thoughts in language, Stöhr noted, and he argued that the structure of thought comes to mirror that of language. Building upon these and similar ideas, Stöhr was early to engage in the "critique of language" subsequently taken up by Fritz Mauthner (1901–1903) and later associated, most famously, with (Hayek's distant cousin) Ludwig Wittgenstein (1922). Like these later Viennese, Stöhr defended the critique of language as a potential bulwark against confused philosophical thinking.[7] Because language and thought are so intimately connected, the careless use of philosophical language can lead easily to confused ideas and pseudo-puzzles, the paradoxical nature of which, the language critics argued, could be dispelled by a deeper appreciation of the intimacy of this connection. Like many later Viennese philosophers, the Logical Positivists most famously, Stöhr was an opponent of traditional metaphysics, arguing against the sort of lazy philosophical inference that moves from the apparent structural similarity of language and thought to ontological posit. Given that its transcendental objects are beyond experience, metaphysical inquiry can neither provide nor uncover knowledge. One cannot know but rather can only have a kind of unprovable faith in a world beyond experience, "a path of faith which his whole constitution obliges him to take" (Stöhr 1921, 36).

Although he lent Hayek a sympathetic ear as the latter developed his preliminary theory of consciousness and encouraged him to publish the work, Stöhr was already gravely ill by the time Hayek arrived at the University. On his own testimony, much of Hayek's psychological learning was autodidactic (Hayek [1952] 2017, 115–116, [1977] 2017, 382). He seemed to rely mostly on the classics of psychology, especially the experimental tradition associated with Hermann von Helmholtz, Wilhelm Wundt, Wundt's students, and the (pre-Logical) positivism of physicist cum philosopher (cum psychologist) Ernst Mach.[8]

Perhaps because Mach was so central to the development of ideas that came to be closely associated with Vienna, several interpreters (de Vries 1994; Birner

1999; Becchio 2011; Ivanova 2016) have focused exclusively on the significance of his sensory psychology for Hayek's theory of mind, despite the fact
that Hayek ([1977] 2017, 382) himself listed among the influences on his theoretical psychology, in addition to Mach, "Wilhelm Wundt . . . William James,
Johannes Müller, and Hermann von Helmholtz."[9] To my knowledge, no one
in the extensive and growing literature on Hayek's theoretical psychology has
asked what Hayek got from the other thinkers mentioned in this quotation or
how their respective ideas related to those parts of Mach's sensory psychology
that influenced Hayek. This is not a chore to be tackled in the present context.[10] However, it is significant that Hayek explicitly declared Helmholtz and
not Mach, "in my opinion, the greatest of them all" ([1977] 2017, 382). In
focusing exclusively on Mach's influence on Hayek's psychology, the perhaps
no less important influence of Helmholtz has been ignored.

It should be remembered that Helmholtz, far more so than Mach, was *the*
international giant of 19th-century science. Originally trained as a medical
doctor, his contributions to fields as diverse as physiology, physics, philosophy,
and psychology effectively set the terms to which other scientists could only
react.[11] Were it not that it rather understates the depth and sheer breadth across
multiple disciplines of Helmholtz's significance, it would be tempting to liken
his influence on the late 19th century to that of Albert Einstein on the early
20th. Of course, none of this is to deny that Mach was an important scientist in
his own right; his influence on Viennese thought in particular was profound.
But, the Prussian Helmholtz's reach was global and palpably felt in Vienna.
Mach (and, for that matter, Einstein) could only react to terms originally set
largely by Helmholtz and scientists he directly influenced, like Heinrich Hertz
and Max Planck.

Hayek's theory of consciousness and the epistemology that follows from it
are children of the Mach-Boltzmann-Stöhr-Schlick line of occupants of the
Viennese chair in the philosophy of inductive sciences. It was in fact Moritz
Schlick, himself a significant Helmholtz scholar, who, according to Hayek
(1994, 64; quoted in Vanberg 2017, 7, fn. 32), "was the first to persuade me
that philosophy could make sense, which until then I had found only in the
works of Ernst Mach."[12] Schlick published the influential *Allgemeine Erkenntnislehre (General Theory of Knowledge)* in 1918. Hayek surely read Schlick's
(1918, 288) pronouncement that "[t]he life of consciousness is . . . only completely knowable insofar as we succeed in transforming introspective psychology into a physiological, natural-scientific psychology, ultimately into a physics
of brain processes." A more succinct expression of his own project in theoretical
psychology is hard to imagine, even though, *contra* Schlick, Hayek ultimately
concluded on the basis of his investigations that consciousness could never be
"completely knowable."

Hayek's conception of knowledge[13]

Hayek's ([1920] 2017) early "Contributions to a Theory of How Consciousness Develops" sought to account for the emergence of consciousness entirely

in terms of the established physiological science of the time. He invoked no wooly metaphysics, no "special psychic capacity for comprehension or . . . special physiological hypothesis," only established "physiological processes that underlie association processes" (Hayek [1920] 2017, 321). Hayek sought to account for the emergence of consciousness entirely in terms of the scientifically established physiological correlates of well-known principles of psychological association (more on which anon).

From the perspective of Hayek's more mature reflections on theoretical psychology in 1952's *The Sensory Order* ([1952] 2017), his early attempt to come to grips with the emergence of consciousness was rather misconceived. In particular, he came to believe that the precise problem his early theory was meant to solve had been poorly formulated ([1952] 2017, 115). "Contributions" attempted to explain the emergence of consciousness, to reconstruct "the functions encompassed by the concept of 'consciousness'." (Hayek [1920] 2017, 321). Three decades later, Hayek explicitly reformulated this as a version of the paradigmatic epistemological problem of the relationship between our sensory experiences and the world external to our senses, that is, the so-called "mind-body problem."

Hayek restated this problem in 1952 in terms of the relations between two "orders," the physical order as described by science and one of its sub-orders, the mental order of everyday sensory experience. Thus, his later account was explicitly ontologically monistic: there is only the physical order.[14] The mental and the physical do not constitute two separate domains, on Hayek's thinking. The mental order is an aspect of the physical. Within the physical order, a mental sub-order can form that, to some extent and in some respects, mirrors the physical order, thus facilitating the planning for action and, ultimately, the effectiveness of the action plans of organisms that possess such mental (or "sensory") sub-orders. An adequate account of the relationship between body and mind must explain the emergence of the sensory sub-order on the basis of laws operating in the physical order.

> *What we call 'mind' is thus a particular order of a set of events taking place in some organism and in some manner related to but not identical with, the physical order of events in the environment.* The problem which the existence of mental phenomena raises is therefore how in a part of the physical order (namely an organism) a sub-system can be formed which in some sense . . . may be said to reflect some features of the physical order as a whole, and which thereby enables the organism which contains such a partial reproduction of the environmental order to behave appropriately toward its surroundings.
>
> (Hayek [1952] 2017, 149; italics in the original)

As we will soon discover, there may be other reasons – pragmatic, methodological – to treat the physical order and the mental (sub-)order as distinct, but this does not imply that they are ontologically distinct.

The concept of knowledge that follows from Hayek's theory of mind and other relevant writings is, as I have put it elsewhere (Scheall 2016), "non-standard."

In his methodological work, Hayek ([1937] 2014, 72–73) argued that the "central problem of economics as a social science" concerns the coordination of knowledge: "[h]ow can the combination of fragments of knowledge existing in different minds bring about results which, if they were to be brought about deliberately, would require a knowledge on the part of the directing mind which no single person can possess?" ([1937] 2014, 76). From this passage, it should be obvious to the philosophically inclined that the meaning that Hayek assigned to the word "knowledge" could not have been the *justified true belief* conception common in the Western intellectual tradition from at least the time of Plato onward.[15] If the fragments of knowledge existing in different minds were justified true beliefs, the coordination problem that Hayek raised would not appear: "The peculiar character of the problem of a rational economic order is determined precisely by the fact that the knowledge of the circumstances of which we must make use never exists in concentrated or integrated form but solely as the dispersed bits of incomplete and frequently *contradictory* knowledge which all the separate individuals possess" (Hayek [1945] 2014, 93; italics added). If all the various bits of knowledge existing in different minds were true, then – though there might be a dearth of knowledge in society and thus some need for learning – there could be no contradictions between them and therefore no need for their resolution via coordination.

That an item of knowledge may not be true is apparent in a number of places in Hayek's writings (see, e.g., [1937] 2014, 62–64, 67–68, 72–76; [1945] 2014, 93, [1952] 2017, 281). Indeed, Hayek's dismissal of the truth condition is an implication of the formulation ([1937] 2014, 72–76) already stated of the knowledge that exists in society at any given time as *fragmented, divided* (or *dispersed among many minds*), and *subjective.*

It is tempting to leap from this denial of the truth condition to the conclusion that, for Hayek, knowledge must have meant *justified belief.* However, whether this is the correct formulation depends on the meaning of *justification* in Hayek's epistemology.

Epistemological normativism vs. epistemological naturalism

As conceived by traditional *normative* epistemologists, especially rationalists like Plato and Descartes, knowledge is a feat, an achievement. To know is for one's beliefs to conform to a particular set of norms or standards, and one knows if and only if these norms are satisfied. According to normative epistemology, there can be no empirical inquiry into knowledge, because "[r]easoning and understanding . . . are subject to appraisal as true or false, right or wrong, valid or invalid" (Hatfield 1990, 1). On a normative conception, one knows to the extent that one's reasons (for believing something true) are adequate, on some to-be-determined criteria of adequacy. The normative epistemological project is that of giving an account of what it means for a believer's reasons to meet the high standards of full-blown knowledge.

Hayek, however, was an epistemological naturalist.[16] Within the naturalist tradition, "[e]pistemology is defined as that discipline which studies exactly how our sense organs construct a picture of the world" (Gontier n.d.). The epistemological naturalist aims to explain knowledge not in terms of reasons for belief and their appropriateness but as the end result of natural processes, namely the organism's (and its species') various engagements with the environment. The modern naturalist tradition in epistemology is often credited to David Hume (1739–1740), who famously sought to develop a "science of man" along the lines of Newtonian physics. More recently, the famous 20th-century philosopher W. V. O. Quine (1969) argued that epistemology could and should be "naturalized," that is, in effect, turned into a kind of scientific psychology.

Whereas normative epistemologists often analyze the mind in terms of "faculties" or abilities – the faculty or capacity of the "intellect," for example, or of "understanding" or "sensation" – naturalists look instead for physical laws or causal mechanisms capable of accounting for mental processes and minimize or deny the role of mental faculties (Hatfield 1990, 2–3). The naturalist seeks, in other words, precisely the sort of empirical explanation of knowledge that normative epistemologists claim to be impossible on the grounds that the sense of knowledge as an achievement, as a sort of faculty for recognizing or grasping the (capital-T) Truth – that is, those properties that are "[t]he essential features of such mental acts" from a normative perspective – "cannot be captured in a naturalistic (nonevaluative) vocabulary that merely describes mental processes and neural mechanisms" (Hatfield 1990, 1).[17]

Within the family of naturalistic epistemologies, Hayek belongs to the branch that explains knowledge in terms of specifically evolutionary processes, such as selection, inheritance, mutation, and adaptation. Evolutionary epistemologists conceive of knowledge as a cognitive relation between an organism and its environment, "[a]ny type of relation that an organism engages in with its environment is understood as a knowledge relation," regardless of whether the organism possesses language and thus the ability in principle to explicitly express their propositional knowledge (Gontier n.d.). From an epistemological perspective,

> Hayek's abiding insight was to emphasize the cybernetic loop of agent ←—→ environment ←—→ agent ←—→ environment through a perennial and mutual process of modification and conditioning; a reciprocal relation between our conceptual creativity and the environment, to intimate, regulate, and inform concepts and action . . . to know is to cognize, and to cognize is to be a culturally-bounded, rationality-bounded, and environmentally-located agent. Knowledge and cognition are thus dual aspects of human sociality.
>
> (Marsh 2010, 115–116)

Naturally, committed epistemological naturalists reject the normativists' assertion of the inadequacy of their conceptual toolkit; it is the normativists, they claim, who err in conceiving of knowledge as some sort of accomplishment of truth-grasping. The inherently evaluative notions of traditional epistemology will, according to the naturalist, eventually be either reduced to (i.e., translated into) the naturalistic terms of some future psychological science or eliminated altogether, cast "to the same dustbin that received 'phlogiston', 'vital spirit', and other outdated or falsified concepts" (Hatfield 1990, 2).[18]

Hayek's ([1952] 2017) attitude on this question was somewhat unique for an epistemological naturalist in that he rejected both the reductionist and eliminativist positions without giving up his naturalism.[19] He was not optimistic about the prospects for future empirical inquiry into the brain's processes to yield a full reduction of mentalistic terms to physicalistic language. Indeed, he ultimately argued that there was a constitutional limit on the brain's capacity to explain its own activities and thus that such a full reduction of the mental to the physical was impossible ([1952] 2017, 295–300). There would always remain an untranslated residue separating mentalistic concepts from their partial physicalistic translations. What's more, even if a full reduction of the mental to the physical were realized, Hayek argued that there would always remain room for the use of mentalistic language inasmuch as social scientists continued to prefer the traditional terms for particular explanatory purposes. Even if the mentalistic concept of, say, human *desire* could be fully reduced to underlying brain processes and neural mechanisms, it is likely that practitioners of the social and behavioral sciences would continue to rely on the mentalistic concept, unless and until the physicalistic translation proved its superiority for their practical purposes. Thus, Hayek rejected the eliminitavist option as well.[20] However, Hayek's dualism was practical and methodological, not ontological; that is, it was an indication of the necessarily deficient state of our knowledge, a marker of our inability to completely explain the relationship between the mental and the physical and not an indication that Hayek believed in some mental realm autonomous from the physical. Hayek avoided taking a firm stand on most ontological matters (see, e.g., Hayek [1952] 2017, 138), but he was quite clear that he meant to be committed to only one "order," namely the physical order investigated by modern scientific methods ([1952] 2017, 290–291):

> While our theory leads us to deny any ultimate dualism of the forces governing the realms of mind and that of the physical order respectively, it forces us at the same time to recognize that for practical purposes we shall always have to adopt a dualistic view. It does this by showing that any explanation of mental phenomena which we can hope ever to attain cannot be sufficient to 'unify' all our knowledge, in the sense that we should become able to substitute statements about particular physical events (or classes of physical events) for statements about mental events without thereby changing the meaning of the statement.
>
> In this specific sense we shall never be able to bridge the gap between physical and mental phenomena; and for practical purposes, including in

this the procedure appropriate to the different sciences, we shall permanently have to be content with a dualistic view of the world.

Association as the principle that explains the complex phenomena of mental life

The relationship between the physical order and sensory sub-order is *complex*, in the sense discussed in Chapter 2. This complexity means that our capacity to explain, predict, and control mental phenomena on the basis of our limited understanding of the underlying physical phenomena from which the former emerge is rather limited. Either our model of the emergence of the mental from the physical is incomplete or we lack knowledge of all of the relevant data with which we would need to populate our model in order to generate a full explanation, or a precise prediction, of particular mental events. We confront significant theory and data problems in theoretical psychology. We cannot, at least not in the current state of science, understand psychological phenomena well enough to predict the particular mental events of an individual human being. We are constrained to pattern predictions and explanations of the principle in the sciences of complex phenomena, including theoretical cognitive psychology and, concomitantly, any naturalistic epistemology derived from such a theory.

The specific principle that Hayek posited to explain the emergence of mental phenomena from physical brain processes was that of *association*. Associationism has a long history in philosophy and psychology. It is through associative processes that, according to most empiricists, the panoply of perceptual experience is built up from the original *tabula rasa* (Hatfield 1990, 6).

Hume was probably the most famous associationist and his exposition of the principles of association the most clearly stated. For Hume (1739–1740), who famously aspired to a Newtonian science of mind, the role of association in human psychology was rather like that of gravity in the physical world. Association was "an attraction or force among ideas whereby they unite or cohere" (Boring [1929] 1950, 191). The laws that, on Hume's system, accounted for the procession of sensory impressions that constitute the mental lives of human beings were laws of association. Hume posited three such laws: *resemblance, contiguity of time and place*, and *causation*. A given sensory impression can trigger further ideas with which it has become "associated" in the experiential history of the organism 1) that resemble the original impression, 2) that have been previously experienced as contiguous in time or place with the previous impression, or 3) that have been previously experienced as connected to the original impression as either its cause or its effect. Of course, Hume famously argued that causation was nothing more than a habit or custom to draw inferences concerning the future from the constant conjunction of impressions that have been previously experienced as contiguous in the past, and thus his principles of association were ultimately twofold, limited to resemblance and contiguity.

Theories of psychological association continued to be developed by empiricists after Hume.[21] Associationism of this late-modern sort reached its apotheosis in Helmholtz's (1924–25) *empiristic* theory of spatial perception. In the

> third or "psychological" portion of his *Physiological Optics* [. . . Helmholtz] attempted to provide explanations of a variety of phenomena of spatial perception by bringing them under psychological laws [of association]; he also sought to extend his naturalistic account of the mind to the domain of "higher" cognition.
>
> (Hatfield 1990, 167)

Empirism (not empiricism) is the denial of the possibility of innate ideas. The central thesis of empirism is that all of an organism's knowledge is acquired over the course of its own lifetime. Empirism is related to empiricism both conceptually and historically but is not identical to it. The debate between *empirists* and *nativists* about the possibility of innate ideas, which concerns the nature of an individual organism's psychological development, should be distinguished from the debate between *empiricists* and *rationalists* about the possibility of knowledge of a mind-independent reality in the absence of experience, a controversy concerning the source(s) of knowledge (Hatfield 1990, 11).[22] "The dispute between rationalism and empiricism concerns the extent to which we are dependent upon sense experience in our effort to gain knowledge" (Markie 2017). Of course, the most natural combinations of these views, and those most widely subscribed to throughout the history of epistemology and psychology, marry empirism to empiricism and nativism to rationalism (Hatfield 1990, Appendix A). However, with the emergence of the theory of biological evolution in the 19th century – which gave the nativists something of an unearned victory in their debate with empirists – the coupling of nativism with empiricism became more than a theoretical possibility.[23] According to this conjunction of theses, some knowledge might be available to the individual organism from birth in virtue of its biological heritage, even though all knowledge is ultimately due to learned experience, albeit partially the learned experience of the species rather than entirely that of the individual organism.[24]

Picking up the threads of Bishop Berkeley's theory of vision, Helmholtz (1924–25) argued that the assumption of an innate capacity to perceive the external world in three dimensions is, whatever the ontological facts, methodologically superfluous.[25] Spatial perception can be fruitfully analyzed as if it were acquired over the course of an organism's individual development via the association of points [*Lokalzeichen*] in a given two-dimensional image with tactile sensations.[26] In Helmholtz's theory of vision, we learn to interpret objects as "out there" in a third dimension by associating what we see in two dimensions with our bodily movements and with what we touch in three dimensions (Hatfield 1990, 174). More exactly, "Helmholtz's theory attempts to explain how we [unconsciously] construct our representation of space from [experience, association, and habit.] According to his theory, we construct it through locating things, by associating the movement of our eyes and bodies with certain sensations from certain locations" (Beiser 2014, 204). According to Helmholtz, the subject tacitly creates the correspondence between sensation and external object via learned but unconscious "inferences."[27] The mind constructs its own internally consistent theory of the world, largely unconsciously, by assimilating and adapting novel sensations to previous experience.[28] Our notions of spatial position and distance, as well as the capacity for stereoscopic binocular vision, are an interpretation of present sensations in the light of past sensations.[29]

That some of this knowledge might be, strictly speaking, native to the newborn infant in the sense that it might have been selected for or inherited from previous generations is irrelevant, given the possibility of explaining the entirety of visual experience on the basis of the *tabula rasa* assumption *plus* associative processes. Relative to nativism, Helmholtz's pragmatic or methodological empirism is at least parsimonious, whatever the facts of the matter, which can never be decided empirically, in any case. Like Helmholtz, Hayek ([1952] 2017, 172–173) also accepted a practical or methodological empirism about innate ideas, but he extended this methodological empiricism beyond visual experience to encompass an explanation of the entirety of sensory experience. Whatever the facts of the matter whether man has inherited ideas from his ancestors, knowledge acquisition can be effectively analyzed entirely on the basis of the *tabula rasa* assumption, and thus nativism is explanatorily superfluous. This is similar to Hayek's ([1952] 2017, 290–291) non-ontological, practical dualism about mind and body, according to which there are good reasons to assume dualism for methodological purposes, despite the ontological fact of the ultimately physical nature of mind.

Though he rejected much of Helmholtz's empirism, Mach ([1886] 1959) also adopted and extended this associationist theory of vision, which Hayek ([1952] 2017, 193) referred to, not entirely felicitously, as the "Berkeley-Helmholtz-Mach" theory of spatial vision.[30] However, for Berkeley, Hume, Helmholtz, Mach, and indeed for all associationists prior to Hayek's generation, the objects of association – the things upon which associative processes operated – were mental objects, ideas, "pure cores of sensation."[31] According to Hayek ([1952] 2017, 266), Helmholtz's "conception of the 'unconscious inference' by which stimuli which do not lead to conscious experience are yet utilized in the perception of a complex position comes very close to the theory developed here." Yet Hayek ([1952] 2017, 266) immediately went on to knock Helmholtz for failing to carry his theory of unconscious inference through to its logical conclusion and thereby giving "support to the conception of a pure core of sensation." Associationism succeeded in explaining the formation of complex perceptions out of simple sensations but treated the latter as given and thus left sensations themselves unexplained.[32] In so doing, sensationist associationists failed to "break the circle in which we move so long as we discuss sensory qualities in terms of each other" (Hayek [1952] 2017, 168). Associationists had in fact not succeeded in accounting for mental phenomena by tracing them back to their physiological correlates. All they had accomplished was to explain one class of mental phenomena (perceptions) in terms of another class of mental phenomena (sensations) plus some laws (of association).[33] Perhaps more to the point, Helmholtz and Mach, two of the 19th century's strictest opponents of unhinged metaphysics – the first usually credited with success-fully undermining Kant's notion of the alleged necessity of Euclidean geometry (Helmholtz 1896) and the second, who showed associationism sufficient to rid Kantian philosophy of what many thought was its last metaphysical vestige, the dreaded *Ding an sich* or "thing-in-itself" (Mach [1886] 1959) – had in fact left a trace of speculative metaphysics in their own respective systems in the form of the untestable posit of elementary sensations.[34]

Part of Hayek's novelty as a theoretical psychologist lay in his extension of associationism to the emergence of the very sensations that had theretofore been conceived as either brute and inexplicable or not in need of explica-tion. He did this by making the objects of association, in the first instance, lie outside the "circle" of the mental order, in the physiological or physical realm. Hayek removed the last remnants of metaphysics from associationism and replaced sensations as the objects of associative processes with the more respectable nervous impulses that were known scientifically to be produced by the impingement of physical stimuli on an organism's receptor organs. Unlike Helmholtz himself, Hayek carried Helmholtzian associationism to its logical conclusion.

Hayekian *a priori* knowledge: pre-sensory linkages

On Hayek's ([1952] 2017, 225–226) naturalistic epistemology, what we con-sider "experience" is just the formation of linkages between neuronal firings. A linkage is formed whenever an organism's central nervous system receives stim-uli from the environment (including the organism's internal environment or *milieu intérieur* [Hayek (1952) 2017, 229]); such linkages are reinforced when-ever the organism re-encounters similar stimuli. Thus, the strongest linkages are those that encode stimuli most frequently encountered.

According to Hayek ([1952] 2017, 224–228, 279–281), *sensory* experience requires *pre-sensory* experience. That is, before we can sense particular sights, sounds, smells, tastes, or touches and before we can internally sense emotions, wants, or intentions, pre-sensory experience must have given rise to a nexus of nascent linkages between particular groupings of neuronal firings. This emer-gent nexus of linkages determines the unique characteristics of different sen-sory qualities. On Hayek's ([1952] 2017, 281–282) account, an organism's mind is an apparatus for classifying environmental stimuli; this pre-sensory nexus determines the criteria of the mind's classifications. More concretely, before an organism can have, say, an olfactory sense experience, the sensory apparatus required for such an experience must be evolutionarily acquired via the pre-sensory experience of its ancestors; if you like, the appropriate equipment – the necessary nervous-system connections between nose and brain – must be in place before such a sensory experience can occur. Without these linkages, an organism cannot have olfactory sense experiences.

Pre-sensory experience essentially regulates sensory experience. However, this does not mean that the sensory apparatus is God-given or otherwise established prior to the species' first encounters with the environment. Neither does it mean that the knowledge encoded by pre-sensory linkages "must also be true of the physical world, that is, of the order of the stimuli which causes our sensations" (Hayek [1952] 2017, 281). Indeed, "knowledge based entirely on experience may yet be entirely false. If the significance which a certain group of stimuli has acquired for us is based entirely on the fact that in the past they have regularly occurred in combination with certain other stimuli, this may or may not be an adequate basis for a classification which will enable us to make true predictions" (Hayek [1952] 2017, 281–282). Thus, Hayek defended a sort of naturalistic falsificationism about both sensory and pre-sensory experience:

> the experience that the classification based on the past linkages does not always work, i.e., does not always lead to valid predictions, forces us to revise that classification. In the course of this process of reclassification we not only establish new relations between the data given within a fixed framework of reference, i.e., between the elements of the relations determining the classes, we are led to adjust that framework itself.
>
> (Hayek [1952] 2017, 282; also see Hayek [1969] 2014 and Lewis 2017, 18)[35]

There is nothing necessary or permanent about these linkages or the networks – the pre-sensory and sensory orders – that eventually emerge from their interrelations. They are contingent and revisable artifacts of an organism's and its species' nervous-system stimulations.

These initial pre-sensory linkages constitute the physiological correlates of *a priori* knowledge on Hayek's epistemology. However, unlike *a priori* knowledge as conceived by rationalists like Mises, these pre-sensory linkages are 1) due to the species' confrontations with the environment and therefore modifiable in virtue of new confrontations with the environment and 2) often known only unconsciously or tacitly; that is, they are often only implicit in the organism's actions and not discursively effable.[36] Hayek constantly emphasized the significance of unconscious knowledge with regard to which we may not be "explicitly aware" but which we "merely manifest . . . in the discriminations which we perform" (Hayek [1952] 2017, 152). It is possible for an individual to possess an item of knowledge without explicitly knowing that they possess this knowledge and thus without being able to state, perhaps even in principle, how they came by this knowledge (Hayek [1962] 2014, 238, 243–245; [1969] 2014, 318). Hayek's friend, the Hungarian-born chemist and philosopher of science, Michael Polanyi (1966), called this "tacit" knowledge. For the British philosopher Gilbert Ryle (1946), this was (non-propositional) "knowledge how" rather than (propositional) "knowledge that."[37]

Hayek versus Mises on matters epistemological, part two

Mises was not silly enough to think that his rationalist apriorism extended very far. He did not believe much was knowable without reference to experience. He did not claim, for example, an ability to guess the results of democratic elections or competitive sporting events just by thinking about them. Indeed, he argued that the only element of (rationalist) *a priori* knowledge in the human cognitive armory was our knowledge of the purposeful, goal-oriented nature of human action (Mises [1949] 1998, 64).[38] However, it is easy to see how the defense he offered of even this limited assertion of rationalist *a priori* knowledge offended Hayek's epistemological sensibilities.

According to Mises' ([1949] 1998, 11) "action axiom," *human action is purposeful behavior.*[39] Mises' apriorism consisted of the claim – the "Reason without Experience" thesis (Scheall 2017a) – that knowledge of this axiom is entirely disconnected from the empirical world, as if knowledge of human action were in no way dependent upon the knower's (or their species') contact with the environment. For example, consider Mises' ([1933] 2003, 13–14) claim that "[i]n all its branches this science [of human action, i.e. what he called "praxeology"] is *a priori*, not empirical."

> Like logic and mathematics, it is not derived from experience; it is prior to experience. It is, as it were, the logic of action and deed . . . in the last analysis, logic and the universally valid science of human action are one and the same . . . [W]hat we know about our action under given conditions is derived not from experience, but from reason. What we know about the fundamental categories of action – action, economizing, preferring, the relationship of means and ends, and everything else that, together with these, constitutes the system of human action – is not derived from experience. We conceive all this from within, just as we conceive logical and mathematical truths, *a priori*, without reference to any experience. Nor could experience ever lead anyone to the knowledge of these things if he did not comprehend them from within himself.

Thus, Mises argued that knowledge of the action axiom is entirely due to reason; in this regard, experience is impotent.

Mises' rationalistic apriorism married the Reason without Experience thesis to the "Greater Certainty" thesis (Scheall 2017a), according to which human knowledge of the action axiom is maximally secure, "apodictically certain."[40] Mises ([1949] 1998, 39–40) claimed that theorems validly deduced from the action axiom are "perfectly certain and incontestable, like the correct mathematical theorems. They refer, moreover with the full rigidity of their apodictic certainty and incontestability to the reality of action as it appears in life and history. Praxeology conveys exact and precise knowledge of real things."

Thus, Mises' conception of *a priori* knowledge was diametrically opposed to Hayek's. The Reason with Experience thesis directly contradicts the Hayekian conception of *a priori* knowledge (i.e., pre-sensory linkages) as a product of the species' confrontations with the environment. The Greater Certainty thesis is inconsistent with both the modifiability of pre-sensory linkages – nothing modifiable can be "apodictically certain" – and the potentially tacit nature of the knowledge they encode: on Mises' apriorism, knowledge of the action axiom is explicit, not tacit. Indeed, there can be no "unconscious inferences" for a rationalist like Mises.

Given that the strength of a linkage is determined by the frequency with which related stimuli are encountered, some of the strongest linkages will encode the most general experiential knowledge, that is, knowledge of encounters with stimuli of any kind. The general presence of environmental stimuli will be uniquely strongly linked in the organism's mind. If this is right, then the Cartesian problem of knowledge of the external world would seem to disappear or, at least, yield somewhat to a naturalist explanation.[41] Our knowledge of the external world is encoded by these strongest – and perhaps also most thoroughly tacit – of all linkages, those in effect reinforced by all of the species' experiences of stimuli beyond the *milieu intérieur*.[42]

Knowledge of human action may well be *a priori* in Hayek's evolutionary sense of *a priori* knowledge. After all, it seems that a set of linkages nearly as strong as those associated with external stimuli must emerge from experiences of the species' and the organism's own actions. Thus, like knowledge of the external world, knowledge of human action may simply be encoded in a set of especially strongly reinforced and perhaps deeply unconscious linkages. But, if so, this knowledge is originally due to and revisable in virtue of contact with the environment; it is neither the product of reason alone nor "apodictically certain." In short, it is not *a priori* in anything like the rationalist sense that Mises ascribed to the action axiom.

Hayek's radical empiricism

Hayek's theory of knowledge extends the typical empiricist treatment of the characteristics of sensory experience as interpretations based on past experience. More exactly, according to Hayek's epistemology, *all* our sensory knowledge consists of interpretations, classifications of environmental stimuli; there is no need on Hayek's account for the standard empiricist postulate of *sensations* ("pure cores of sensation") as the fundamental objects of interpretation: "the same [associative] processes which are known to modify and alter the qualitative attributes of sensations can also account for the initial differentiation" (Hayek [1952] 2017, 172). It is in this respect that Hayek's epistemology can be fairly considered a radical empiricism: Hayek's rejection of the fundamentality of sensations is not a denial of empiricism but a result of "a more consistent and radical application of its basic idea," that is, the basic idea that experience emerges from the operation of laws of association (Hayek [1952] 2017, 285). Hayek turns the "Berkeley-Helmholtz-Mach" theory of spatial perception into a general account of all sensory experience. "The account of the determination of the spatial order of perception by the coordination between the various sense modalities and the kinesthetic sensations is of course merely one particular instance of the theory of the determination of sensory qualities developed here" (Hayek [1952] 2017, 265).[43] For Hayek, mental life is association, as it were, *all the way down* (or, at least, all the way down until one reaches the originating physical stimuli).

Epistemic justification and Hayek's non-standard conception of knowledge

The extended historical and conceptual excursions of the last few sections serve to clarify the background necessary to understand the relationship between Hayek's theoretical psychology and the concept of epistemic justification. It is not for me to settle the dispute between epistemological normativists and naturalists over the possibility of an empirical science of mind.[44] Neither is it for me to take a position on the naturalists' best strategy – reductionism, eliminativism, or Hayek's practical dualism – for dealing with normative mentalistic discourse. What is important to note is that, on Hayek's naturalist epistemology, the intrinsically normative concept of epistemic justification – the notion that some bits of evidence, some reasons for belief, are sufficient to raise mere (true) belief to the level of full-blown knowledge – is reduced as far as possible to the natural mechanism, namely association, that explains the principle of mental phenomena.

According to Hayek ([1952] 2017, 279–282), all beliefs are either possessed by an individual organism as a consequence of its own interactions with the external environment (i.e., ontogenetically) or acquired from its ancestors in virtue of their interactions with the external environment (i.e., phylogenetically). That is, all beliefs ultimately originate in some such encounters with the environment in the organism's developmental history, broadly construed. If a belief is justified to the extent that it is a consequence of either ontogenetic or phylogenetic interactions with the environment that give rise to associations between neuronal firings, then, as all beliefs are obtained in this way, all beliefs are justified beliefs and, therefore, all beliefs are, for Hayek, items of knowledge.

However, an artifact of modern epistemology, originally due to its founder, Descartes, and long overdue for excision from the canon, assumes the infallibility of knowledge of one's own mental states and thus makes epistemic justification hinge on the ability to explicitly state reasons for, evidence in support of, one's beliefs. On this conception of justification, even if you believe something true and have reasons for believing as you do, unless you can state your reasons in full, you do not have knowledge. If a belief is justified (and thus counts as knowledge) only to the extent that the individual can explicitly state how the belief was acquired – that is, only as far as the organism can give an explicit account of the environmental interactions that gave rise to the neuronal associations that encode the belief – then only those of the individual's beliefs that satisfy this condition qualify as knowledge. That this conception of justification is untenable from Hayek's perspective is clear both from his excoriating criticisms of the Cartesian tradition in epistemology, especially its assumption of the infallibility of knowledge of one's own mental states (Hayek [1964a] 2014, 41–43; [1967b] 2014, 293, 302; [1970] 2014, 340–341), and also from his recurrent emphasis upon the tacitness, the unconscious nature, of much human knowledge.

Thus, if the justification requirement of the standard definition of knowledge means that, in order to count as knowledge, a belief must be discursively justifiable by the individual epistemic subject, then, since Hayek accepted the tacitness of much knowledge (and, thus, denied that knowledge required discursive justification), he also rejected the justification condition for knowledge, and, therefore, all beliefs qualify as knowledge on his epistemology. On the other hand, if justification instead means merely that a belief must be a consequence of some set of encounters with the environment in the developmental history of the individual believer in order to count as knowledge, then, since all beliefs trivially satisfy this condition on Hayek's theoretical psychology, all beliefs are justified, and therefore all beliefs are knowledge. Either way, for Hayek, "knowledge" is nothing more than a synonym for "belief."

For Hayek, knowledge includes both scientific/theoretical knowledge ("of general rules") and particular/empirical knowledge (of "circumstances of time and place") (Hayek [1945] 2014, 95), as well as "all that we call skills" (Hayek [1962] 2014, 233) and everything that in the system of another thinker might fall under the heading of mere beliefs, including a person's "views," "opinions" ([1946] 2014, 115–116), "expectations" ([1937] 2014, 64), and "information" ([1967] 2014, 292), as well as "customs," "habits" ([1962] 2014, 246), and "rules of conduct" ([1967] 2014, 292). In the end, "'knowledge' of the external world which such an organism possesses consists in the action patterns which the stimuli tend to evoke" (Hayek [1969] 2014, 320). An organism's knowledge of – its beliefs about – the external world consists of its responses to it.

However, Hayek did not mean only the organism's intersubjectively observable responses – if he had, his epistemology would have been a kind of behaviorism – rather, he meant *all* of an organism's responses, observable and otherwise, behavioral and beyond, external and internal, real and merely potential. An individual's knowledge of the world is constituted not only by its observable behavior but by all of the myriad ways it is *disposed to act in the world* in response to environmental stimuli (Hayek [1969] 2014). Expressed a bit differently, an individual's beliefs are the cognitive ingredients of their engagements with the world, the suppositions, both tacit and explicit, of the plans they might make for acting in and interacting with the environment.

Subjective data and objective data

The various plans that individuals make are, of course, based on their personal knowledge or beliefs, their "subjective data," in Hayek's ([1937] 2014, 60; italics added) terms, that is, "the things as they are *known to* (or *believed by*) him to exist." At any given time, an individual's subjective data and therefore the plans of action based upon these data will be, at best, only partially consistent with the "objective data," that is, the facts of the external environment, including the subjective data (and therefore the plans) of other individuals in the environment. "[O]ne of the main problems [the social sciences] have to answer" is how plans based upon the subjective data of different individuals, partially inconsistent with each other and with other facts of the external environment, come to be coordinated with these objective data (Hayek [1937] 2014, 63).

The social sciences have to explain how individual beliefs, all acquired in virtue of either the individual organism's or its ancestors' interactions with the environment, come to be internally consistent, mutually consistent, and adequate to other external circumstances and thus how plans based on these beliefs come to be mutually consistent and adequate to other external circumstances, that is, how plans become, in the absence of further changes in the data, *actionable*. A person's subjective data are coordinated with the objective data when environmental stimuli evoke from the person action patterns that are compatible with the stimuli themselves, including those stimuli related to the action patterns that environmental stimuli evoke in other persons. Knowledge need not be true. Rather, knowledge must *permit successful plan-based action*. One knows to the extent that one can design, implement, and deliberately (i.e., without need for the intervention of spontaneous forces) realize the goals of an action plan, and one's knowledge consists of the explicit and implicit (unconscious or tacit) assumptions of action plans that can be designed, implemented, and deliberately realized. The Hayekian epistemological and social-scientific project is to describe the environmental, psychological, and social processes whereby beliefs come to be sufficiently well adapted to relevant circumstances to permit successful plan-based action.

Hayek's epistemology makes knowledge the ingredients of an effective plan of action, the effectiveness of which does not depend on the mediation of luck, fortune, or any other spontaneous forces. In effect, Hayek replaces the truth and justification conditions of the traditional justified-true-belief definition of knowledge with a criterion of *actionability*. Knowledge, on Hayek's conception, is ultimately actionable belief; knowledge is belief that can be put to work in the service of deliberately realizing the believer's goals.[45]

Hayekian political epistemology

Thus, on Hayekian political epistemology, with respect to some potential policy goal, policymakers know to the extent that they can design, implement, and deliberately (i.e., without need for intervention of spontaneous forces) realize the goal – that is, inasmuch as they can form, even if only in principle, an actionable plan for the realization of the goal – and their (policy-relevant) knowledge consists of everything that is assumed, implicitly or explicitly, in their actionable political plans.

Reflection and foreshadow

Mises' socialist calculation argument is a political-epistemological argument to the effect that the policymaker in a fully collectivized socialist state is necessarily ignorant of knowledge required to make central economic planning effective. However, as Hayek (1994, 72–73) recognized, Mises' political-epistemological argument does not sit comfortably upon its rationalist-apriorist base. Given Mises' rationalist apriorism – given that he accepted the possibility of discovering apodictically certain axioms entirely through rational reflection – his argument was vulnerable to an imaginary socialist apriorist who simply and stubbornly countered with an insistence either upon the *a priori* axiom that *policymakers are epistemically privileged if not policy-omniscient* or upon the policymaker's own ability to introspect *a priori* knowledge adequate to effective central planning.

Silly though such a counterargument might seem, the point is not whether it is silly (there are probably only degrees of silliness when it comes to arguments for rationalist *a priori* knowledge, in any case), but that Mises' commitment to rationalist apriorism would have prohibited him from arguing against such a claim on anything other than further *a priori* grounds. He could not, in particular, have made an empirical case against such an imaginary socialist, given his apriorism. As Mises ([1933] 2003, 30; 1962, 18, 71, [1949] 1998, 64) was fond of pointing out with regard to the action axiom, rationalist *a priori* knowledge is not intersubjectively testable; it is a mistake to claim to evaluate *a priori* knowledge against the empirical evidence. If it was a mistake for others to argue against the action axiom on empirical grounds, it would have been a mistake for Mises to offer an empirical argument against the imaginary socialist's assertions of empirically immune knowledge. Hoisted by his own epistemological petard, Mises could have countered such a make-believe socialist interlocutor only with further assertions of *a priori* knowledge, the inevitable result being further assertions of *a priori* knowledge from the interlocutor, and so on.[46]

If political epistemology is not to descend into interminable disputes over claims to rationalistic *a priori* knowledge, the question of whether a policymaker possesses the knowledge to realize a policy goal must be conceived, at least in principle, as amenable to empirical analysis. Of course, the mere possibility of bringing empirical evidence to bear to settle some dispute is not sufficient to avoid controversy in some fields. Political epistemology is no different in this regard. There is no reason to think that arriving at a consensus with respect to the political-epistemological facts should be any easier than it is in other fields of social inquiry. However, to build political epistemology on a rationalist-apriorist foundation is to make dogmatism the only possible response to disagreement about these facts.

It is interesting to note that Mises' socialist calculation argument actually rests much more securely on a *Hayekian* epistemological foundation that places the possibility of deliberately planning successful action at the core of the very concept of knowledge. That is, Mises' argument is better read as a political-epistemological argument to the effect that the policymaker in a fully collectivized socialist state is necessarily ignorant *in Hayek's sense of ignorance*, that is, in the sense of failing to possess the ingredients of an actionable (central) plan, which is to say, a central plan conducive to social order and successful plan-based action across society. On this way of conceiving the epistemological foundations of Mises' socialist calculation argument, central economic planning fails – ultimately – because it hinders the correspondence of individual sub-jective knowledge with the objective data; under central economic planning, environmental stimuli tend to evoke action patterns from persons that prove incompatible in some way with the stimuli themselves, including but not lim-ited to those stimuli due to the action patterns of other persons.

As long as human beings are not gods, we cannot expect omniscience and omnipotence – the only real *solution* to the problem of policymaker ignorance – from human policymakers. We must accept that there are only less-than-perfect approaches to the problem and seek to mitigate it as far as possible rather than solve it once and for all. In the next two chapters, I consider two (non-mutually exclusive) ways of analyzing the problem of policymaker ignorance. These two methods, in turn, imply two (again, non-exclusive) ways of possibly moderating the deleterious effects of policymaker ignorance in the real world. Both of these analytical and practical approaches to the problem, which given their non-mutual-exclusivity, might be combined in practice, have their roots in Hayek's ideas.

My primary goal in these final two chapters is to consider tools and methods that might serve the development of political epistemology as both a theoreti-cal and an empirical discipline. Given the limited attention that has heretofore been paid in the social-scientific and philosophical literatures to the problem of policymaker ignorance and the methods of its possible mitigation, these last two chapters of the book are necessarily more speculative and tentative than the chapters that have preceded them. My goal is to encourage further political-epistemological inquiry, whether by Austrian economists or others, not to dic-tate the path such inquiry must take. What I offer in the next two chapters are mere suggestions for getting this inquiry off the ground. I have no idea what course political epistemology might ultimately take in the future. Indeed, if it means that the problem of policymaker ignorance is finally recognized for what it is, namely the fundamental problem of politics and political inquiry, I will have accomplished my primary goal in this book, and, if subsequent political-epistemological investigation travels paths to the analysis and mitigation of the problem of policymaker ignorance radically different from those described in the next two chapters, I will be only too happy to admit that my present self was too dim to see the future.

Notes

1 Economics was part of the law curriculum at the University of Vienna at the time of Hayek's matriculation. Hayek would complete a second doctorate, this time in political

science, in early 1923, immediately before leaving Vienna for a year-and-a-half long trip to the United States (Hayek 1994, 64).

2 On the relationship, personal and intellectual, between Mises and Hayek, see Caldwell (2004, esp. 147–149)

3 In several places, Hayek emphasized the significance of his theoretical psychology for his work in the social sciences. Viktor Vanberg's (2017, 25ff) introduction to the *Collected Works* edition of *The Sensory Order* summarizes these comments. See, for example, Hayek's (1979, 199f., fn. 26) discussion in *Law, Legislation, and Liberty*:

> My conception of evolution, of a spontaneous order and of the methods and limits of our endeavors to explain complex phenomena have been formed largely in the course of the work on [theoretical psychology]. As I was using the work I had done in my student days on theoretical psychology in forming my views on the methodology of the social sciences, so the working out of my earlier ideas on psychology with the help of what I had learned in the social sciences helped me greatly in all my later scientific development.

Vanberg's (2017, 26; italics in the original) introduction offers a convincing (to my mind) argument that Hayek's theoretical psychology "provides, as characterized by Hayek himself, an essential *foundation* of his comprehensive social theory[.]"

4 On both of these counts, I think Boettke's (2018) recent book on Hayek leaves much to be desired. Boettke neglects Hayek's theoretical psychology and epistemology. This is problematic, not only because it implicitly denies both of my two central theses concerning Hayek's career, but because the central purpose of Boettke's book is "the refinement and articulation of *epistemic institutionalism*" (Boettke 2018, xviii; italics in the original). Boettke apparently believes that epistemic institutionalism can proceed without a grounding in epistemology. I have argued in a review of Boettke's book that epistemic institutionalism must be rather empty without epistemology (Scheall 2019c). How can we investigate the social institutions that best serve our epistemic purposes without a theory of what knowledge is and of how it is acquired, that is, without an epistemology?

5 Also see Gamble (2006, 111–112): Hayek's "theory of knowledge provides a thread which runs through almost all his work, the organizing idea which he spent fifty years exploring through a variety of intellectual projects . . . At the heart of every Hayek problem is his theory of knowledge, which became the pivot of his thought."

6 It is a bit odd that Lavoie ([1985b] 2016, 87, fn. 20) acknowledged that "Hayek's theory of knowledge is the foundation of all his work, including his critique of central planning," but failed to recognize how thoroughly this fact undermined the "Lavoie-Boettke line" that Hayek's critique of central planning *could*, much less that it *should*, "be understood as essentially an elaboration of the meaning that Mises originally attached to his own words." If Hayek's critique of central planning is built on his epistemology, as both Lavoie and I would agree that it is, then Hayek's critique has a rather different meaning than Mises' critique, founded as the latter is on a rationalistic apriorism, and the Lavoie-Boettke line cannot be rationally sustained.

7 Stöhr "wrote: 'If there were no words, there would be no nonsense, or at worst there would be errors. . . . Nonsense cannot be thought, it can only be spoken'. Today, this sounds like vintage Wittgenstein" (quoted in Sigmund 2017, 90; quotation from Stöhr 1910).

8 "[O]n some occasions an empirical and naturalistic stance toward the mind was adopted in order to alter philosophy itself. Indeed, during the late nineteenth and early twentieth centuries the experimental approach to the mind was advanced in order to replace the outdated and prescientific approach allegedly pursued by philosophers" (Hatfield 1990, 13).

9 Regarding Mach's influence on *fin de siècle* Vienna, see Chapter Two of Sigmund (2017).

10 I had originally intended to include in the book a more comprehensive analysis of Hayek's epistemology and philosophy of science. However, this would have taken the discussion too far afield from my main concern with political-epistemological issues.

Some readers may be rather exhausted by even the relatively limited discussion in the present chapter of Hayek's theoretical psychology and the epistemology that follows from it. Such readers might skip straight to the sub-section titled "Subjective Data and Objective Data."

11 On Helmholtz's life, career, and influence, see Cahan (2018).

12 "Perhaps no single academic did more to keep Helmholtz's name alive in the interwar period than Schlick" (Cahan 2018, 752). Schlick was "the heir apparent to the tradition of philosophical physicists, a tradition founded by Hermann von Helmholtz, the icon of 19th Century physics and . . . continued by [Helmholtz's] student and (later) colleague [and Schlick's mentor, Max] Planck" (Oberdan 2017). Schlick co-edited Helmholtz's (1921) *Schriften zur Erkenntnistheorie* (translated as *Epistemological Writings*) and was the "first to attempt a systematic formulation of the picture of knowledge implicit in Helmholtz's writings" (Coffa 1991, 172).

13 This section reproduces parts of an argument previously published in Scheall (2016).

14 This monism is present in Hayek's earlier paper on consciousness, too, but is rather less explicit than in *The Sensory Order*. Indeed, some care must be taken to avoid reading a kind of ontological dualism into the 1920 argument. This is largely a consequence of the less careful way that Hayek framed the problem in the early paper. Although that essay ultimately identifies the mental process of *uptake into consciousness* with the physical process of *facilitation* or *smoothing*, whereby physiological linkages between ganglion cells are formed in an organism's brain, and thus commits Hayek to only a single process, Hayek's initial framing of the problem left open the possibility that these processes were conceived as ontologically distinct.

15 According to the traditional conception of knowledge, a subject *S* knows proposition *P* if and only if 1) *P* is true, 2) *S* believes *P*, and 3) *S* is justified in believing *P*. It has been generally accepted among traditional epistemologists, at least since Gettier (1963), that this standard definition is in need of some supplementation. However, no consensus concerning the auxiliary conditions both necessary and sufficient for knowledge has yet been realized. I am not interested in the present context in the question whether Hayek's non-standard conception of knowledge has any bearing on the Gettier problem as it is typically understood.

16 "Hayek is through and through a naturalist, a position he has consistently held throughout his career. Hayek fully acknowledges that consciousness is a natural phenomenon" (Marsh 2010, 128).

17 Gary Hatfield's (1990) *The Natural and the Normative: Theories of Perception from Kant to Helmholtz* is an excellent source on the history of this dispute, which continues to this day.

18 Quine (1969) is "[t]he father of eliminativism" (Hatfield 1990, 260).

19 Hayek's position is close to P. F. Strawson's (1985) "soft naturalism," which "does not try to reduce our description of ourselves to the purely physical vocabulary of the hard naturalist, accepting instead a framework for description that is implicit in the culture to which we belong" (Hatfield 1990, 261).

20 For more on Hayek, reductionism, and eliminativism, see Lewis (2017)

21 See Boring ([1929] 1950, Chapters 10–12)

22 Beiser (2014, 203): "While the nativists hold that space is an innate intuition, which is simple, given and unanalysable, the [empirists] hold that it is constructed from experience, association, and habit." Turner ([1994] 2016; also see Hatfield 1990, 179–195) tells the story (beautifully, I might add) of the debate between Helmholtz and Ewald Hering over empirism and nativism. It should be noted that few empirists would deny that some mental capacities, if only the ability to form associations, are innate, and that no nativists would deny that some capacities are learned. The distinction is thus more one of degree than a dichotomy.

23 The nativists' victory was unearned because they postulated innate knowledge without providing a mechanism capable of explaining it. According to this critique, "nativism

cheats by simply assuming what it needs to produce the explanation it wants. In simply assuming an innate ability, nativism refuses to undertake the honest work required to show how an ability could be acquired through experience" (Hatfield 1990, 151; also see 188–195). Nativists left innate knowledge a mystery, if not a mysticism, frequently attributing it to God's grace. Except perhaps by accident, they never conceived of anything like the evolutionary mechanisms that might account for innate knowledge in a scientifically respectable way. "[P]rior to Darwin, there was no generally accepted means for explaining innate adaptive mechanisms" (Hatfield 1990, 191). Herbert Spencer's (1870–1872) evolutionary psychology "was essentially a resolution" of nativism and empirism: "Spencer simply substituted phylogenetic origin for ontogenetic origin in many cases. What is empiristically derived in the race may nevertheless be native in the individual, he might have said" (Boring [1929] 1950, 243). Similarly, Hayek was an empirist inasmuch as he accepted that all of the "relations between stimulation and perceptual experience [are] alterable" (Hatfield 1990, 184). However, he also believed that alterations in these relations typically occur only in the developmental history of the species and only rarely, if ever, in the life of an individual organism. In this regard, he was a nativist, albeit one cognizant of evolutionary biology (see Hayek [1952] 2017, 172–173).

24 For reasons that should be rather obvious, the conjunction of empirism and rationalism, which implies both the impossibility of innate knowledge and the possibility of non-experiential knowledge, has never attracted many adherents among the scientifically minded, although someone who accepts the possibility of religious epiphany or born-again conversion might subscribe to some such view.

25 Helmholtz "did not believe that the nativistic theory could be disproved . . . In general he believed that the nativistic view was unnecessary and gratuitous, that the development of perceptions in experience is to a certain extent demonstrable, and that there is no need of hypothesizing in addition another ground of perception unless positive evidence can be adduced for it" (Boring [1929] 1950, 306).

26 Berkeley (1790); also see Hatfield (1990, 41–43). Like Hayek ([1952] 2017, 226), Helmholtz "contended that originally such signs are without . . . meaning, which they attain as a result of subsequent physiological processes" (Hatfield 1990, 172).

27 On this point, Helmholtz differed from Kantians and neo-Kantians (with whom he was sometimes associated) in two respects. First, "[i]n attributing [unconscious] inferences to spatial perception, Helmholtz was effectively saying that they are not really the immediate given intuitions that strict Kantians made them out to be." Second, for Helmholtz, "the basic axioms of Euclidean geometry are not *a priori* truths about the structure of space . . . [I]t is only a contingent feature of our spatial world that the Euclidean axioms apply to it" (Beiser 2014, 204). A key figure in the development of non-Euclidean geometries, Helmholtz (1896) is often credited with having effectively countered the Kantian "thesis that the Euclidean axioms are necessary consequences of an *a priori* transcendental form of intuition" (Beiser 2014, 205).

28 Helmholtz "characterized the psychological processes underlying perception as unconscious inferences, and he emphasized the role of active experience in the formation and testing of such inferences" (Hatfield 1990, 167). According to Helmholtz, "we learn to see . . . [and] vision results from judgments, conclusions, and deliberations of which we are not conscious" (Hatfield 1990, 196; see Helmholtz 1896 and Hatfield 1990, 195–208 for a summary of Helmholtz's theory of unconscious inference).

29 It was Helmholtz's student and laboratory director, Wilhelm Wundt, who originated the theory of unconscious inference (Hatfield 1990, 198). However, Wundt (1873–1874) later rejected unconscious inferences (Boring [1929] 1950, 309; Boring credits Helmholtz, not Wundt, with originating the theory) when he realized how far the possibility of unconscious mental processes limited the value of the introspective method he recommended for the so-called "experimental" tradition from which modern scientific psychology (eventually, toward the end of Wundt's life) emerged (Kusch 1995, 135). The

introspective method presumed the infallibility of knowledge of one's own mental states and thus was plainly inconsistent with the possibility of unconscious inferences. On the emergence of scientific psychology from philosophy, physics, and physiology, see Boring (1942 and [1929] 1950).

30 "[A]nyone who, in spite of repeated protests from myself and from other quarters, identifies my view with that of Berkeley, is undoubtedly very far removed from a proper appreciation of my position" (Mach [1886] 1959, 361)

31 Throughout the early-modern period at least, there was "nearly universal agreement regarding the characteristics" of the sensory "given": "The predominant view was that it is a [two-dimensional] mental representation of the retinal image" (Hatfield 1990, 35; also 46).

32 Nineteenth-century psychology of the sort that influenced Hayek typically conceived of perceptions as either simple aggregates of distinct sensations or emergent products of combinations of sensations. On historical conceptions of the relationship between sensations and perceptions, see Boring (1942 and [1929] 1950) and Hatfield (1990, Appendix B).

33 For example, Helmholtz's sensations were "mental states varying only in quality and intensity" (Hatfield 1990, 209).

34 Mach's rejection of metaphysics is well known. On Helmholtz's negative attitude toward metaphysics, see Hatfield (1990, 165): Helmholtz wanted to "banish metaphysics from philosophy once and for all [and] held that epistemology alone is the proper subject matter of philosophy." Rather like Hayek ([1952] 2017, 138, 285, 290), Helmholtz rejected both idealism and materialism as "equally metaphysical" (Hatfield 1990, 194).

35 A naturalized falsificationism or, perhaps better, a physiological Humeanism: a "characteristic feature of early naturalized accounts of the mind," for example, Hume's, was that, like Hayek's naturalized epistemology, "they posited belief-producing processes that were neutral with respect to whether the beliefs produced are true or false . . . So far as we can rationally determine, the processes that yield beliefs in matters of fact (that go beyond current and remembered sensory impressions) are equally capable of producing true or false beliefs. Hume of course did not deny that some ways of inculcating customs or habits have been more success-promoting than others in the past, that is, have proven to be better at predicting the course of subsequent impressions; he spoke of a 'harmony,' established over time, between the regularities of nature (as manifest in patterns of related impressions) and the associative regularities of ideas. But, famously, it was one of Hume's central tenets that the formation of associative connections in the previously most successful manner is not inconsistent with future falsehood" (Hatfield 1990, 26–27).

36 Hayek's friend and fellow Viennese, Konrad Lorenz (1941), one of the fathers of ethology and co-winner of the 1973 Nobel Prize in Physiology, "is famous for reinterpreting Kant's synthetic *a priori* claims."

> No longer are the inborn categories regarded as evidently true, rather, they are understood to be "ontogenetically *a priori* and phylogenetically a posteriori". This means that an individual organism is born with innate dispositions. These innate dispositions are acquired phylogenetically, through the evolution of the species, by means of the mechanism of natural selection. Most importantly, these dispositions are fallible, because they are the result of selection, not instruction. That is, these dispositions are adaptations, and natural selection only weeds out maladaptive organisms, which results in the survival of the adaptive ones.
>
> (Gontier n.d.)

Hayek's very similar conception of *a priori* knowledge is implicit in his 1920 paper on consciousness.

37 As noted in Chapter 1, and in keeping with Hayek's conception, I use "knowledge" throughout the present work to encompass both non-propositional knowledge-how and propositional knowledge-that.

38 It should be noted that something like an evolutionary, non-rationalist account of *a priori* knowledge can be found in places in Mises' writings (see, e.g., Mises [1949] 1998, 35, 85–86; 1962, 14–16). However, this account is so sketchy and manifestly inconsistent with other passages that surround it in the relevant texts, which seem to deny experience a role in the construction of *a priori* knowledge and appear to double-down on rationalist apriorism, that it is difficult to take seriously. I have argued that these passages reveal Mises' deeply set confusion regarding the contemporary epistemology of his day (Scheall 2017b).

39 Parts of the rest of this paragraph and the next are taken from Scheall (2017a).

40 More exactly, according to the Greater Certainty thesis, which has been accepted by several prominent economists throughout the history of the discipline (see Scheall 2017a), knowledge of human action is more, if not maximally ("apodictically"), certain, as compared to knowledge of the assumptions of explanations of natural phenomena, because humans can acquire knowledge of human action by internal reflection or introspection, whereas knowledge of the assumptions of explanations of natural phenomena requires sensory or external observation. I have argued that the Greater Certainty thesis is a non sequitur (Scheall 2017a). It hinges on an undefended and, in light of modern cognitive psychology, indefensible assumption that internal reflection on mental states is a more secure source of knowledge than external observation.

The original source of the Greater Certainty thesis may well have been Wilhelm von Humboldt (1767–1835), brother of the great naturalist Alexander von Humboldt (1769–1859). According to Beiser (2011, 174–175) Wilhelm von Humboldt argued that "the inanimate world . . . will remain utterly alien to us. . . . However, the human world is our home, familiar and accessible to all of us, because we all share it from within. Here . . . Humboldt had reversed the traditional order of precedent that had favored the natural over the human sciences. Now, it seemed, on the basis of empathetic understanding, the human sciences could know reality more directly than the natural sciences." Whether Humboldt was its original source, the Greater Certainty thesis was a widely held article of faith among German historicist philosophers (Beiser 2011, 315, 336, 344), although Dilthey eventually came to express some doubts about it (Beiser 2011, 340). Note that what I call the Greater Certainty thesis, Markie (2017) calls "The Superiority of Reason Thesis: The knowledge we gain in subject area S by intuition and deduction or have innately is superior to any knowledge gained by sense experience."

Hayek (1978b, 137) rejected Mises' epistemology, at least in part, on the grounds that he "never could accept the . . . almost eighteenth-century rationalism in his [Mises'] argument." It is interesting to consider what Hayek found anachronistic, that is, an artifact of the 18th century, in Mises' epistemology. Hayek did not elaborate this point, but it is worth noting that "[t]he standard of science in the eighteenth century was certainty; probability, no matter how high, did not suffice because it allowed for the possibility of doubt, which it was the very purpose of science to remove. Science, [the influential German philosopher, Christian] Wolff insisted, required demonstration from true premises, all of which are incontrovertible, based on immediate sense experience or the law of contradiction" (Beiser 2011, 59), a proposition that Mises seemed inclined to accept. Mises did not require all of the premises of an economic explanation to be incontrovertibly true, but he seemed to think the alleged incontrovertibility of the action axiom somehow significant for and the axiom itself the necessary starting point of economic science (Scheall 2017a), a position sufficiently anachronistic in the wake of the Darwinian and Einsteinian revolutions to explain Hayek's hesitancy. As I have argued elsewhere, Mises did not seem to understand the extent to which these and other scientific, and philosophical, developments made his apriorism untenable (Scheall 2017b).

This may fail to account for everything that Hayek found anachronistic in Mises' epistemology. It is tempting to speculate that Hayek also rejected Mises' ([1933] 2003) apparent and anachronistic reliance on a kind of Kantian "pure" intuition for knowledge of the action axiom (the history of the slow death of Kantian pure intuition is retold in

Coffa [1991]), a notion that has no place in Hayek's epistemology. "Intuition is a form of rational insight. Intellectually grasping a proposition, we just 'see' it to be true in such a way as to form a true, warranted belief in it" (Markie 2017). It seems that Mises accepted the "Intuition/Deduction Thesis" (Markie 2017), a hallmark of rationalism, according to which "[s]ome propositions in a particular subject area, S [i.e., economics/praxeology], are knowable by us by intuition alone; still others are knowable by being deduced from intuited propositions." Mises might also have accepted something like the "Innate Knowledge Thesis: We have knowledge of some truths in a particular subject area, S, as part of our rational nature" (Markie 2017). In any case, it is clear that Hayek rejected both the notion that certainty is the relevant criterion of scientific knowledge and that scientific method requires incontrovertibly true premises, not to mention intuition as a source of knowledge of such premises. Indeed, he denied that there are premises which cannot be controverted in future.

41 Adolf Stöhr, Hayek's philosophical psychology teacher at the University of Vienna, argued that a person could at best have a kind of unprovable faith in the external world, "a path of faith which *his whole constitution* obliges him to take" (1921, 36; italics added). Similarly, Helmholtz, who argued early in his career that causality was an *a priori* principle sufficient to support knowledge of the external world (1896, 116), "came to realize the full force of the notion that the [causal] law cannot be justified empirically . . . and adopted a position according to which we accept the causal law on faith, as a guiding principle in our comprehension of appearances" (Hatfield 1990, 169).

42 Naturally, on such a conception, our knowledge of the boundary between the internal and external environments is just a consequence of the emergence of appropriate linkages.

43 In a previous era, Helmholtz believed that his theory of unconscious inference, plus laws of association, accomplished a similar unification of all mental life (Hatfield 1990, 204).

44 The existence of modern cognitive psychology and cognitive science would seem to be evidence that supports this possibility, even if the success of these fields is open to discussion.

45 Similarly, Helmholtz "maintained that our ideas can possess no more than a 'practical' correspondence with the world, and that the only comparison possible between ideas and things is in terms of the guidance our representations provide us for engaging in actions that bring about a desired result (in the form of an expected group of new sensations)" (Hatfield 1990, 209–210).

46 Imagine a debate on the foundations of economics between Mises and Martin Hollis and Edward J. Nell, authors of the Marxian and decidedly un-Austrian, but no less aprioristic, *Rational Economic Man* (1975).

5 Political order and disorder as epistemic phenomena

The *epistemic-mechanistic* approach to the problem of policymaker ignorance investigates, both empirically and theoretically, any devices, mechanisms, or processes that might promote the orderliness of the political domain, that is, that might function to coordinate the knowledge and thereby improve the actionability of the plans of policymakers and constituents alike. The epistemic-mechanistic approach is concerned with how knowledge is communicated between constituents and policymakers and with how this communication might be improved so that actors in the political domain can adjust their plans to relevant circumstances. In the present chapter, I offer a meta-theory of the epistemic-mechanistic approach. That is, I do not posit or theorize about specific mechanisms that might serve the epistemic requirements of an ideal political order. Rather, I try to state clearly the problems that such mechanisms must address and describe what an adequate theory would look like.

Knowledge, planning, social order, and epistemic mechanisms

I have argued in previous work (Scheall 2015b) that Hayek's later methodological writings (see esp. Hayek [1937] 2014, [1945] 2014, and [1975] 2014) lead to an epistemic theory of order and disorder in the economy and, in particular, to the epistemic theory of industrial fluctuations discussed in Chapter 2. Together with my co-authors, William Butos and Thomas McQuade, I later extended the epistemic theory of economic order into a fully general epistemic theory of *social* order that considers the conditions under which the subjective data of the individuals operating in various social domains might come to correspond to relevant objective data and thus the conditions under which the plans of individuals in these domains might become more actionable and the relevant domain itself more orderly (Scheall, Butos, and McQuade 2019). For an individual's knowledge to become better coordinated with external circumstances, including the knowledge of other individuals, there must be mechanisms in place, as there are in several social domains but not in others, that signal the individual *what to do* in response to changing circumstances in the environment about which they would otherwise, in the absence of such mechanisms, remain ignorant. Thus, the epistemic theory bears important implications for the conditions under which this tendency toward social order might be hindered or even reversed. In domains where there are no such epistemic mechanisms or their operation is somehow encumbered, individuals do not receive appropriate signals about what to do in response to changing circumstances in the environment and thus cannot adjust their plans to the new circumstances effectively. Their expectations tend to be disappointed and further disorder results. The epistemic theory explains both order *and* disorder in various domains of society.

According to the epistemic theory, policies fail, political plans are disappointed, and constituents become disenchanted with policymakers because we lack mechanisms that could serve to coordinate the knowledge and thus the plans of policymakers and their constituents. Such mechanisms as exist in political contexts to convey knowledge between relevant actors serve their epistemic function poorly. Consequently, one of the main tasks of political epistemology is to consider the conditions under which political life might become more orderly and the operation of various mechanisms that might, at least in theory, facilitate the coordination of individual knowledge and thus the making of actionable plans in the political realm.

On Hayek's conception of knowledge, being able to plan and act effectively on the basis of one's plans – which is to say, *knowing* – is intimately connected with the capacities of other persons to plan and act effectively. The knowledge possessed by any one person is closely connected with, and in part determined by, the knowledge possessed by other people. Unless a person's subjective data are compatible with the subjective data of other people whose plans are relevant to the person's own, none of these people will be able to deliberately realize the goals of their plans. As atypical as it might seem to anyone familiar with the history of traditional epistemology, Hayek's conception of knowledge loses some of its eccentricity when considered from the perspective of his treatment of economic equilibrium or "order" (Hayek [1968] 2014, 308–309).

> For a society . . . we can speak of a state of equilibrium at a point of time – but it means only that compatibility exists between the different plans which the individuals composing it have made for action in time. And equilibrium will continue, once it exists, so long as the external data correspond to the common expectations of all the members of the society.
>
> (Hayek [1937] 2014, 64)

Economic order is a condition in which everyone in the economy possesses all of the knowledge required to plan and act effectively on the basis of their plans. It is a condition in which everyone can act without bumping painfully into the furniture of the world, including each other.

The central problem of economics, according to Hayek, is to explain how this condition might come to pass or, more exactly, how a tendency toward this condition, even if it is never fully realized, might operate in the economic

domain. We have good reasons to think such a tendency exists in many different contexts in the economic realm. The existence of a tendency toward order
is the best explanation of the observed fact that *consensuses* often emerge, that is,
that people often come to hold similar (or at least compatible) beliefs concerning the value of particular goods. Were no such tendency at work in market
economies, it would not be unusual to observe, say, two gas stations across the
street from each other selling indistinguishable gallons of gas for wildly different
prices. That this almost never happens in market economies is strong evidence
for the presence of a tendency toward economic order. Economics investigates
the processes by which the plans of various individuals with respect to production and consumption become more (or less) actionable, given the fragmented
and dispersed nature of the subjective data upon which plans are based. On
Hayek's conception, in particular, given the story he tells about how individuals
acquire knowledge from and about the environment over the course of their
(phylogenetic and ontogenetic) developmental history, economics investigates,
theoretically and empirically, any *mechanisms* that serve to facilitate (or hamper)
the coordination of individuals' subjective knowledge concerning the supply
of and demand for various goods with the external environment, including
the subjective knowledge of other individuals. Of course, Hayek ([1945] 2014)
was famous for pointing out the knowledge–coordinating function in the economic domain of an unconscious system of spontaneously adjusting prices.
Changing prices tell people what to do in response to changes in circumstances
that would otherwise, without access to the price system, likely fall outside
their epistemic purview.

The epistemic theory of the trade cycle discussed in Chapter 2 (also see
Scheall 2015b) is an implication of Hayek's account of economic order and
the epistemic function of the price system. Anything that interferes with the
capacity of the price system to reflect changes in relevant circumstances also
hinders its knowledge-coordinating function and thus contributes to the disappointment of individuals' plans and to economic *disorder*. Falsely believing that
they know more than they do (i.e., operating under a pretence of knowledge)
about the theory and empirical conditions of economic order, policymakers
act in ways that either directly or indirectly impede the price system's capacity
to reflect changes in relevant circumstances and thereby hamper its knowledge-
coordinating function, contribute to the failure of economically relevant plans,
and engender economic disorder.

The general epistemic theory of social order and disorder that I subsequently
developed with Butos and McQuade simply generalizes the epistemic theory
of industrial fluctuations to social domains other than the economic. According
to this epistemic theory, order emerges in some social domain – be it the economy, science, politics, or society itself – to the extent that the subjective data
upon which the plans of individuals operating in this domain are based correspond with the objective data, that is, are mutually compatible with each other
and adequate to relevant circumstances in the physical environment. Order in
some domain of society simply means that, absent changes in the environment,

the individuals acting in this domain will all be able to implement and deliberately realize the goals of their respective plans – in other words, that these people *know* in the Hayekian sense of knowledge. It follows that social disorder in some domain is also epistemic. The epistemic theory implies that disorder will emerge in some domain if either no mechanism exists to coordinate knowledge or an epistemic mechanism exists but some exogenous forces act upon it in a way that overrides its endogenous operation. Social disorder indicates a lack of knowledge in the relevant sense: it is an indication that the subjective data of the individuals in the domain are either intersubjectively or externally uncoordinated and that some of their plans are destined to fail. The evidence of social disorder is disappointed expectations and failed plans, and the extent of social disorder is measured by the degree of this disappointment and failure (Scheall, Butos, and McQuade 2019).

Of course, no one thinks it is practically possible in the world outside theoretical models to realize social order perfectly in any particular domain, much less across the whole of society.[1] The objective data to which individuals must adapt their subjective data (and thus their plans) change continuously, far too rapidly and unpredictably to allow cognitively limited individuals to faultlessly accommodate their plans. Moreover, the temptation to interfere with the endogenous operation of epistemic mechanisms is too strong to resist for some people exogenous to the relevant processes, often (but not necessarily) policymakers operating under a pretence of knowledge. However, nothing in the epistemic theory of social order requires that perfect order be a realistic possibility in any domain of society. The actionability of plans is not dichotomous but a matter of degree. Where individuals are less than omniscient and omnipotent, the disappointment of plans is an unavoidable aspect of social life.

On this conception, the social sciences, in general, are concerned with the theoretical analysis of any epistemic mechanisms that might operate in different domains of society, as prices operate in the economic realm, to either facilitate or hinder the coordination of individual knowledge with relevant circumstances. The social sciences are further concerned with the empirical investigation of any mechanisms that actually serve this function in various social domains. Perfect social order is never the measure by which the effectiveness of such mechanisms is to be judged. The evaluation of epistemic mechanisms is always relative and never absolute. What matters is how well some mechanism coordinates knowledge and facilitates the making of actionable plans in a particular domain as compared to other possible mechanisms or to the absence of epistemic mechanisms altogether.

Further epistemic requirements of social order

As already noted at several points in the book, Hayek ([1945] 2014) argued that an unconscious system of spontaneously adjusting prices is a necessary element in minimizing the disappointment of expectations in the economic domain. Of course, knowledge of constantly changing prices is necessary but not sufficient for individuals to adapt their economic plans to new circum-stances.[2] Individuals also require knowledge of conditions that can be assumed to change less frequently than prices. For example, they require knowledge of the external world and of other minds, in particular, knowledge of other market participants and relevant external circumstances, including knowledge of prevailing social and legal institutions and knowledge of any pertinent rules of social conduct, as well as knowledge of relevant scientific facts and theories (Hayek [1961] 2014; also see Vaughn 1999). It is reasonable to assume that similar "background" knowledge is required for social order in domains other than the economic, as well.

Rules of social conduct and the contents of accepted science change over time but typically not as frequently as the conditions that underlie ever-changing commodity prices (Lavoie [1985] 2016, 82). What matters for the purposes of planning and effective plan-based action, of course, is how well subjective data concerning these background conditions correspond to rele-vant environmental circumstances. There are epistemic mechanisms that serve the actionability and thus the tendency toward order in many domains. Thus, in domains where social disorder is observed in the form of disappointed expectations and failed plans, it may be either that this relatively stable back-ground knowledge is poorly coordinated with the objective data, in virtue of the meagerness of the epistemic mechanisms that serve this function, or that the epistemic mechanisms that function to coordinate knowledge concerning more variable foreground circumstances are absent, feeble, or malfunctioning in virtue of exogenous interference. The cause of a disappointed plan, in other words, may lie in the inadequacy of either the actor's background or fore-ground knowledge or, more exactly, in the deficiencies of relevant epistemic mechanisms.

For social order to emerge, any relevant systems of rules of social conduct must be both reasonably well adapted to external physical circumstances and subscribed to by individuals in the relevant society to an adequate degree. Sys-tems of rules of social conduct may be acquired either genetically or culturally (Hayek [1967a] 2014, 278). Among culturally transmitted systems of rules, Hayek distinguished between those that are deliberately designed and those that emerge or develop over time without design. It often happens, of course, that the members of a society follow rules of conduct that have long been followed by previous generations of the same society and that have been handed down as a kind of cultural inheritance. It also happens that, in order to improve the like-lihood of their own society's survival, the members of a society come, deliber-ately or otherwise, to emulate the rules of seemingly more successful societies.[3] Hayek denoted the social orders that emerge from deliberately constructed systems of rules as "organizations" (Hayek [1967a] 2014, 278n) and the orders that emerge out of unconsciously evolved systems of rules as "spontaneous orders" (Hayek [1967a] 2014, 286). Such social orders as we observe in the real world are usually the results of both human design and human action; that is, they emerge out of combinations of, and the interactions between, genetically and culturally transmitted – some imposed and some evolved – systems of rules.[4] In any case, because their members confront comparative difficulties in making actionable plans and coping with the environment, societies that follow rules maladapted to their environment are less likely to persist than those that follow well-adapted systems of rules of conduct. Systems of rules of social conduct are ultimately tested for their environmental suitability in the crucible of natural selection.

Well-adapted systems of rules thus serve a number of epistemic functions. They express knowledge about the past effectiveness of different social practices in various contexts and, like price changes, economize on the knowledge about such practices that would otherwise be required to adjust one's plans to the environment. For example, the general and typically unspoken rules common in many Western societies concerning proper (and improper) behavior at the dining table tell diners what (not) to do, what sort of behavior "works" and, especially, does not "work," in such contexts, and save much of the cognitive labor that would otherwise be involved in deciding how to respond to a fellow diner's request to pass the butter.

To facilitate social order, the scientific presuppositions that enter into individuals' action plans must likewise be adapted to the physical environment – which is not to say that they must be *true*, but merely that they must be suitable for the purposes of planning and action in the relevant context – and broadly, if not necessarily universally, shared among other individuals in the environment. The processes whereby scientific beliefs come to be adapted to relevant objective data and the role that epistemic mechanisms play in securing this result are discussed later in the present chapter, so I will save this topic for that time. Suffice it to say for present purposes that the actionability of plans and thus the degree of order in any particular social domain requires more than a well-functioning epistemic mechanism that communicates knowledge of vacillating foreground circumstances relevant to planning and action in the given domain. It also requires well-coordinated background knowledge and thus well-functioning epistemic mechanisms to secure this coordination between the subjective data of actors in the relevant domain and the objective data. Of course, the objective data of any given domain include all of the epistemic mechanisms that serve to coordinate relevant knowledge, whether of background and relatively stable conditions or of foreground and relatively variable circumstances; thus, social disorder might manifest because one or more of these mechanisms is maladapted to some other epistemic mechanism. To take an obvious example, there may be some tension, in various pertinent contexts, between the epistemic function of the price system and the epistemic mechanisms, to be considered in greater detail subsequently, that serve to coordinate scientific knowledge.

How prices tell you *what to do*

Hayek's ([1945] 2014, 99–100) famous "tin example" illustrates the price system's role in the coordination of economically relevant knowledge and thus its essential role in the maintenance of economic order.

Assume that somewhere in the world a new opportunity for the use of some raw material, say, tin, has arisen, or that one of the sources of supply of tin has been eliminated. It does not matter for our purpose – and it is very significant that it does not matter – which of these two causes has made tin more scarce. All that the users of tin need to know is that some of the tin they used to consume is now more profitably employed elsewhere and that, in consequence, they must economize tin. There is no need for the great majority of them even to know where the more urgent need has arisen, or in favor of what other needs they ought to husband the supply. If only some of them know directly of the new demand, and switch resources over to it, and if the people who are aware of the new gap thus created in turn fill it from still other sources, the effect will rapidly spread throughout the whole economic system and influence not only all the uses of tin but also those of its substitutes and the substitutes of these substitutes, the supply of all the things made of tin, and their substitutes, and so on; and all this without the great majority of those instrumental in bringing about these substitutions knowing anything at all about the original cause of these changes. The whole acts as one market, not because any of its members survey the whole field, but because their limited individual fields of vision sufficiently overlap so that through many intermediaries the relevant information is communicated to all. The mere fact that there is one price for any commodity – or rather that local prices are connected in a manner determined by the cost of transport, etc. – brings about the solution which (it is just conceptually possible) might have been arrived at by one single mind possessing all the information which is in fact dispersed among all the people involved in the process.

Hayek thus describes how the price system conveys indirect knowledge concerning changes in either the supply of or the demand for tin, changes initially known directly by only a few individuals uniquely proximate to these changes, to market participants further removed, who would otherwise likely remain ignorant of them, and how this knowledge diffuses across worldwide markets not only for tin but also for its substitutes and complements. The changing prices of tin on world markets communicate to users of tin how to adjust their planned uses to whatever changes have caused its price to fluctuate without any need for the users to possess direct knowledge of these changed circumstances. Prices economize on the knowledge required to plan effectively.

It is worth pondering the tin example, or one very much like it, at greater length in order to see more clearly how prices tell economic actors what to do in response to changes in relevant circumstances in order to coordinate their plans moving forward with those of other actors.

Forget about tin. Consider the current state of the market for your favorite beverage, whether coffee, tea, or something rather more inebriating. Whatever your preferred tipple, it probably cannot be produced without at least one key ingredient: coffee requires coffee beans, tea cannot be made without tea leaves, wine requires grapes, beer and whiskey require wheat, gin production needs juniper berries, and so on. Chances are, if the price system has been working effectively heretofore, your consumption plans with respect to your favorite beverage are reasonably well adapted to relevant circumstances, for example, your own budget and personal tastes, the budgets and tastes of other consumers, the existing supply of the essential ingredient(s) of the beverage, and, importantly, expectations concerning the future supply of and future demand for this ingredient. The market for your favorite beverage is likely to be relatively orderly.

However, suppose that these expectations concerning the future supply of and future demand for the key ingredient of your favorite beverage turn out to be wildly mistaken and that either some weather-related event wipes out half of next year's crop of the required ingredient or a new demand for it appears that manifests the same effect on the supply available for beverage production. Whatever degree of social order prevailed in the beverage market before this new circumstance appeared has, for the moment at least, been confounded. If a similar degree of order is to return, market participants cannot all plan to consume the same quantity of the beverage as before and must adapt their plans moving forward to the new condition. Provided that the price system is functioning properly, it does not matter – and, as Hayek says in the tin example, "it is very significant that it does not matter" – whether the cause of the newfound scarcity of the ingredient originates on the supply or the demand side of the market for the ingredient, because price changes will communicate to participants in the beverage (and other relevant) markets what they must do to adapt to this new circumstance.

More carefully, if the supply of the ingredient available for production of the beverage is limited due to crop failure, the initial owners of the available stock of the resource as it emerges from nature, directly knowledgeable as they are of this crop failure, will immediately raise their asking prices for the surviving crop in an effort to maintain profits. Alternatively, if the supply of the ingredient available for beverage production is limited because of a new, previously unforeseen demand for the essential ingredient, these newcomers to the market, directly knowledgeable as they are of this new demand, will offer bids above the prior equilibrium price in an attempt to attract adequate supplies of the resource for this new use. Either way, in the face of increased competition for a relatively limited supply of the ingredient, producers of goods intermediate between the raw resource and the final forms in which it is consumed will have to raise their bid prices in order to secure a supply adequate for their purposes. Confronted with higher factor prices, these producers will in turn increase their asking prices for their respective intermediate goods in order to maintain their own profits. Of course, these higher factor prices will ultimately be reflected in higher market prices for whatever consumption goods the essential ingredient figures as an input. Thus, whether the initial impulse originates in a more limited supply or a new source of demand, other things equal, prices will rise to inform consumers of the beverage what they must do to adapt their plans to the new circumstance, namely either 1) consume less

of the beverage, 2) curb consumption of some other good in order to maintain their prior level of consumption of the beverage, or 3) enlarge their budgets in order to maintain prior consumption of the beverage without curbing
consumption of other goods. Of course, not every consumer can successfully
maintain their prior consumption level of the beverage in the manner of one of
the latter two options. *Ex hypothesi*, under the new circumstances, there simply
is not enough of the essential ingredient to go around.[5] Thus, the price of the
beverage will continue to rise to encourage more consumers to adopt the first
course of action until something approaching order is restored.

Now, consider the same scenario, but in circumstances where prices either
do not exist (as far as this is conceivable) or the prices of the resource at various stages of the production process have been dictated exogenously on the
basis of considerations other than the supply of and demand for the resource.
How will consumers of the beverage learn what to do to adapt their consumption plans to the new circumstances, that is, to the newfound relative
scarcity of the essential ingredient available for beverage production? It might
be tempting to respond, especially in today's day and age, that the requisite
knowledge is easily discoverable via sources other than price signals, say, the
Internet or cable news. One might think that a few clicks of the mouse or a
few turns of the television channel are all that would be required to learn that
torrential rains had destroyed the entire annual South American coffee crop
or that an equivalent quantity of coffee beans would be dedicated to some
previously unforeseen use moving forward. But, even granting the dubious
assumption that the Internet or cable news is a reliable source of knowledge
that economic circumstances have changed, it is preposterous to think that this
is all the knowledge (that and *how*) beverage consumers need to adjust their
plans to the changed circumstances.

Unlike the previous scenario, where there was no need for consumers to
know whether the relevant change originated on the supply or demand side
of the market, in this revised scenario, it might make a significant difference to
how consumers should adapt their plans to the new circumstances whether
the change originated on one or the other side of the market. More exactly,
the nature and extent of the changes that consumers would have to make to
coordinate their plans in this new environment would hinge crucially on their
knowledge of relevant price *elasticities*. Prices may not exist as such or, alternatively, might not be permitted to fluctuate in this revised scenario, but this does
not mean that implicit price elasticities would not exist. If the conditions that
would otherwise determine the prices of the ingredient at various stages of the
production process should change, then, even if prices do not exist as such or
are artificially held constant by government fiat, to the extent that the implicit
price elasticity of supply differs from the implicit price elasticity of demand –
in layman's terms, to the extent that the resource's supply and demand curves
have different slopes, implying that supply and demand are distinctly sensitive
or responsive to changes in the (implicit) price of the good – then whether
the change originated on the supply or the demand side would bear different

implications for how consumers should adapt their plans to the new circumstance moving forward.

However, neither Google nor CNBC has figured out yet how to express price elasticities in a way conducive to the epistemic requirements of plan adaptation in this second scenario. In other words, without knowledge of the relevant elasticities, merely knowing that a drought had wiped out half of the next crop of the essential ingredient or that the supply of the ingredient available for beverage production had been similarly depleted by a new source of demand would do little to help beverage consumers adapt to the new circumstance. Indeed, even knowledge of these elasticities, which would, at best, tell consumers of the effect of the change on the total quantity of the ingredient available, would not inform them of its unique significance for their own beverage-consumption plans moving forward, that is, for what they must do to adapt to the new circumstances.

In the sense that in neither case could market participants adapt their plans to changed conditions, the case in which prices simply do not exist is similar to the one in which prices are pre-determined and manipulated by exogenous forces. However, the two cases are different in that, in the no-price case, there would be *no signals* telling market participants what to do to adapt to new circumstances, whereas, in the manipulated-price case, there would be *misleading signals* betraying market participants into maladapting their plans to the new conditions. In the first case, market participants would be given no idea what to do; in the second, they would be given the wrong idea what to do.

Following this discussion, it is perhaps easier to see how, on the epistemic theory of industrial fluctuations discussed at length in Chapter 2, prices that have been pre-determined by forces and for reasons exogenous to the market contribute to economic disorder. When, for example, monetary policymakers manipulate loan markets to ensure a particular interest rate (or range of interest rates) for extra-economic reasons, they express misleading signals to everyone in these markets regarding relevant objective data. The subjective data of market participants fail to correspond to the objective data, and market participants are misled into maladapting their plans. Economic crisis strikes when market participants sooner or later realize their errors, as they eventually must, given that policymakers are not knowledgeable enough to maintain the required deception in perpetuity. The recession is, first, the dawning realization of many individuals across the economy of the inevitable disappointment of various of their economic plans and, second, their flailing efforts to gain a better grasp on and adapt their plans to the objective data.

How reputation signals tell scientists (and others) *what to do*

My colleagues and co-authors, Thomas McQuade and William Butos (2003; also see Butos and McQuade 2012), have argued that a mechanism exists that plays a knowledge-coordinating and knowledge-economizing role in the scientific domain similar to the epistemic function served by prices in market contexts. This epistemic device coordinates the beliefs of scientists relative both to each other and to the ultimate arbiter of scientific success, the external environment. In plain language, it is in virtue of this system that a consensus emerges in a scientific discipline or field, and it is this system that ensures a degree of correspondence between a consensus and relevant objective data that promotes the actionability of plans based upon the consensus belief. According to Butos and McQuade (2012), the "publication-citation-reputation" (PCR) system of modern science provides price-like signals to individual scientists that tell them, in effect, what to do to coordinate their activities with other scientists in their respective scientific (sub-)domain (and often across different scientific domains). The pattern of *citations*, positive or negative, that follow upon the *publication* of an article in a scientific journal, thereby serving to either strengthen or weaken the publishing author's *reputation*, provides crucial indicators to other scientists concerning trends in the formation and destruction of science-relevant beliefs (also see Lavoie [1985] 2016, 84). The PCR system is a weathervane that indicates the direction in which the prevailing winds of science are blowing. It communicates to other scientists their peers' evaluations of both *theories* and of the *evidence* for, or against, said theories and provides knowledge to scientists that they require to adapt their plans to prevailing circumstances.

Scientists are no more gods than are policymakers. Scientists do not have privileged access to the facts of the world, not even in their particular scientific domains. However, they do have a PCR system that expresses in economized form their peers' judgments about these facts and the relative significance of competing theoretical explanations in light of the empirical evidence. The PCR system assists scientists in adapting their own individual beliefs to these judgments. It is an aspect of the tentative and fallible nature of science that these judgments are tentative and fallible as well and in constant need of revision, as both the pertinent objective data and subjective judgments about the objective data change over time. However, the PCR system ensures that, at any given time, the subjective data of individual scientists are mutually coordinated and correspond well enough to external circumstances for the purposes of plan-based action in the scientific domain and, often, beyond it.

The manner in which the PCR system informs scientists what to do in their particular domains in response to new circumstances is analogous (though not identical) to the way that the price system instructs market participants what to do to adapt their economic plans to new data. Imagine that a new theory has been published to account for some important phenomena. There are many reasons, and many ways in which, the theory might be subsequently used, extended, defended, criticized, pursued, adopted, or rejected, in whole or in part. In most empirical disciplines, of course, one of the foremost reasons a theory is either accepted or rejected concerns how well it is judged to both stand up against the observable evidence and explain the relevant phenomena. But non-empirical considerations such as how a theory is judged in terms of

its simplicity, elegance, prospective fruitfulness, parsimony, ease of use, mathematical tractability, and conservatism (i.e., the extent to which it preserves
the existing body of accepted scientific assumptions) – not to mention various
social factors, such as peer pressure and pecuniary incentives – can be relevant
to theory choice and may count as reasons to accept or reject a theory. In
general, however, the theory will be either neglected or cited, either positively or negatively. Neglect of a theory typically does not burnish an author's
reputation, but whether it damages or indifferently affects it is likely to be a
contingent matter, dependent on particular circumstances. Positive and negative citations, on the other hand, directly affect the reputation of the theory
and its author, and, in turn, further affect the author's subsequent chances for
professional success, acquiring research funding, publishing new research, and
so on. The PCR system

> ensures that what is ultimately accepted as scientific knowledge has been
> exposed to the daylight of rational scrutiny. The scientific knowledge
> that emerges from the PCR process has been subjected to, criticized from
> the perspective of, and deemed in acceptable conformance with, the
> assessment standards of the relevant scientific community. It is through the
> PCR process that scientific error (or, worse yet, deliberate fraud) is identified
> and corrected.
>
> (Scheall, Butos, and McQuade 2019, 1–2)

The PCR system informs scientists what their peers think of the new theory
and, to some extent at least, why they judge the theory as they do. It is then
up to individual scientists to adapt their plans in light of a better understanding
of the consequences of either accepting, neglecting, or rejecting the new theory. Science "involves an interpersonal process of persuasion . . . More often
[scientific consensus] is the result of heated arguments about the interpretation advanced by rival theories and subtle hints that the new theory somehow
explains better" (Lavoie [1985] 2016, 14; see also 63).

   Much like prices, reputation signals economize on the knowledge required
to effectively adapt one's plan to new conditions. So long as the system is left to
itself and not exogenously forced into channels different from those it would
take if left to scientists in the relevant domain, many individual scientists will
be able to adapt to the reception of a new theory without having to read its
original published version. The PCR system tells scientists what they need to
know about a theory to adapt their plans to it, even if they lack first-hand
knowledge of its content. If only a few scientists read a new publication and
proceed to cite it, positively or negatively, and if other scientists respond to this
signal appropriately, by either adopting, rejecting, or neglecting its content,
then "the effect will rapidly spread throughout the whole . . . system and influence" the subsequent evaluation of the theory and related (complementary or
competing) theories. In this way, a scientific consensus is formed, sustained,
and, sooner or later, undermined and overturned. "The whole acts as one"

scientific community, "not because any of its members survey the whole field, but because their limited individual fields of vision sufficiently overlap so that through many intermediaries the relevant information is communicated to all" (Hayek [1945] 2014, 99–100).[6]

As noted previously, elements of scientific knowledge typically form part of the background knowledge required for successful plan-based action in society. Thus, to the extent that an unmanipulated PCR process promotes the orderliness of scientific domains and so the actionability of the knowledge that emerges therefrom, it also promotes knowledge coordination, the making of actionable plans, and therefore the orderliness of the broader society beyond science. To take an obvious example, various elements of Newtonian physics enter into the background knowledge required to act effectively in the (macro-)physical world. Whether one plans to throw a baseball, shoot a gun, or send a rocket to the moon, knowledge of Newtonian principles, if perhaps only superficial, is conducive to the success of related plans. More to the point, the comparative orderliness of the scientific domain of macro (not micro!) physics serves the orderliness of domains that employ, if only in the background, the knowledge that emerges from this domain.

The epistemic theory of social order implies that exogenous interference with the spontaneous operation of an epistemic mechanism – attempts to override or hinder its operation for the sake of ends unrelated to its epistemic purpose – contributes to failed expectations and social disorder. Unfortunately, just as the price system can be exogenously abrogated or manipulated for non-economic reasons, the PCR system can also be overridden to serve interests other than the traditional values of science. Plans for economic activity based on a manipulated price system or made in the absence of a price system are more likely to fail, other things equal, as are plans made without recourse to a spontaneously adjusting PCR process.

Just as it is often (though not necessarily) policymakers operating under a pretence of knowledge who, wittingly or not, override the epistemic function of the price system, it is typically (though not always) policymakers with misplaced faith in their own knowledge of the relevant objective data, that is, of the scientific facts, who manipulate the PCR system for ends unrelated to science as traditionally conceived. In principle, the PCR process might be manipulated by exogenous forces emerging from either government or corporate, public or private, interests. As a matter of fact, in many modern scientific contexts, there are exogenous forces acting from all directions on scientists and scientific practice at all times. These forces are not dangerous to science *per se* provided that their combined effect on the PCR process is more or less neutral. Exogenous interference in scientific domains becomes dangerous when *particular* interests, unbalanced and not neutralized by competing interests, are able to hijack the PCR process and decide its results. For this reason, there should be special concern about the effects of governments and political activity on scientific practice. Only governments, super-governmental organizations, and their various agencies possess sufficient coercive power to, at almost any time and place, override the interests of all other comers and impose their will on some scientific domain. What's more, governments are often the main funders and regulators, and are frequently significant beneficiaries, of scientific research. Government officials can leverage these institutional functions to enforce their particular visions of the scientific facts.[7] Private interests, on the other hand, tend to be in competition with each other, and the net effect of their competing efforts to bend science toward their special concerns is often neutral.

In any case, the knowledge exemplified in a scientific consensus is likely to be less actionable when it has been determined from outside the PCR process and imposed on the relevant scientific domain (also see Lavoie [1985] 2016, 84). When this happens, it is not only the orderliness of the relevant scientific domain that is threatened but the orderliness of other realms of society, the members of which use the results of science as assumptions in their action plans. Scientific disorder threatens social order.

An example of the potentially dangerous influence of government on the PCR process and of government's unique capacity to override even powerful private interests can be found in my co-authored paper with Butos and McQuade. In "Social and Scientific Disorder as Epistemic Phenomena, or the Consequences of Government Dietary Guidelines" (Scheall, Butos, and McQuade 2019), upon which parts of the argument of the current chapter are based, we offer a relevant case study that illustrates the epistemic theory of social order and disorder and the frequently deleterious consequences of the problem of policymaker ignorance.

Briefly, before the late 1970s, the U.S. federal government had never taken much of a stance on the wisdom of any particular dietary advice and had not interfered to any considerable degree with the PCR process of nutrition science. No consensus had yet emerged concerning the "fat hypothesis" (the proposition that the dietary fat we consume is the primary cause of obesity, coronary heart disease [CHD], diabetes, and a whole host of other maladies) and the competing "carbohydrate hypothesis" (the view that consuming carbohydrates is the main cause of these conditions). Each view had its defenders in nutrition and related scientific fields. Neither group was able to convince or otherwise impose its views on the other, and research on both hypotheses proceeded concurrently. What's more, as might have been expected, competing private interests – on one side, in support of the fat hypothesis, the sugar and processed-food industries and, on the other, in support of the carbohydrate hypothesis, the meat, egg, and dairy industries – had been fighting an interminable range war over their rival hypotheses. Their competing efforts to influence the science of nutrition, obesity, and heart and kidney disease had, to that point in time, had little net effect one way or the other.

Then, unfortunately for the health of several subsequent generations of Americans, federal policymakers got it in their heads that their remit encompassed the proffering of healthful dietary advice. Worse – for had they accurately assessed their ignorance, they might have been incented to do *something else* – policymakers succumbed to the pretence that they knew enough to determine the appropriate content of this advice, despite the apparent absence of any consensus in nutrition science. Federal policymakers simply *chose* a winner in the debate, ignored countervailing voices and the absence of decisive evidence, and subsequently imposed and enforced their preferred hypothesis through control of much of the research funding in relevant fields. Given their ignorance of a consensus endogenously determined in a spontaneously adjusting PCR process, policymakers could have realized the goal of proffering healthful dietary advice only if spontaneous forces, perhaps luck, had intervened. Tragically – the word is not inappropriate – it is now apparent four decades after the first statement of federal dietary guidelines that relevant policymakers were neither uniquely knowledgeable nor especially lucky. The PCR process that otherwise might have eventually led spontaneously to an undistorted consensus has only slowly overcome the exogenous pressure to conform to the government's priorities. Many Americans adopted the federal government's advice in their plans of dietary action. They tended to conform their eating behavior to the government's advice to consume more carbohydrates and less dietary fat. "But the plans went astray and social disorder in the domain of diet and nutrition followed: the incidence rates of obesity, CHD, and diabetes – the very conditions the politicians ostensibly meant to ameliorate – either rose or failed to fall over this time" (Scheall, Butos, and McQuade 2019, 14).

An unmanipulated PCR system is a mechanism for coordinating the subjective data of individual scientists with relevant objective data. It serves the actionability of individuals acting in the scientific domain and therefore functions to make science more orderly. To the extent that scientific presuppositions enter into the action plans of individuals outside the scientific domain, the degree of scientific order or disorder serves to either promote or hinder the orderliness of other domains as well. Thus, a PCR system that has been either abrogated or manipulated in favor of particular interests is a mechanism for disorder in the scientific domain and beyond.

Political order and disorder

A well-ordered political domain would be one in which all political actors, policymakers and constituents alike, could coordinate their knowledge intersubjectively and relative to other relevant environmental conditions. Political order would mean that each political actor possessed an internally consistent belief system compatible both with the belief systems of other political actors and with other relevant external circumstances. An orderly political domain would be one where disappointment was minimized because all political actors could make and effect actionable plans. More to the point, for there to be a tendency toward order in some political context, epistemic mechanisms must exist that serve to coordinate the initially uncoordinated subjective data with politically-relevant objective data.

Unfortunately, the common mechanisms of democratic political contexts tend to be meager epistemic devices.[8] Standard voting mechanisms convey knowledge to policymakers concerning their constituents' political priorities but (at best) only in a limited, nebulous, and easily defeated form.[9] Policymakers can also acquire limited evidence of their constituents' priorities from public opinion polls, but, again, only in a vague, confused, and changeable form: public opinion often changes from one day to the next, while even the notion that a particular survey accurately reflects public opinion *at a given time* is often a dubious proposition. Policymakers can acquire anecdotal evidence of their constituents' political priorities from direct contact with individual voters, but it is treacherous to draw inferences from such limited samples to the whole population of constituents. Historical trends might provide some knowledge of constituents' political priorities, but, unless there is special reason to think particular trends have not changed, extrapolations from past to future are infamously problematic. In short, standard democratic mechanisms convey little of the knowledge of constituents' priorities that policymakers require to realize policy goals associated with these preferences. Political order requires more effective mechanisms than are commonly found in democratic contexts for the communication of constituents' demands to policymakers.

Furthermore, assuming for the moment an epistemic mechanism that communicates actionable knowledge to policymakers of their constituents' political priorities, such a mechanism would provide little or none of the non-propositional know-how that political order requires. At best, it would tell policymakers *that* their constituents want some end to be pursued, but knowing that constituents demand the pursuit of a particular policy goal does not mean that policymakers know or could learn from this mechanism *how* to deliberately realize these goals. Even if policymakers possessed perfect knowledge of their constituents' demands, they might not possess knowledge of means adequate to deliberately realize related goals. When constituents demand the pursuit of policy goals the realization of which requires more knowledge than policymakers possess, there are few mechanisms the latter can rely upon to surmount their epistemic burdens. The so-called "experts" that policymakers often turn to in this regard are not omniscient in their domains but often fail to possess knowledge required to realize a policy goal (Koppl 2018). True, experts may know more than policymakers about various phenomena, but this is saying very little in many cases. A marginal improvement upon policymakers' manifest ignorance does not imply the adequacy of expert knowledge for the purposes of effective policymaking. Given their ignorance, when policymakers do pursue policy goals that constituents demand – say, when under the pretense that their knowledge is adequate to the realization of some such goal – there should be little surprise when these goals are not realized. Typical democratic mechanisms do a poor job of telling policymakers *what to do* to meet their constituents' demands. These mechanisms unambiguously express neither knowledge *of* constituents' policy demands nor knowledge *how* adequate to realize them. There should be little wonder that constituents' expectations of even the most admired politicians are frequently disappointed. Of course, such disappointment is, from a political-epistemological perspective, the manifestation and empirical marker of political disorder.

To the extent that policymakers recognize their ignorance in this regard, they confront a disincentive to pursue the policy goals set for them by their constituents. If policymakers know that they do not know either what these goals are or how to realize them, there should be little surprise when they opt to do *something else* other than pursue the policies demanded by their constituents. On the other hand, if policymakers fail to recognize the meagerness of democratic mechanisms in expressing their constituents' policy preferences or fail to appreciate their ignorance of the means required to realize goals associated with these preferences – if they succumb to the pretence that they possess the knowledge required to realize their constituents' policy demands – then they face an incentive, unwarranted given their impoverished epistemic circumstances, to pursue policy ends that they cannot deliberately realize.

Inasmuch as respect for democratic ideals requires that constituents' political priorities guide policy decisions, that is, to the extent that being a good democratic policymaker means realizing or at least seeking to realize, the goals associated with constituents' priorities, these ideals will not be well served without epistemic mechanisms that effectively convey relevant knowledge from constituents to policymakers, because policymakers will be disincented from pursuing and, in any case, will not be able to deliberately realize constituents' demands. As ever, epistemic considerations are logically prior to moral considerations. Democratic ideals will be respected only if policymakers know how to do so or spontaneous forces act to mitigate their ignorance. Respecting democratic ideals is not as simple as instituting a majoritarian system but requires creative thought about different democratic institutions capable of improving upon the knowledge-coordinating and knowledge-economizing properties of majoritarian democracy. Those truly committed to the ideals of democracy – civil rights, popular sovereignty, self-determination, due process, equality under the law, and so on – should not confuse the *means* of democracy for its *ends*. It is important to ask whether and to what extent common democratic mechanisms are effective means to the end of realizing the goals associated with these ideals. The answer depends to a large degree on how well these mechanisms convey relevant knowledge from constituents to policymakers. If there is anything to the present argument, affirmative answers to this question are dubious.

However, it is no less important to recognize that, while democratic mechanisms do a poor job telling policymakers what to do to meet their constituents' demands, they are no more effective at communicating knowledge from policymakers to constituents that the latter need to adapt their plans to relevant circumstances. Indeed, there is *no* apparent mechanism whatever that communicates knowledge to constituents concerning the kinds of policies that are actually within the ken and control of policymakers. There is nothing that conveys to constituents knowledge concerning the epistemic capacities of policymakers or knowledge of the epistemic requirements of different possible policy pursuits. Constituents are largely ignorant of the epistemic burdens that their policy demands place on policymakers. Thus, constituents have little under-standing of the policy goals that policymakers can learn enough to deliberately realize and those objectives that, because they exceed the capacities of cogni-tively limited policymakers, can be realized only if spontaneous forces inter-vene. Neither do constituents have much knowledge of any spontaneous forces that might intervene to moderate the effects of their epistemically burdensome policy demands. If standard democratic institutions leave policymakers largely ignorant of their constituents' policy demands and how to realize them, these institutions leave constituents in a state of blind darkness about the likely realiza-tion, deliberate or spontaneous (or some combination of the two), of various potential policy pursuits. In short, constituents do not know very well what to do to avoid placing insurmountable epistemic burdens on policymakers; nei-ther do they know what to do to demand policies that might be realizable with the assistance of spontaneous forces. All of which is to say that constituents do not know what to do avoid circumstances in which their policy demands are likely to be disappointed.[10]

Political order requires epistemic mechanisms that both convey to constitu-ents what they need to know to demand realizable policies and communicate to policymakers what they need to know to realize constituents' policy demands. Unfortunately, the epistemic requirements of political order do not end there. In order to minimize political disappointment, particularly in the medium to long run, constituents require a mechanism that informs them of the policy goals that policymakers actually pursue at any given time. As already noted, policymak-ers can often accrue the same benefits by merely pretending to pursue a policy goal as they can by actually pursuing it. They can form "blue-ribbon panels" and "watchdog committees" to conduct research on various social problems; they can conduct "feasibility studies" to investigate potential solutions; they can hire "experts" or "put their best people" on a problem; they can make insincere efforts at policymaking, then claim to have been thwarted by the dastardly devils of the rival faction or party; they can do all of this without ever actually making a substantive policy decision and without ever appearing to the voting public to have had any but the best intentions. In other words, policymakers can be skillful bullshit artists.[11] Same as it ever was, to be sure. However, in the modern age of 24-hour news, overtly biased journalism, politicians with sizable media budgets, and deranged social media bombardments, it is perhaps easier than ever for those in positions of power to manipulate constituents into mistakenly thinking their interests are being pursued. When the benefits to be expected from bullshitting are roughly equivalent to those of the more epistemically burdensome task of earnestly trying to meet constituents' policy demands, we are likely to discover a big steaming pile of political bullshit. More to the point, constituents need a way to distinguish bullshit from earnestness, if their plans are not to be disappointed when they eventually discover the ruse that their demands were actually being pursued by policymakers.

Finally, political order requires a mechanism that informs constituents not only of the policy goals that policymakers actually pursue but of the costs of these pursuits and of the extent to which they succeed in their pursuits. Obviously, there is room for considerable disappointment of political expectations if it is discovered, say, that some policy goal has been pursued at a cost that exceeds its estimated cost by orders of magnitude or that some goal has been pursued but not realized.

Reflection and foreshadow

The epistemic-mechanistic approach to the problem of policymaker ignorance investigates various devices whereby knowledge might be conveyed to both constituents and policymakers that each group requires to ensure that excessively epistemically burdensome policies – read: polices likely to fail unless spontaneity saves them – are neither demanded by constituents nor pursued by policymakers. Mechanisms that communicate relevant knowledge between constituents and policymakers are necessary for a tendency toward order to be present in some political domain. Political order requires epistemic devices that convey to both individual policymakers and constituents what to do to make actionable plans in the prevailing political environment. In particular, an orderly political domain requires epistemic mechanisms that communicate to policymakers knowledge concerning 1) the policy goals demanded by constituents; 2) means adequate to the deliberate realization of these goals, if any such means exist; and 3) any spontaneous forces that might serve to mitigate the effects of their (policymakers') ignorance. Moreover, political order requires mechanisms that communicate to constituents knowledge concerning 4) the epistemic capacities of policymakers, 5) the epistemic requirements of different potential policy goals, 6) any spontaneous forces that might serve to mitigate the effects of policymaker ignorance, 7) the policy goals that policymakers actually pursue at any given time, 8) the costs of and 9) the degree of success or failure of policymakers' policy pursuits. Such mechanisms would allow policymakers and constituents alike to acquire the knowledge necessary to adjust their subjective data to the relevant objective data, including – indeed, especially – the subjective data of other political actors.

Unfortunately, the mechanisms that typically exist in democratic political contexts ostensibly to convey knowledge between political actors are quite inadequate to the requirements of a tendency toward political order. Extant voting mechanisms do not suffice to mitigate the problem of policymaker ignorance or its deleterious consequences. However, the analysis of the present chapter has, I hope, at least shown the sort of epistemic mechanisms that political order requires. If I haven't offered a theory of political order, replete with posits of specific devices capable of conveying the required knowledge from constituent to policymaker and back again, I have at least provided a theory of such a theory, a meta-theory, if you will, of political order.

In a more advanced state of political-epistemological inquiry, the epistemic-mechanistic approach would probably also involve either the testing of such devices in real-world natural experiments, which, of course, might prove very difficult, if not impossible, in practice (but such are the complex phenomena of society) or the theoretical analysis of their operation in various model settings.[12]

In order to avoid misinterpretation, it is important to emphasize again that nothing in the argument of this section should be read as an attack on the ideals that "government of the people, by the people, and for the people" is intended to serve. Rather, it is an argument that the standard mechanisms of democracy are not always – indeed, perhaps only rarely – effective in this regard. If we are serious about upholding democratic ideals, if we mean to pay more than mere lip service to these ideals, we need to think creatively about mechanisms that might ensure that goals associated with these ideals are actually pursued and realized.

Notes

1 Social order across the whole of society would mean the coordination of knowledge and thus the presence of epistemic mechanisms to facilitate this coordination, both within and across *all* domains of society.

2 Indeed, trivially, individuals need not only knowledge *of* changing prices but also knowledge *how* to adjust their plans to changing prices appropriately.

3 The "chiefly negative (or prohibitory) rules of conduct which make possible the formation of social order are of three kinds . . . (1) rules that are merely observed in fact but have never been stated in words;. . . (2) rules that, though they have been stated in words, still merely express approximately what has long before been generally observed in action; and (3) rules that have been deliberately introduced and therefore necessarily exist as words set out in sentences" (Hayek [1970] 2014, 343–344).

4 "[T]he degree to which outcomes are unintended is a continuum" (Schmidtz 2012).

5 Also see Lavoie ([1985b] 2016, 75; italics in the original):

> [W]hen a rival outbids me for a factor of production (say, by pushing its price so high that I can no longer afford to use this factor in my own project), he is . . . *informing* me. He is telling me that this factor has more highly valued uses than the one to which I would have put it. When the bidding of thousands of participants instead of just two is involved, the informing process is still going on, but it is now the scattered bits of knowledge from all the participants that combine to produce a price that is informative, in turn, to each of them. It is only by being informed in this way – by the contrary tugging of all of one's rivals – that any one producer can be said to know what he is doing.

6 "There is a network of overlapping specialties in the scientific community in which border contributions meet the pressure of criticism from related scholars, but in which no one scientist can possibly understand the whole" (Lavoie [1985b] 2016, 64).

7 The infamous case of Trofim Lysenko and the tragic tale of the consequences of the Soviet government's interference in mid-20th-century biological and agronomic science is an especially egregious example of this phenomenon.

8 In the present section, I focus on the epistemic properties of voting mechanisms and other devices commonly found in democratic contexts, as these are the most obvious examples of mechanisms potentially capable of conveying relevant knowledge between political actors. I have little to say about any mechanisms that might communicate knowledge between constituents and policymakers in non-democratic contexts.

9 The problem may be even more profound: the famous "impossibility theorem" associated with Nobel Prize-winning economist Kenneth Arrow (1950) shows that, given a

few fairly plausible assumptions, no voting system can translate the preferences of individual voters into a preference ranking for the entire constituency.

10 "Democratic decision-making needs to recognize its own fallibility, and hence needs to institute feedback mechanisms by which it can learn how to devise better solutions and correct its course in light of new information about the consequences of policies" (Anderson 2006, 12).

11 In the sense of Harry Frankfurt's (2005) *On Bullshit.*

12 Shane Ralston (2012) argues for a (John) Deweyan-Hayekian theory of *democratic experimentalism.* Also see Dewey (1976), (1981a), (1981b), (1981c), and Anderson (2006).

6 Hayekian political epistemology as a science of the limits of deliberate political action

> If we are to understand how society works, we must attempt to define the general nature and range of our ignorance concerning it. Though we cannot see in the dark, we must be able to trace the limits of the dark areas.
> – F. A. Hayek, *The Constitution of Liberty* ([1960] 2011)

In this last chapter, I explore the possibility of a *constitutional* approach to the problem of policymaker ignorance. The ultimate aim of such an approach, as its name implies, is the crafting of a political constitution, either merely in theory or also in practice, that mitigates the effects of policymaker ignorance as far as possible.[1] A constitutional approach to the problem of policymaker ignorance investigates the limits of deliberate political action – more exactly, the epistemic capacities of human policymakers and the kinds of policy goals deliberately realizable on the basis of these capacities – and therefore, *ipso facto*, the range of policy goals realizable only if spontaneous forces intervene. That is, if we define the range of goals that policymakers can deliberately achieve on the basis of their epistemic capacities, at the same time, we also define the range of goals that they cannot deliberately achieve, the goals that require the assistance of spontaneous forces of some kind(s) and to some extent if they are to be realized at all. Beyond investigating the goals that can and, because of policymaker ignorance, cannot be deliberately realized, a constitutional approach investigates the nature and extent of whatever spontaneous forces might operate in a given political-institutional environment to mitigate the consequences of policymaker ignorance. A constitutional approach thus provides essential knowledge about the possibilities for the realization, deliberate or spontaneous, of various potential policy goals.

On a constitutional approach, mitigating the problem of policymaker ignorance means constraining policymakers to the pursuit of policy objectives the realization of which they can at least contribute to, given their limited knowledge and learning capacities. We cannot make policymakers truly omniscient and omnipotent, but we might limit their range of political motion to pursuits with respect to which their epistemic capacities are adequate, making them, in effect, *functionally omniscient and omnipotent* with respect to their specifically political decisions. We cannot give policymakers all the knowledge and abilities they might need to solve any problem come what may, but we might limit the problems under their purview to those they can contribute to mitigating on the basis of their knowledge and learning capacities. Such a constitution would constrain both policymakers from pursuing and constituents from demanding the pursuit of objectives to which political action could not make a positive contribution.

At the same time, such a constitution would go a long way toward mitigating the ancillary problem of policymaker incentives: in a world of functionally omniscient and omnipotent policymakers, where policymaking was constrained to the pursuit of policy goals policymakers could actually help realize on the basis of their epistemic capacities, ignorance of either their constituents' interests or of means adequate to realize related objectives could not distort policymakers' incentives. In such a world, in effect, the constitution would treat as politically relevant only a subset of constituents' overall interests, in particular, those interests associated with policy goals that policymakers could help realize on the basis of their epistemic capacities. In such a world, not everything would be political. Only those objects with regard to which politics could make a positive contribution, as determined by political-epistemological inquiry, would be potential objects of political concern.

In order to get at some of the issues relevant to the constitutional approach to the problem of policymaker ignorance, I return once again to the relationship between Hayek and Keynes. Policymaking contexts in which the business-cycle and macroeconomic theories of Hayek and Keynes are potentially relevant constitute empirical case studies for political epistemology. I do not mean to pretend that political epistemology has it within its power to conclusively settle the Hayek-Keynes debate, but we might use its tools to determine whether policymakers are epistemically equipped to deliberately promote economic order using one or the other theory as a policy instrument. Perhaps more importantly, whether we ever actually succeeded in making such a determination, Hayekian political epistemology clarifies what would be required to do so.

Hayek versus Keynes yet again

For all the heat that the Hayek-Keynes debate generated between the two principals, it shed remarkably little light on the facts of the business cycle and macroeconomy. Eighty-odd years after the debate petered out, the respective intellectual descendants of Hayek and Keynes almost invariably interpret the Great Depression, and related events such as the more recent "Great Recession," to support their preferred theoretical perspective. I have argued that this conflict will never be resolved on the basis of either the empirical evidence or the methodological precepts subscribed to by members of the rival camps (Scheall 2015e). Both theories are so underspecified that whatever happens come what may, whatever evidence is observed, both can be interpreted as having survived the gauntlet of empirical falsification; there is no evidence that must, on pain of irrationality, compel a defender of one theory to reject it in favor of the other. Moreover, the two schools follow distinct methodologies that provide little common ground for the emergence of consensus.

In the present sub-section, I modify this prior assessment somewhat. I still believe that the evidence will never tell us which theory is *true*. However, from the perspective of Hayekian political epistemology, the truth of a theory is immaterial. What matters for the purposes of political epistemology is not the truth of a theory but the contribution it makes to the actionability of plans. Can a theory be used to build a plan that can be acted upon to deliberately realize a goal? A false theory simply makes for, or at least tends to make for, less actionable plans. Put another way, epistemic burdens tend to be heavier where only false theories are available for the purposes of planning, because more knowledge needs to be acquired to overcome such falsity. False presuppositions need not be fatal to a plan of action but might mean instead merely that more knowledge must be acquired to compensate. What matters in the present context is whether either Hayek's theory or Keynes' theory provides theoretical knowledge that, in conjunction with the available empirical data, can yield predictions of a degree adequate to the kind and extent of social control required to realize what Keynes called "full-employment equilibrium" (or, for Hayek, economic order.)[2] Are plans of economic policymaking founded upon Hayek's theory more or less actionable than plans of economic policymaking built upon Keynes' theory? More to the point, what are the relative epistemic burdens of actionable plans built upon each theory; which epistemic burden is heavier for ungodlike cognitively limited human policymakers to carry?

I doubt that a general answer, much less a consensus on a general answer, to this question is likely to emerge anytime soon. However, the concepts of Hayekian political epistemology can at least help us come to grips with some of these issues. We may at least get some empirical purchase on whether, in a particular context, policymakers possess the knowledge required to use one theory as a policy instrument more effectively than the other. That is, we may be able to use political epistemology to empirically investigate the epistemic burdens that economic policymakers confront with respect to Hayek's and Keynes' competing theories of industrial fluctuations and unemployment. We may be able to understand – perhaps not definitively, but some understanding is better than none – whether policymakers can acquire the knowledge necessary to use one or the other theory to deliberately realize and maintain equilibrium and, if not, whether any spontaneous forces exist in relevant environments to mitigate the effects of policymaker ignorance.

A general schema for empirical political epistemology

On Hayekian political epistemology, whether policymakers can deliberately realize a policy goal depends on whether they can acquire adequate general and particular knowledge. The theoretical constructions upon which policymakers rely and the empirical data that they insert into these constructions must be sufficiently comprehensive to yield predictions "full" enough for the degree of social control required to deliberately realize the relevant policy goal. If either the available theories or the data are deficient in this respect, then the relevant goals cannot be deliberately realized; they can be realized, if at all, only if spontaneous forces of some kind intervene to some extent.

Thus, in any given policymaking context, the first question of empirical political epistemology is whether there is a theory that implies that the desired policy goal might be deliberately realized via particular policy means. Is there an extent theory that, in effect, implies *policy P is a means to the realization of policy goal G?* If the answer to this question is no, then either the goal must be given up as an appropriate end of deliberate political action and left to spontaneous forces to realize (or not), or such a theory must be found, unless policymakers are just to make guesses unguided by theoretical knowledge in the hope that some guesses turn out "lucky," which is just another way of leaving the realization of the relevant goal to spontaneity. In any case, if a theory appropriate to the deliberate realization of the goal is not available, political epistemology must turn to ask whether any theories of the required kind are under development – are policymakers likely to *learn* an adequate theory in the foreseeable future? – and whether any spontaneous forces operate in the relevant context to mitigate the effects of policymaker ignorance.

If a theory can be found that implies policy means to realize the relevant goal, the second question to consider concerns the theory's adequacy as a policymaking instrument. In particular, it must be asked whether the theory adequately encompasses what is already known about the potential causes of, or whether it ignores factors believed to play a causal role in, the phenomena to be addressed via policy. It is important to ask, in other words, whether the theory is sufficiently comprehensive as a theory of the relevant phenomena or whether it leaves potential causal factors out of the picture. To the extent that a theory ignores causal factors that actually do figure in the manifestation of the phenomena, it exhibits the "theory problem" discussed in Chapter 2, and the theory will systematically fail as a tool of explanation and prediction, and therefore as an effective instrument of social control and deliberate policymaking. Again, a negative answer to this question means either that a supplementary theory sufficiently comprehensive to encompass what is known about the potential causes of the phenomena must be discovered or that political-epistemological inquiry must turn to investigate whatever spontaneous forces might operate in the prevailing circumstances to mitigate the effects of policymaker ignorance, that is, which might function to ensure that, where the relevant phenomena are caused by considerations beyond the scope of the theory, the effects emanating from these neglected causal factors are neutralized, despite policymakers' ignorance.

Political epistemology is concerned with all of the combinations of ways – that is, on the basis of current knowledge, future knowledge, or spontaneous forces – that policymaker ignorance might be surmounted or its effects mitigated, and political-epistemological inquiry must push in all of these directions to the exclusion of none. Political epistemology must ask about the knowledge that exists, the knowledge that might soon be within policymakers' grasp, the mechanisms whereby policymakers might learn knowledge required of effective policy action, and the consequences of action on an inadequate epistemic basis. Political epistemology is, among other things, a science of all of the various sciences relevant to policymaking, which investigates the knowledge produced by and the epistemic progress of these sciences and, especially, the adequacy of their knowledge products for policymaking purposes. Empirical political epistemology is concerned with any theory and data problems in these sciences and, especially, with the implications of these problems for policymaking, that is, with the manner and degree to which theory and data problems in policy-relevant sciences confound policymaking efforts to deliberately realize various policy goals.

If it has been determined that the available theoretical knowledge is adequate to policymakers' task in the context under investigation, the next question is whether sufficiently extensive data of the right kind, that is, of a kind that can be, in effect, "plugged" into the relevant theory to yield a prediction of a sufficiently high degree, are available. There must be both data of a kind appropriate to the terms of the relevant theoretical construction and, of course, enough of these data. As discussed previously, to the extent that data are lacking for some potential causal factors that actually figure in the manifestation of the phenomena, the conjunction of theory and data will systematically fail to predict to a sufficiently high degree for the purposes of effective policymaking. Again, if it turns out that the data are insufficient in this regard, if it turns out either that data of the right kind, given an otherwise adequate theory, are not available or that the extant data contain gaps with respect to potential causal factors, then either adequate data must be found or political epistemology must ask whether any spontaneous forces in the prevailing environment might operate to mitigate the effects of this ignorance.

It is possible to deliberately realize a goal, any goal, via policymaking if and only if all of these epistemic conditions are met, that is, if and only if policymakers possess both a theory and data sufficiently comprehensive to make, implement, and effect a plan for the realization of the relevant goal.[3] Empirical political epistemology is primarily concerned with investigating whether and to what extent these conditions are satisfied in particular cases.

As shown in Chapter 1, policy options that policymakers judge to bear a comparatively heavy epistemic burden rank lower in their initial incentive structures and thus are less likely to be chosen, other things equal, than policy options judged to bear lighter epistemic burdens. Policies succeed either because they are founded on adequate knowledge or because spontaneous forces operate to mitigate policymaker ignorance; policies fail to realize their goals because they are based on an inadequate epistemic basis and spontaneous forces are unable to mitigate this ignorance. Thus, we can infer policymakers' initial epistemic conditions from instances of policy success and failure, and, if we can get an adequate grasp on policymakers' epistemic conditions at the time a policy is made, we can (pattern) predict its success or failure.

As an empirical matter, it seems as if it is often easier to discover ignorance than to recognize knowledge; it is often easier to tell when someone does not possess an item of knowledge than to determine when they do. In general, it should be relatively easy to negatively determine that policymaker knowledge is inadequate to deliberately realize some policy goal than to positively determine that a conjunction of theoretical and empirical knowledge is adequate. What's more, as ignorance is the original and typical state of mankind and its tokens, knowledge being a far more special case in the course of human affairs, the class of goals with respect to which policymaker knowledge is inadequate is likely to forever dwarf the much smaller class of goals with respect to which policymaker knowledge is sufficient. For these reasons, the value of empirical political epistemology is likely to be more negative than positive, that is, to consist more often in the knowledge that policymakers probably *cannot* deliberately achieve some goal on the basis of their extant knowledge and learning capacities and only relatively rarely in the knowledge that they likely can deliberately realize some goal. Political epistemology is less likely to tell us which policy goals can be deliberately realized than those that cannot and therefore require the intervention of spontaneous forces for their realization.

The Hayek-Keynes debate through the lens of political epistemology

This schema for empirical political epistemology sheds some light on the Hayek-Keynes debate and, in particular, on the question of the relative epistemic burdens policymakers confront in adopting one theory rather than the other as a policy instrument to deliberately realize and maintain full-employment equilibrium. Although political epistemology probably cannot settle the debate, it provides resources for predicting and explaining economic policymakers' policy decisions and the success or failure of these decisions.

According to Hayek's theory of the business cycle, in both its earlier version and its later "epistemic" version, under conditions of recession or inflation or, more generally, under conditions of relative economic disorder – keeping in mind that, on Hayek's conception, the economy is always in some degree of disorder, if, thanks to the spontaneous forces of the price system, typically tending toward greater order – there is no positive measure policymakers might adopt to deliberately realize more orderly economic conditions. To promote economic order, the best policy is a negative one, namely either a pure do-nothing or a do-nothing-but-remove-obstacles policy. According to Hayek's theory, the economic policymaker in a disorderly economic environment must either leave economic order to the price system or remove barriers to its effective spontaneous operation.

As noted in Chapter 3, to the extent that a policy is aimed at a particular end, it bears an epistemic burden. In order to deliberately realize the end via some policy – even if the policy is "doing nothing" – policymakers must at least know that it is an effective means to the relevant end. Thus, even a pure do-nothing policy bears an epistemic burden when it is intended to manifest particular results. In the present case, economic policymakers need to know that economic order will be promoted by doing nothing.[4] As always, this requires adequate theoretical and empirical knowledge. If a pure do-nothing policy is adopted as a means to promote greater economic order, policymakers must possess a theory of the spontaneous-ordering forces of the price system (presumably, Hayek's theory of the operation of these forces) and of any other spontaneous forces that might operate to promote, or hinder, economic order in the given context. Policymakers must also possess the empirical knowledge that their particular circumstances of time and place are apt for the application of this theory, that is, that, in the given context, relevant spontaneous forces are functioning the way the theory implies they must function in order to promote economic equilibrium. Policymakers must know that there are no hindrances in the environment to the effective operation of spontaneous forces. Without this knowledge – if policymakers do not know that relevant spontaneous-ordering forces operate without hindrance in the given environment – they cannot adopt a pure do-nothing policy as a means to deliberately realize the end of promoting economic order but must rely on other spontaneous forces that they do not understand if economic order is to be promoted.

If a do-nothing-but-remove-obstacles policy is adopted instead, policymakers need a theory of any spontaneous forces that might operate to promote, or hinder, economic order in the given context, as well as a theory adequate to both identify and remove obstacles hindering these spontaneous forces – they need to know both what relevant hindrances look like and how they might be removed – and they need empirical knowledge that relevant circumstances of time and place are apt for the application of these theories. Removing hindrances need not be a simple matter. Where various interests are vested in the continuation of particular hindrances – say, particular price controls or barriers to entry – policymakers need to know how to overcome these interests in order to remove the relevant obstacles. Without this knowledge, the intervention of yet other spontaneous forces that policymakers do not understand is required to remove obstacles that hinder the effective operation of either the price system or any other spontaneous forces that might serve to promote economic order.

So, we understand the epistemic burdens of policymaking according to Hayek's theories of industrial fluctuations. They are the epistemic burdens of do-nothing and do-nothing-but-remove-obstacles policies. Without the theoretical and empirical knowledge required to surmount these burdens, policymakers cannot deliberately realize the policy goal of promoting economic order in the face of recession or inflation via such policies but have to rely on other spontaneous-ordering forces to ensure the effective operation of the spontaneous-ordering forces of the price system. Among the most important items of knowledge for would-be do-nothing policymakers to acquire, obviously, is Hayek's theory of the price system and, more generally, the Hayekian theory of social order developed in Scheall, Butos, and McQuade (2019). This theoretical knowledge would put policymakers in a better position to determine empirically whether, to what extent, and what kind of spontaneous-ordering forces are operating in their institutional environment, in particular, whether the price system is functioning properly and what barriers, if any, might be hampering its functioning. Though it would not be sufficient by itself, such knowledge would go some way toward surmounting the epistemic burdens of would-be do-nothing economic policymakers.

Unlike Hayek's theory of the cycle, Keynes' ([1936] 1973) macroeconomic theory implies that there are positive measures that policymakers can adopt to deliberately realize and maintain full-employment equilibrium. In particular, according to Keynes and his followers, policymakers can use a combination of monetary and fiscal policies to deliberately close the so-called "output gap" between *actual* and *potential* gross domestic product that constitutes involuntary unemployment according to the Keynesian way of thinking.

The epistemic burden of deliberately realizing full-employment equilibrium encompasses the knowledge that economic policymakers require that they do not already possess in order to use these policy means to close an output gap. As so many others have with respect to their own favored policy recommendations, Keynes assumed without argument or evidence that policymakers could acquire the knowledge necessary for the effectiveness of his policy suggestions.[5] It is for empirical political epistemology to determine whether, how far, and under what conditions, if any, this assumption holds. Given Keynes' theory, the relevant questions concern its adequacy as an explanation of involuntary unemployment – that is, does it encompass all of the potential causes of or does it ignore factors believed to play a causal role in unemployment? – and the adequacy of the data available to plug in to the theory.

As we have seen in Chapter 2, Hayek always held that, because it ignored the causal influence of capital phenomena on fluctuations in economic activity, Keynes' theory was deficient *qua* theory and that, therefore, it could not provide the general theoretical knowledge that policymakers required for effective macroeconomic management. In order to use Keynes' theory to deliberately manage the macroeconomy effectively, either policymakers need to know that Hayek's criticism here is invalid, that is, either that Keynes' theory does encompass the effects of capital or that capital bears no causal effects on cyclical phenomena, or they need to know an auxiliary theory that can be paired with Keynes' theory to encompass the causal effects of capital on involuntary unemployment. Without this knowledge, policymakers cannot use Keynes' theory to deliberately close an output gap and eradicate involuntary unemployment. If both Hayek's criticism hits the mark and no such auxiliary theory exists, then using Keynes' theory as a policy tool to close an output gap is potentially quite treacherous, because related policies will neglect whatever effects capital has on economic fluctuations. If policymakers do not know that Keynes' theory encompasses all of the relevant causal factors of involuntary unemployment, they will be able to close an output gap only if, say, they get lucky and guess an appropriate policy or other spontaneous forces intervene to mitigate the consequences of their ignorance.

Although Keynes did not explicate this fact and few later Keynesians have recognized it, the theoretical knowledge required to use Keynes' positive policymaking approach to deliberately realize and maintain full-employment equilibrium extends far beyond mere knowledge of Keynes' theory (Scheall 2015e). First, there is the problem that Keynes' theory implies an array of different combinations of fiscal and monetary policy measures that *might* effectively counter an output gap. There is no reason to think that all of these policy combinations are equally effective against any output gap whatever; indeed, there are reasons to think that some policy combinations are plainly ineffective and others perhaps even counterproductive. Thus, in order to deliberately manage the macroeconomy, economic policymakers need some supplementary theory that offers better guidance than Keynes' theory provides for distinguishing effective, ineffective, and counterproductive policy combinations.[6]

Second, assuming a theory of the latter kind, even the theoretically best policy will fail in practice if it is poorly designed, improperly implemented, or incompetently administered. Thus, the would-be Keynesian policymaker also needs a theory of phenomena about which Keynes' macroeconomic theory is completely silent, namely the effective design, implementation, and administration of public policy. Indeed, a similar epistemic burden potentially attaches to all policies except pure do-nothing policies. We already know how to design, implement, and administer doing nothing, but we may not know how to design, implement, and administer a positive policy that effectively "does something." In other words, even if Hayek's criticism of Keynes' supposed theory problem, that is, its lack of a capital-theoretic foundation, is invalid, other theory problems nevertheless remain. The Keynesian approach definitely lacks theories of specific policy combinations and their design, implementation, and administration adequate to the deliberate realization of full-employment equilibrium. Without these auxiliary theories, policymakers cannot use Keynes' theory to deliberately narrow an output gap and can realize this goal only if spontaneous forces intervene to mitigate the effects of their ignorance. Recall that the first question of political-epistemological inquiry is whether a theory exists that implies *policy P is a potential means to the end of policy goal G.* Without these supplemental theories, Keynes' theory does *not* imply a policy means to the relevant end; it implies, rather, the mere *possibility* of some such policy and leaves the policymaker otherwise ignorant of specific details.

Whatever theory problems Hayek thought he had found in Keynes' macroeconomic approach paled next to the data problems he attributed to it. The empirical knowledge required to implement Keynes' policy recommendations in practice, Hayek argued, exceeded the epistemic capacities of human policymakers. The aggregative data available to policymakers in the form of GDP figures and gross measures of total production, consumption, investment, and so on were no substitute for the detailed knowledge of relative prices that Hayek thought necessary to make policymaking of a Keynesian variety minimally effective. Economic fluctuations, Hayek believed, always originated in particular sectors (usually especially capital-intensive sectors) of the economy. Without knowledge of both the sector in which the disturbance originated and the course of its propagation throughout the economy, it was not enough for policymakers to know merely that an output gap of a particular magnitude existed. Indeed, mere knowledge of the extent of an output gap was not only largely irrelevant but potentially dangerous to the goal of realizing full-employment equilibrium, because policymaking on this epistemic basis, if misdirected at inappropriate sectors (or, in Hayek's terms, at inappropriate stages of the structure of production) of the economy, could reinforce, rather than reverse, the effects of the original disturbance.

On the assumption that they know Keynes' theory is adequate, in order to use his policy approach to deliberately realize and maintain full-employment equilibrium, policymakers need to know that the data available to them are adequate to calculate the magnitude of an output gap and that no other data unavailable to them are relevant to full-employment equilibrium, that is, they need to know that, contra Hayek, Keynes' system is not beset with data problems. If they do not possess this knowledge, they will be able to use Keynes' theory to realize full-employment equilibrium only if, say, luck intervenes to mitigate the effects of their ignorance, that is, only if they are fortunate that Hayek's claims of Keynes' data problems miss their target (though they remain ignorant of this) or they make lucky guesses about the nature and extent of the gap to be closed.

Thus, we understand the epistemic burdens of policymaking according to Keynes' macroeconomics. In addition to knowledge of Keynes' theory, policymakers require knowledge of its explanatory adequacy. They need to know that the theory does not leave out causal factors. They also need theoretical knowledge adequate to distinguish combinations of fiscal and monetary policy as effective, ineffective, or counterproductive relative to the goal of realizing and maintaining full-employment equilibrium. They also require theories of policy design, implementation, and administration adequate to this goal. Assuming they possess this theoretical knowledge, policymakers need to know that there are no data problems to be overcome in applying these theories to economic conditions, that the data available to them can be plugged into the relevant theories to generate predictions of a sufficiently high degree for the kind and extent of social control required to deliberately close a given output gap. Without the theoretical and empirical knowledge required to surmount these epistemic burdens, policymakers cannot deliberately realize, but have to rely to some extent on spontaneous-ordering forces to ensure, full-employment equilibrium.

So, we have some understanding of the different epistemic burdens involved in economic policymaking in either a Hayekian or Keynesian vein. The questions naturally arise: is a negative Hayekian do-nothing (or do-nothing-but-remove-obstacles) policy more or less epistemically burdensome than a positive Keynesian "do-something" policy? Which kind of policy is typically judged by policymakers to be more epistemically burdensome, and how do these latter assessments affect the incentives that economic policymakers confront to adopt one policymaking strategy rather than the other? If there is anything to my argument in Chapter 1, then policymakers are less inclined to pursue policy goals that they evaluate as relatively epistemically burdensome, other things equal (which is not to say that they may not gin up a public charade of their pursuit of epistemically burdensome policies). We can infer from this, together with the fact that, at least when confronted with apparent economic disorder in the last century or so, economic policymakers have tended to pursue, if not Keynes' specific policy recommendations, some positive policy strategy more assimilable to the Keynesian do-something than to the Hayekian do-nothing approach. It would seem, in other words, that policymakers have tended to evaluate Keynesian do-somethingism as less epistemically burdensome, other things equal, than Hayekian do-nothingism. Are these fair appraisals by policymakers of their actual epistemic circumstances? Is the epistemic burden of doing nothing, or doing nothing but removing obstacles to the effective functioning of the price system, heavier or lighter than the epistemic burden of acquiring the theoretical and empirical knowledge required to design, implement, and administer a positive policy that results in full-employment equilibrium?

There is no single univocal response to this question, of course, as the epistemic burdens of these respective strategies depend on the knowledge that policymakers already possess. An epistemic burden, recall, is the knowledge someone requires to deliberately realize some goal *that they do not already possess*. So, at least in principle, we might imagine policymakers who already know much of what they need to know to use one or the other theory to deliberately realize economic order or particular circumstances in which it is relatively easier to surmount the epistemic burden of one strategy than to overcome the burden of the other strategy. However, it is not necessary to resort to such special assumptions to explain why policymakers have, whatever the facts of their epistemic circumstances vis-à-vis the competing policy strategies, tended to evaluate Keynesian do-somethingism as less epistemically burdensome than, and thus have tended to prefer it to, Hayekian do-nothingism. It is possible to explain these choices without resorting to the assumption that policymakers are better equipped epistemically (either *ab initio* or in certain circumstances) to effectively pursue the Keynesian approach. We can assume that economic policymakers are about equally ignorant with respect to both strategies – indeed, we might even assume that they are more ignorant relative to the epistemic requirements of the Keynesian strategy than they are relative to those of the Hayekian strategy – and still use political-epistemological notions to explain their seeming preference for doing something rather than nothing.

The first point to note here is that, as Hayek ([1975] 2014) argued in "The Pretence of Knowledge," the Keynesian approach has always been *advertised* as a simple recipe for policymaking success. Whether they actually possess the required knowledge or not, policymakers have been led to believe either that they do possess it or that it is conveniently within their cognitive reach. If policymakers suffer from a pretence of knowledge concerning the Keynesian approach, as Hayek argued that they do, then their preference for it is explained. Regardless of actual epistemic circumstances, if policymakers believe that Keynesian do-somethingism is comparatively less epistemically burdensome than Hayekian do-nothingism, it will rank higher in their initial preference rankings and, other things equal, be more likely to be chosen as a policy strategy.

The second point to keep in mind is that other things are definitely not equal when it comes to the benefits policymakers can expect to accrue from "doing something" rather than "doing nothing" to address a social issue. Even if policymakers judge a do-nothing policy far less epistemically burdensome than a do-something policy, so profound are the benefits which typically redound to policymakers who are judged by constituents to be "doing something" to address a social issue, as compared to the significant costs to policymakers believed by constituents to be "doing nothing," that these differences can explain policymakers' choices. Indeed, policymakers' efforts to "do something" need be neither successful nor even terribly earnest for them to accumulate these profound benefits. If my argument in the first chapter is sound, then epistemic burdens determine whether a course of action appears as an option and, if so, where it is ranked, in a decision-maker's *initial* incentive structure. This does not mean that epistemic burdens alone *determine* decisions. The initial, pre-conscious ranking of an option in an actor's incentive structure, as determined by the actor's comparative epistemic burdens with respect to various courses of action, can be (and, presumably, often is) overridden by other, non-epistemic considerations. Policymakers might evaluate doing nothing to be much less burdensome than doing something and thus might rank the first above the second in their initial incentive structures. However, if the benefits, in terms of public approval, popularity, praise, power, whatever, of doing something outweigh the relative epistemic ease of doing nothing, then (other things equal) the policymaker is likely to choose to do something rather than nothing. Policymakers will opt for the Keynesian strategy regardless of their assessment of its comparative epistemic heaviness, because, so long as they are seen to be either doing or trying to do something, they can reasonably expect this strategy to pay off for them. None of this means that non-epistemic considerations are ever logically prior to epistemic burdens; it merely means that, in isolation, epistemic burdens are not fully determinate for decision-making.

Of course, it is entirely possible that these two causes interact. It may be that policymakers tend to prefer the Keynesian approach both because they suffer from a pretence of knowledge with respect to it and because they recognize the relative benefits of being seen by constituents to be either doing or trying to do something. Indeed, in many contexts, the best option for policymakers would seem to combine the often lower epistemic burden of doing nothing with the general benefits of being seen by constituents to be doing something to address social issues. That is, the best option for policymakers who think that they know enough to do nothing, but not enough to do something effectively, may well be to pretend to do something while, in fact, doing nothing. As discussed elsewhere in the book, this is perhaps all the easier in modern media environments, where it seems relatively easy for policymakers to broadcast their concerns for various social problems without in fact doing anything substantive to address them. In general, there would seem to be a built-in bias toward *pretending to do something*, a policy that combines a minimal epistemic burden with the significant benefits of public approbation.

There is a very real sense in which the Hayek-Keynes debate is nothing more than a disagreement between two competing and irreconcilable political-epistemological perspectives, "a difference between the self-confident rationalist of Edwardian Cambridge [Keynes] who saw no limits to knowledge, and a more modest, but equally scientific, man [Hayek] who saw a large part of social life as simply not explicable in terms of a simple dichotomy between the true and the false that physical science provides" (Barry 1979, 173). Empirical political epistemology does not allow us to definitely resolve this disagreement. It does not permit us to decide once and for all whether it is better for policymakers to be "self-confident rationalists" or "more modest" in their self-evaluations of their own epistemic capacities. However, in this subsection, I have tried (and hopefully succeeded) to show that empirical political epistemology provides resources relevant to understanding the particular choices of economic policymakers and the reasons these decisions succeed or do not.

A constitutional approach to the problem of policymaker ignorance

Readers familiar with the Hayek-Keynes debate and the extended, and still ongoing, discussion between Austrians, Keynesians, and their respective intellectual allies concerning the wisdom of political intervention in the economy might be surprised to learn the extent to which the two principals to the debate actually agreed on various methodological and important political-economic matters. For example, Hayek and Keynes agreed about the general approach that Britain should take to fighting inflation and financing World War II (Keynes 1940; Hayek [1966] 1978). If they disagreed about each other's theories, they nevertheless agreed on the methodological significance of economic theorizing, against those who argued for a less theoretical approach to economics, like German Historicist and American Institutionalist economists (Caldwell 2019b, 8). Both were skeptical of the value of econometrics (Keynes 1939; Hayek [1975] 2014). They also agreed about the long-range significance of ideas over vested interests in shaping the course of human society (Keynes [1936], 1973, 383–384; Hayek [1944] 1991, 36–37).[7]

The letter that Keynes ([1944] 1971) sent to Hayek praising (with qualifications) the argument of *The Road to Serfdom* ([1944] 2007) provides some idea of the extent of their agreement on various matters, but the letter offers an even richer understanding of their political-epistemological disagreement. Keynes apparently read the book in early summer 1944, while sailing to America to participate as Britain's lead representative in the international discussions that led to the Bretton Woods agreement, and he wrote to Hayek upon arrival in the States. Keynes' letter began with fulsome praise for *The Road to Serfdom*: "In my opinion it is a grand book [. . .] Morally and philosophically I find myself in agreement with virtually the whole of it: and not only in agreement with it, but in deeply moved agreement." However, he soon came to "what is really my only serious criticism of the book."

> You admit here and there that it is a question of knowing where to draw the line [i.e., between government planning and individual planning]. You agree that the line has to be drawn somewhere, and that the logical extreme is not possible. But you give us no guidance whatever as to where to draw it. In a sense this is shirking the practical issue. It is true that you and I would probably draw it in different places. I should guess that according to my ideas you greatly underestimate the practicability of the middle course. . . . I should therefore conclude your theme rather differently. I should say that what we want is not no planning, or even less planning, indeed I should say that we almost certainly want more. But the planning should take place in a community in which as many people as possible, both leaders and followers, wholly share your moral position. Moderate planning will be safe if those carrying it out are rightly orientated in their own minds and hearts to the moral issue. This is in fact already true of some of them. But the curse is that there is also an important section who could almost be said to want planning not in order to enjoy its fruits but because morally they hold ideas exactly the opposite of yours, and wish to serve not God but the devil. . . . What we need is the restoration of right moral thinking – a return to proper moral values in our social philosophy. If only you could turn your crusade in that direction you would not feel quite so much like Don Quixote.

It is hard to imagine better evidence of Keynes' "self-confident rationalism" about political epistemology. Indeed, like so many other writers on these subjects, Keynes could see only the problem of policymaker incentives – all that seemed important to him was that "leaders and followers" shared a particular moral vision relative to which policymakers were "rightly oriented." He just assumed that rightly oriented policymakers (indeed, he assumed that all policymakers, even those oriented toward the "devil") would possess the knowledge required to successfully realize the goals implied by their respective moral perspectives. Keynes failed utterly to recognize the problem of policymaker ignorance, much less its logical priority to the problem of policymaker incentives. As hard as it is to imagine, given his obvious worldliness and, especially, his direct experience in the British government, Keynes apparently remained forever innocent that policymaking could go quite awry where policymakers with no desire to be anything but rightly oriented toward their constituents were ignorant of the relevant moral vision or of policy means adequate to realize goals associated with it.

How Hayek should have responded to Keynes' challenge

Hayek spent much of his subsequent career trying to answer Keynes' challenge. As discussed in Chapter 3, in later works like *The Constitution of Liberty* (Hayek [1960] 2011) and, especially, *Law, Legislation and Liberty* (Hayek 1973, 1976, 1979), Hayek tried to identify the social institutions most conducive to an effective liberal order. He tried to provide the guidance that Keynes requested as to where to "draw the line" between collective and individual planning. Unfortunately, he did so in a way that ignored the lessons of the political-epistemological approach he had previously applied to central planning and countercyclical economic policymaking. The stance that Hayek adopted in these works implicitly reverted to the false assumption of the primary significance of the problem of policymaker incentives. I showed previously that Hayek's arguments, especially in *Law, Legislation, and Liberty*, fail, at least from a political-epistemological perspective. Hayek offered little reason to think that the epistemic burdens of policymaking either *within* his ideal institutional arrangement or *aimed at realizing* such an arrangement could be carried by human policymakers. Unfortunately, perhaps because he did not follow the logic of his political-epistemological approach through to its limit, Hayek apparently failed to notice that this approach leads naturally to an answer – or at least to the promising beginnings of an answer – to Keynes' challenge.

First, Hayek might have responded that Keynes' challenge was rather misconceived. Given the experientially contingent and culturally conditioned nature of the success or failure of different social institutions – that is, the empirical fact that some institutions "work" in one cultural context but fail in others – he might have argued that no single univocal response should be expected to the question where to draw the line between government planning and individual planning. The best way(s) to draw this line in some particular cultural context is more likely to be discovered via experience than known *a priori*. Thus, in order to determine the better and worse ways for a society to delineate the public and private realms – the demarcations that "work" more or less well for the society and its members – requires extensive empirical and historical analysis.

In particular, Hayek might have argued that Keynes' challenge could not be given a rational answer without reference to the results of empirical political epistemology. The limits of what can be deliberately achieved via policymaking and, at the same time, the range of goals that can be realized only if spontaneous forces intervene, are determined by the nature and extent of policymaker ignorance, the primary object of empirical political epistemology. Thus, any response to Keynes' challenge that ignores empirical political epistemology is an attempt to delineate the realm of government action without regard for what can and cannot actually be deliberately achieved via government action. It is an attempt to answer Keynes' challenge while stumbling around in pitch darkness, without regard for highly relevant empirical evidence.

Of course, by itself, empirical political epistemology is non-normative; in isolation, it implies nothing about the best form of government or about how we ought to draw the line between government planning and individual planning. Nonetheless, it supplies data crucial to any rationally grounded response to Keynes' challenge. When the question is which goals we should assign to policymakers and which goals should be left to individuals – which is in effect what Keynes is seeking when he asks how the line between government planning and individual planning should be drawn – it is important to determine what policymakers can and cannot deliberately achieve, a determination that can be made only through empirical political epistemology. In short, Hayek might have responded that he lacked much of the data required to answer Keynes' challenge rationally – and that, so too, of course, did Keynes himself and anyone else who might try to respond to the challenge without regard for political-epistemological considerations.

Second, Hayek might have countered Keynes' challenge by noting that it is more important to define the region in which the line should *not* be drawn than it is to know exactly where it *ought* to be drawn and that warning against dangerous ways of drawing the line was precisely the purpose of *The Road to Serfdom*. In other words, Hayek might have rejected Keynes' notion that he was "shirking the practical issue" by giving "no guidance whatever" where exactly to draw the line between government planning and individual planning. Nothing could be more practical, in the first instance, than avoiding disaster, and *The Road to Serfdom* was about nothing if not avoiding disaster. But, more to the present point, Hayek might have noted the significance of empirical political epistemology to the investigation of the disastrous – or just merely ineffective – ways of drawing the line. If we want to avoid political disaster or even just political futility, then we need political epistemology. Inasmuch as we care about realizing our goals, we should avoid drawing the line between government planning and individual planning in a way that hinders the realization of our goals. In particular, to the extent that we care about realizing our goals, we should avoid assigning goals to policymaking that are more effectively realized spontaneously, and we should avoid leaving goals to spontaneous forces that are more effectively realized via policymaking. As a science that investigates the limits of deliberate policymaking and the spontaneous forces that might assist in realizing goals with respect to which policymaker knowledge is inadequate, empirical political epistemology is of fundamental importance here. "Keynes wanted to know exactly how one could tell *good* government intervention from *bad*" (Caldwell 2004, 289). If it says nothing further in response to Keynes' challenge, political epistemology at least answers that government interventions destined to fail because they require more knowledge than policymakers can acquire and available spontaneous forces are inadequate to the realization of relevant goals are bad interventions.

As political-epistemological inquiry progresses, we should learn more about how to divide the class of potential policy ends between those that can be deliberately realized via political action and those that can be realized, if at all, only if spontaneous forces intervene. In particular, such analysis should gradually (if probably no better than roughly) partition the entire class of policy goals into several sub-classes, that is, 1) goals realizable deliberately, but not spontaneously; 2) ends realizable either entirely deliberately or entirely spontaneously; 3) goals realizable through a combination of deliberate action and spontaneous forces; 4) objectives realizable spontaneously, but not deliberately; 5) goals not realizable at all. A completed empirical political epistemology would allow us to determine precisely which goals are more effectively realized via government planning and which goals are more effectively realized spontaneously. That is, at the end of inquiry, a finished political epistemology would allow us to respond to Keynes' challenge in the way(s) most conducive to the realization of our goals. If we care about realizing our goals, this is probably the best answer that can be given to Keynes' challenge.

Functional omniscience and omnipotence

Of course, as potential policy ends vary from one place and time to another, and as human cognitive capacities change (if only slowly and gradually), there will never be a completed political epistemology. But, in the present state of obliviousness to policymaker ignorance, that political epistemology can never be completed is beside the point. Physics is not complete, but we still find it useful. The purpose of political-epistemological inquiry is less to complete such a scientific program than to start it: the goal is to gather as much relevant knowledge as possible about what can be achieved through political action and thus, hopefully, to contribute to an improvement of political decision-making, if not immediately, then in the medium to long run. As in most things, it is unwise to make the perfect the enemy of the good. The fact that political epistemology can never be completed is no reason not to complete it as far as practicable.

On the epistemic-mechanistic approach to the problem, discussed in Chapter 5, the goal is the discovery of mechanisms, in theory and, ultimately, in practice, that will facilitate the communication of knowledge between policymakers and constituents so as to improve the actionability of their respective plans and thus promote the orderliness of the political domain. On the epistemic-mechanistic approach, in other words, the goal is to improve the knowledge of political actors, policymakers and constituents alike. On a constitutional approach to the problem of policymaker ignorance, on the other hand, the epistemic capacities of political actors are taken as given, more or less, and the relevant goal is to constrain political action to areas where it can be effective on the basis of these capacities. The knowledge acquired via empirical political epistemology, however partial and incomplete, could be used to mitigate the problem of policymaker ignorance by drawing (or re-drawing) the lines of a political constitution that would limit deliberate political action to those realms where it is comparatively more effective than spontaneity. In particular, mitigating the problem of policymaker ignorance via the constitutional method would involve constraining policymakers to the pursuit of policy goals that they could contribute to realizing on the basis of their knowledge and learning capacities. The constitutional approach would assign to policymakers the pursuit of goals they could help realize and prohibit them from the pursuit of goals they could not help realize. The constitutional approach would limit policymakers to the first three of the five aforementioned sub-classes of policy goals – that is, to goals realizable deliberately, but not spontaneously; to goals realizable either entirely deliberately or entirely spontaneously; and to goals realizable through a combination of deliberate action and spontaneous forces – and prevent policymakers from pursuing goals in the last two sub-classes, namely objectives realizable spontaneously, but not deliberately, and goals that are not realizable at all.

A constitution that limited policymakers to the pursuit of goals that they know enough to (at least help) realize would not make them any smarter or more capable than they already are, but it would limit their range of political motion to pursuits with respect to which their epistemic capacities are more or less adequate. In other words, we cannot make policymakers omniscient and omnipotent, but we might come close to making them *functionally* omniscient and omnipotent with respect to policy-related decisions. The goal would be to limit their policy options to those pursuits with respect to which their epistemic capacities are sufficient to make a positive contribution and keep them away from policy pursuits with respect to which their epistemic capacities are inadequate.

Nearly as important as keeping policymakers from pursuing policy goals that they cannot contribute to realizing, such a constitution would further serve the goal of political order by preventing constituents from demanding the pursuit of political objectives that, because of the nature and extent of their ignorance, policymakers cannot contribute to realizing. Political disorder has multiple sources. Political expectations and plans of political action fail not only because policymakers take on more than their epistemic capacities permit; they fail also because constituents demand that policymakers take on more than their epistemic capacities permit. A constitution that kept policymakers from policy pursuits beyond their epistemic capacities would mitigate both of these causes of political disorder.

Policymaker ignorance would be minimized as far as humanly possible in a world of functionally omniscient and omnipotent policymakers. Given the logical priority of the problem of policymaker ignorance to that of policymaker incentives – in particular, given the fact that ignorance affects incentives but not the other way around – mitigating the problem of policymaker ignorance (via either the constitutional approach or the epistemic-mechanistic approach) would contribute to mitigating the problem of policymaker incentives as well. Where policymakers are knowledgeable in policy-relevant respects – as indeed they would be in either a context where epistemic mechanisms functioned to communicate knowledge between policymakers and constituents or a context in which policymakers' range of political motion was constrained to goals they could help realize on the basis of their epistemic capacities – ignorance cannot distort policymakers' incentives.

Reflection

We can use Hayek's epistemological system to empirically investigate the knowledge required to deliberately realize various policy ends and the epistemic capacities of policymakers. In particular, we can investigate the theoretical and empirical knowledge required to realize various policy goals, and we can inquire about the theoretical and empirical knowledge that policymakers actually possess. We can use Hayek's epistemology, in other words, to get some (perhaps only tenuous) empirical grasp on the epistemic burdens that policymakers confront with respect to various policy objectives and thus on the extent to which spontaneous forces are required to realize different policy goals.

The nature and extent of policymaker ignorance sets boundaries around what can be deliberately realized via political action. We need to understand policymakers' epistemic capacities, because these determine the policy goals that can be deliberately realized and, at the same time, *ipso facto* define the range of policy goals that can be realized only if spontaneous forces intervene. Moreover, we need to figure out how policymakers assess their own knowledge with respect to various policy goals, because, whatever the epistemic facts, these self-assessments serve to determine the ends that policymakers actually pursue.

Empirical political epistemology is a descriptive discipline concerned with the knowledge required to realize various policy goals, the knowledge that policymakers can actually acquire, the consequences of policy actions taken on an inadequate epistemic basis, and thus the operation of any spontaneous forces that might serve to mitigate the consequences of policy actions taken on an inadequate epistemic basis. In response to Keynes' challenge to delineate the realm of government planning from that of individual planning, Hayek might have argued that, if we care about the realization of our goals, the line separating the realm of goals planned for by policymakers and the realm of goals planned for by individuals should not be drawn beyond the limits of what policymaking can deliberately achieve, which is ultimately a matter for empirical political epistemology to determine. The nature and extent of policymaker ignorance set limits around the goals that can be deliberately realized via policy means. Beyond these limits are goals that can be realized only if spontaneous forces intervene to some extent or other. Goals that require the intervention of spontaneous forces should not be left entirely to policymakers. It is empirical political epistemology that determines which goals are beyond the ken and control of policymakers. Empirical political epistemology might be used to write or revise a constitution that ensured policymakers' functional omniscience and omnipotence and that thereby mitigated both the problems of policymaker ignorance and the secondary problem of policymaker incentives.

Notes

1 In Chapter 3, I endorsed the arguments of Devins, Koppl, et al. (2015) against constitutional design. I should emphasize that the arguments of the present chapter are subject to the qualifications elucidated in that paper.

2 According to Keynes' ([1936] 1973) argument in his famous *General Theory of Employment, Interest, and Money*, economic equilibrium did not mean, as it meant for the so-called "classical" economists whom he claimed were his targets, a condition of zero involuntary unemployment. It was possible, according to Keynes, for the macroeconomy to "equilibrate" at a level of significant involuntary unemployment. Thus, on a Keynesian picture, the goal of macroeconomic demand management is not equilibrium *per se*, but *full-employment* equilibrium. As we have had several occasions to discuss, Hayek conceived of economic equilibrium/order as a condition in which everyone's plans are realized and no one's expectations are disappointed. Thus, although he thought a state of equilibrium a (useful) fiction, that the economy was always in disequilibrium, and, at best, tending toward equilibrium, Hayek rejected the notion that, *in* economic equilibrium, there could be involuntary unemployment, a condition which implies the disappointment of the expectations of the involuntarily unemployed. Since, by definition for Hayek, there cannot be involuntary unemployment in a state of economic equilibrium/order, this state is just what Keynes called full-employment equilibrium. What Keynes would have considered a state of under-employment equilibrium, on the other hand, Hayek would have just called disequilibrium/disorder.

3 That these conditions are necessary for the success of deliberate policy action should be rather obvious; that they are also sufficient is perhaps less apparent. Given the way that I have defined the relevant terms, if policymakers possess adequate theoretical and empirical knowledge, including all relevant propositional knowledge-that and non-propositional know-how, then they can deliberately realize a policy goal.

4 Naturally, if doing nothing is not actually meant to realize any end and is not aimed at particular results, then policymakers do not confront this epistemic burden.

5 "[I]n its practical application," Keynes' macroeconomic theory "does depend upon a benevolent and fully-informed economic manager" (Barry 1979, 122–123).

6 There is, of course, an extensive literature, but no consensus, on the policy implications of Keynes' theory (see Scheall 2015e).

7 On the intellectual and personal relationship between Hayek and Keynes, see Caldwell (2019a).

Reflection and foreshadow

What the argument is and what the argument is not

The present work is an attempt to establish the significance of a problem that has previously been largely ignored and a plea for further inquiry into its many aspects and implications, including the spontaneous forces required to realize policy goals with respect to which policymaker knowledge is inadequate. Policymaker ignorance is the ultimate constraint on our political ambitions: we cannot get beyond the limits set by policymakers' limited epistemic capacities to realize whatever social goals we might like, unless spontaneous forces intervene. Our failure heretofore to recognize the logical priority of the epistemic in (political) decision-making has led us to place the normative cart before the epistemic horse that must drive policymaking if it is to be effective. It has confused us into thinking we can make rational decisions concerning what we ought to do through political action without first determining what political action can and, more importantly, cannot accomplish. Our long-held, but clearly mistaken, belief in the priority of the problem of policymaker incentives has been a constant cause of government failure and a significant source of constituent disappointment.

The main implication of the priority of the epistemic in political decision-making is that, *ceteris paribus*, the relative epistemic burdensomeness of competing policy goals serves to determine the goals that policymakers pursue. There is a tendency for policymakers (indeed, given the general problem of ignorance, there is a tendency for all of us) to pursue the epistemically easy. If policies demanded by constituents are relatively more burdensome than other potential policy pursuits that constituents demand less, then, other things equal, so much the worse for constituents and their policy preferences. Indeed, this is true of even the most ostensibly constituent-minded policymakers. If policymakers do not know how to be constituent-minded, they will not be constituent-minded (barring the intervention of luck, fortune, or other spontaneous forces), even if they are otherwise inclined and fully motivated to pursue their constituents' interests. In the presence of policymaker ignorance, even the most altruistic policymakers by natural bent might appear quite venal, because seemingly venal policies are the only ones they know enough to pursue. "The notion that there are principled, publicly-minded policymakers who will pursue their constituents' interests come what may is terribly quaint" (Scheall 2019a).

However, as we have seen, it is no less an error to treat all policymakers as "knaves" and assume *a priori* that they always act venally. The extent to which policymakers pursue self-interested rather than constituent-minded objectives can be explained in terms of the nature and extent of the ignorance they must overcome in order to pursue one kind of policy rather than the other. What's more, if we assume that all policymakers are knaves and should be treated as such for the purposes of analyzing political decision-making, we will systematically fail to account for cases in which policymakers are truly constituent minded, except with the lame explanation that relevant constituents in such cases must prefer the same policy goals as their venal political representatives. The public-choice economist inclined to start from Hume's maxim can instead start from Scheall's maxim – "All persons are ignoramuses; the nature and extent of their ignorance serves to determine the extent of their knavery" – and arrive at the same conclusions.

Indeed, there is no need for political analysis of any stripe to assume anything in particular about the nature of policymakers' motivations. Rather, the quality of these motives inversely correlates with the weight of policymakers' epistemic burdens, which can be investigated empirically. Starting from an empirical inquiry into the nature and extent of policymakers' ignorance to realize various ends should contribute to a deeper understanding of the connections between political knowledge, political incentives, policy pursuits, and social outcomes.

When trying to explain government failure and constituent disappointment, a key consideration is the space separating the epistemic requirements of the policies most extensively and most intensely demanded by constituents and the epistemic capacities of policymakers. If the epistemic burdens of constituents' preferred policies greatly exceed those of other potential policy pursuits less demanded by constituents, policymakers will tend to ignore the former in favor of the latter. But, in any case, given the comparatively heavy epistemic burdens of realizing constituents' demands, related policies will tend to fail, unless spontaneous forces intervene. The height of political expectations directly correlates with the extent of political disappointment. Where government failure and constituent disappointment are observed, we will often discover constituents demanding relatively epistemically burdensome policy pursuits. Constituents are their own worst enemies when they demand epistemically burdensome policy objectives. Other things equal, we should expect to find more simplistic than more ambitious policymaking.[1]

Related to this, there is a tradeoff between effective government and ambitious government. Policymakers are likely to be quite successful, and government is likely to be quite effective, where policymaking is constitutionally constrained to the relatively epistemically simple and rather less successful where policymakers are permitted to pursue the epistemically fanciful.

> We can have a government that is effective in the sense that it regularly meets policy objectives or we can have a government that is ambitious in the sense that it permits the pursuit of comparatively epistemically burdensome policy objectives, but we cannot have both. Until policymakers approach omniscience and omnipotence, governments of the latter kind will always be less effective – they will tend to achieve their objectives less regularly – than will governments of the former kind.
>
> (Scheall 2019a)

Anyone expecting policymakers to forthrightly address complex problems – especially when they can garner similar benefits by simply pretending to address complex problems – does not understand how ignorance distorts incentives.

In the absence of some epistemic mechanism that informs them of the goals that policymakers in fact pursue, constituents should not infer from the mere appearance of policymakers pursuing complex policy objectives that they in fact pursue these objectives earnestly rather than disingenuously. In today's media-driven age, it is relatively easy to playact at constituent-mindedness. Take, for example, the farce that became known as Obamacare. The relevant question is whether the law that was ultimately passed and soon became known by this colloquialism was a legitimate attempt by policymakers to meet their constituents' demands for a health-care system that covered more patients at lower (individual and collective) cost – in which case, given the recognized failure of the policy as designed, passed, and implemented, to realize this goal, policymakers must be judged to have fallen into a pretence of knowledge – or whether it was a cynical ploy by policymakers, who recognized the inadequacy of their knowledge to realize the goal, to make constituents think their policy demands were being earnestly pursued. I posit no particular answer to this question here but merely note the relevance of political-epistemological considerations to any explanation of constituent dissatisfaction with the results of the relevant legislation.[2] Had the adequacy of the theoretical and empirical knowledge upon which the policy was built been queried in advance of its making, its ultimate failure might have been predicted. What's more, had constituents not demanded such an epistemically burdensome policy in the first place – it may well be impossible to cover more patients at lower cost to both individuals and the country as a whole – they would likely have been less disappointed with the consequences of whatever less ambitious law might have otherwise been passed.

Something similar to this brief political-epistemological take on Obamacare might be given of the George W. Bush administration's incompetent escapades in Iraq. Of course, it was Donald Rumsfeld who gave us the famous phrase "unknown unknowns," translated here in Hayek's terms as the "pretence of knowledge." Either the Bush administration fell into the pretence of knowledge that Rumsfeld diagnosed; that is, they did not know that they did not know there were no weapons of mass destruction to be found in Iraq, or invading the country on the supposition of the existence of such weapons was a cynical ploy to convince American voters that the Bush administration was earnestly trying to solve the problem of international terrorism, which administration officials in fact recognized on some level they were too ignorant to solve. Knowing that they would be punished by constituents for doing nothing to address this problem in the wake of 9/11 and that they did not possess the knowledge and capacities to address it effectively, administration officials decided to do *something else*: make it appear to constituents that the administration was earnestly trying to protect them from international terrorists.

The problem of policymaker ignorance is not the unique property of any one political party, persuasion, or procedure. That we may not know enough to realize our goals is inherent in our seemingly permanent circumstances as cognitively limited human beings in a constrained and complex world. That our political surrogates may not know what our goals are or how to realize them is intrinsic to surrogate decision-making. As we have seen, the problem of policymaker ignorance can arise at all points across the political spectrum. It is almost certainly very difficult to deliberately realize the goals of socialist central planning and other forms of government intervention without some assistance from spontaneous forces. Yet, even if the relative epistemic simplicity of policymaking is an implication of an effective liberal order, as we have also seen, realizing and sustaining an effective liberal order need not be epistemically simple. The epistemic superiority of a particular political system cannot be established *a priori*. *The only attitude that political-epistemological considerations support* a priori *is skepticism in the absence of evidence of the adequacy for realizing relevant policy objectives of either policymakers' epistemic capacities or extant spontaneous forces.*

Beyond aiming to establish the importance of and pleading for inquiry into the problem of policymaker ignorance, the book argues for the relevance of Austrian School arguments, tools, and concepts, first, to the original recognition of the problem (to the limited extent it was previously noticed at all) and, second, to the future analysis of and attempts to mitigate the problem. I have argued that Austrian economists have come closer to recognizing the problem of policymaker ignorance than any other political thinkers, without recognizing its complete generality across the political spectrum and thus its relevance for their own preferred liberalism. I have offered some suggestions for how political-epistemological inquiry might proceed using Hayekian tools, but I do not mean to predetermine how it must proceed. I am more concerned that the problem finally be recognized as significant, to encourage research on the problem, however it might proceed, than I am in dictating methods to potential colleagues.

It should perhaps be emphasized, if it has not been apparent to this point, that the argument presumes nothing about the nature and extent of policymaker ignorance either in general, other than the manifest fact that human policymakers are neither omniscient nor omnipotent, or in particular instances. I have not argued that policymakers are *completely* ignorant, that they do not know *anything*. Presumably, they do know some things, about as much, I would guess, as average people. Indeed, I have meant to appeal throughout the book for empirical inquiry into the nature and extent of policymakers' knowledge and capacities for learning in order to clarify what can be deliberately achieved via political action and what requires the intervention of spontaneous forces. This is how decision-making proceeds outside of surrogate cases: we always determine, if only pre-consciously, what we can do before we consider what we ought to do. Political-epistemological inquiry could only improve political decision-making and the effectiveness of policymaking and serve to limit constituent disappointment.

Notes

1 It is interesting to note a unique aspect of the *ceteris paribus* assumption in the context of discussions of policymaker ignorance and its effects. The future development of Hayekian political epistemology should involve loosening this simplifying assumption. However, it is not the case that making the analysis more complex in this way will necessarily weaken the conclusions of the present simplified analysis. Dropping the assumption that other things are equal means that the policymakers' decision context is complexified along with the analyst's investigative context. In other words, allowing other factors to vary might increase rather than diminish certain of the policymakers' epistemic burdens. Loosening the *ceteris paribus* assumption as Hayekian political-epistemological inquiry proceeds may well bolster the current argument.

2 Of course, the explanations are not mutually exclusive. The correct answer might be: "a little of both."

Bibliography

Anderson, Elizabeth. 2006. "The Epistemology of Democracy." *A Journal of Social Epistemology*, 3(1–2), 8–22.

Arrow, Kenneth. 1950. "A Difficulty in the Concept of Social Welfare." *Journal of Political Economy*, 58, 328–346.

Bader, Ralf M. 2011. "The Framework for Utopia." In R. M. Bader and J. Meadowcroft (eds.), *The Cambridge Companion to Nozick's Anarchy, State, and Utopia* (pp. 255–288). Cambridge: Cambridge University Press.

Barnes, Barry and David Bloor. 1982. "Relativism, Rationalism and the Sociology of Knowledge." In M. Hollis and S. Lukes (eds.), *Rationality and Relativism* (pp. 21–47). Cambridge, MA: MIT Press.

Barone, Enrico. [1908] 1935. "The Ministry of Production in the Collectivist State." In F. A. Hayek (ed.), *Collectivist Economic Planning*. London: Routledge.

Barry, Norman P. 1979. *Hayek's Social and Economic Philosophy*. London: Macmillan.

Bateman, Victoria. 2018. "John Maynard Keynes." In Jonathan Conlin (ed.), *Great Economic Thinkers*. London: Reaktion Books.

Bauer, Otto. 1919. *Der Weg zum Sozialismus*. Vienna.

Becchio, Giandomenica. 2011. "A Note on the Influence of Mach's Psychology in *The Sensory Order*." In L. Marsh (ed.), *Hayek in Mind: Hayek's Philosophical Psychology*. Bingley, UK: Emerald.

Beiser, Frederick C. 2011. *The German Historicist Tradition*. Oxford: Oxford University Press.

Beiser, Frederick C. 2014. *The Genesis of Neo-Kantianism, 1796–1880*. Oxford: Oxford University Press.

Berkeley, George. 1790. *An Essay towards a New Theory of Vision*. Dublin: Aaron Rhames, for Jeremy Pepyat.

Besch, Thomas A. 2011. "Factualism, Normativism and the Bounds of Normativity." *Dialogue*, 50(2), 347–365.

Birner, Jack. 1999. "The Surprising Place of Cognitive Psychology in the Work of F. A. Hayek." *History of Economic Ideas*, 7(1–2), 43–84.

Boettke, Peter. 2018. *F. A. Hayek: Economics, Political Freedom, and Social Philosophy*. London: Palgrave Macmillan.

Boettke, Peter and Peter Leeson. 2004. "Liberalism, Socialism, and Robust Political Economy." *Journal of Markets and Morality*, 7, 99–111.

Boettke, Peter and Peter Leeson. 2006. "Liberal Tolerance as Robust Political Economy." In G. Moreno-Riano (ed.), *Tolerance in the 21st Century: Prospects and Challenges*. Lanham, MD: Lexington Books.

Boettke, Peter and Virgil H. Storr. 2015. "Foreword." In Don Lavoie (ed.), *Rivalry and Central Planning*. Arlington, VA: Mercatus Center.

Boring, Edwin G. [1929] 1950. *A History of Experimental Psychology*, 2nd edn. New York: Appleton-Century-Crofts.

Boring, Edwin G. 1942. *Sensation and Perception in the History of Experimental Psychology*. New York: Appleton-Century-Crofts.

Brennan, Jason. 2016. *Against Democracy*. Princeton, NJ: Princeton University.

Bronk, Richard. 2013. "Hayek on the Wisdom of Prices: A Reassessment." *Erasmus Journal for Philosophy and Economics*, 6(1), 82–107.

Brutzkus, Boris. 1935. *Economic Planning in Soviet Russia*. London: Routledge.

Buchanan, James. 1969. *Cost and Choice: An Inquiry in Economic Theory*. Chicago, IL: University of Chicago Press.

Burczak, Theodore A. 2006. *Socialism after Hayek*. Ann Arbor, MI: The University of Michigan Press.

Burke, Edmund. [1774] 1999. "Speech on American Taxation." In Edward Payne (ed.), *Select Works of Edmund Burke*. Indianapolis, IN: Liberty Fund.

Butos, William N. and Thomas J. McQuade. 2012. "Nonneutralities in Science Funding: Direction, Destabilization, and Distortion." *Journal des Economistes et des Etudes Humaines*, 18(1), 1–26.

Cahan, David. 2018. *Helmholtz: A Life in Science*. Chicago, IL: University of Chicago Press.

Caldwell, Bruce. 1995. "Introduction." In *The Collected Works of F. A. Hayek, Volume IX: Contra Keynes and Cambridge: Essays, Correspondence*. Indianapolis, IN: Liberty Fund.

Caldwell, Bruce. 1997. "Introduction." In B. J. Caldwell (ed.), *The Collected Works of F. A. Hayek, Volume X: Socialism and War* (pp. 1–50). Chicago, IL: The University of Chicago Press.

Caldwell, Bruce. 2004. *Hayek's Challenge: An Intellectual Biography of F. A. Hayek*. Chicago, IL: University of Chicago Press.

Caldwell, Bruce. 2010. "Introduction." In *The Collected Works of F. A. Hayek, Volume XVIII: Studies on the Abuse and Decline of Reason, Text and Documents*. Chicago, IL: The University of Chicago Press.

Caldwell, Bruce. 2014. "Introduction." In *The Collected Works of F. A. Hayek, Volume XV: The Market and Other Orders* (pp. 1–35). Chicago, IL: The University of Chicago Press.

Caldwell, Bruce. 2019a. "Keynes and Hayek." *History of Political Economy*, 89–94.

Caldwell, Bruce. 2019b. "*The Road to Serfdom* after 75 Years." *Center for the History of Political Economy at Duke University Working Paper Series 2019–13*, August 2, 2019. Retrieved from SSRN: https://ssrn.com/abstract=3431183 or http://dx.doi.org/10.2139/ssrn.3431183

Cannan, Edwin. [1893] 1917. *A History of Theories of Production and Distribution*, 3rd edn. London: P. S. King.

Chomsky, Noam. 2008. "Interviewed by Joe Walker." *Joe Walker Blog*, November 14, 2008. Retrieved from https://chomsky.info/20081114/. Accessed September 22, 2019.

Coase, Ronald H. [1991] 2016. "The Institutional Structure of Production." In P. Boettke, S. Haeffele-Balch, and V. H. Storr (eds.), *Mainline Economics: Six Nobel Lectures in the Tradition of Adam Smith* (pp. 63–77). Arlington, VA: Mercatus Center.

Coffa, Alberto J. 1991. *The Semantic Tradition from Kant to Carnap* (Linda Wessels, ed.). Cambridge: Cambridge University Press.

Colonna, Marina and Harald Hagemann. 1994, *Money and Business Cycles, Volume 1 of the Economics of F. A. Hayek*. Aldershot, UK: Edward Elgar.

Cooper, Neil. 1966. "Some Presuppositions of Moral Judgments." *Mind*, 75(297), 45–57.

Cottrell, Allin. 1994. "Hayek's Early Cycle Theory Reexamined." *Cambridge Journal of Economics*, 18(2), 197–212.

Cowen, Nick. 2018. "Robust against Whom?" In S. Horwitz (ed.), *Austrian Economics: The Next Generation* (Advances in Austrian Economics, Vol. 23, pp. 91–111). Emerald Publishing Limited. https://doi.org/10.1108/S1529-213420180000023008

Crutchfield, Parker and Scott Scheall. 2019. "Epistemic Burdens and the Incentives of Surrogate Decision-Makers." *Medicine, Health Care and Philosophy*, 22(4), 613–621. https://doi.org/10.1007/s11019-019-09899-2

de Vries, Robert P. 1994. "The Place of Hayek's Theory of Mind and Perception in the History of Philosophy and Psychology." In J. Birner and R. van Zijp (eds.), *Hayek, Coordination and Evolution: His Legacy in Philosophy, Politics, Economics and the History of Ideas* (pp. 311–322). London: Routledge.

DeCanio, Samuel. 2014. "Democracy, the Market, and the Logic of Social Choice." *American Journal of Political Science*, 58(3), 637–652.

Den Uyl, Douglas J. and Douglas B. Rasmussen. Manuscript. "The Perfectionist Turn: From Metanorms to Metaethics, Chapter 12".

Devins, Caryn, Roger Koppl, Stuart Kauffman, and Teppo Felin. 2015. "Against Design." *Arizona State Law Journal*, 47(3), 609–681.

Dewey, John. 1976. "Valuation and Experimental Knowledge." In J. A. Boydston (ed.), *The Middle Works of John Dewey, 1899–1924* (Vol. 13, pp. 3–28). Carbondale, IL: Southern Illinois University Press.

Dewey, John. 1981a. "Creative Democracy: The Task before Us." In J. A. Boydston (ed.), *The Later Works of John Dewey, 1925–1953* (Vol. 14, Essays, pp. 224–230). Carbondale, IL: Southern Illinois University Press.

Dewey, John. 1981b. "Freedom and Culture." In *The Later Works of John Dewey, 1925–1953, Volume 13*, ed. J. A. Boydston, 65–188. Carbondale, IL: Southern Illinois University Press.

Dewey, John. 1981c. "The Public and Its Problems." In J. A. Boydston (ed.), *The Later Works of John Dewey, 1925–1953* (Vol. 2, pp. 235–372). Carbondale, IL: Southern Illinois University Press.

Dickinson, H. D. 1933. "Price Formation in a Socialist Community." *Economic Journal*, 43(170), 237–250.

Dickinson, H. D. 1939. *Economics of Socialism*. Oxford: Oxford University Press.

Dobb, Maurice. 1933. "Economic Theory and the Problem of a Socialist Economy." *Economic Journal*, 43(172), 588–598.

Driver, Julia. 2011. "Promising Too Much." In H. Scheinman (ed.), *Promises and Agreements* (pp. 183–197). Oxford: Oxford University Press.

Durbin, Evan. [1936] 1968. "Economic Calculus in a Planned Economy." In *Problems of Economic Planning* (pp. 140–155). London: Routledge & Kegan Paul.

Easterly, William. 2002. *The Elusive Quest for Growth: Economists' Adventures and Misadventures in the Tropics*. Cambridge, MA: MIT Press.

Easterly, William. 2006. *The White Man's Burden: Why the West's Efforts to Aid the Rest Have Done So Much Ill and So Little Good*. New York: Penguin.

Easterly, William. 2015. *The Tyranny of Experts: Economists, Dictators, and the Forgotten Rights of the Poor*. New York: Basic Books.

Ebenstein, Alan. 2001. *Friedrich Hayek: A Biography*. New York: St. Martin's Press.

Ebenstein, Alan. 2003. *Hayek's Journey: The Mind of Friedrich Hayek*. New York: Palgrave Macmillan.

Engels, Friedrich. 1884. "Preface to 1st German Edition." In *The Poverty of Philosophy*, Karl Marx. Moscow: Foreign Languages Publishing House.

Feyerabend, Paul. [1975] 2010. *Against Method*. New York: Verso.

Figes, Orlando. [1996] 2017. *A People's Tragedy: The Russian Revolution, 1891–1944*, 100th Anniversary edn. New York: Penguin.

Francis, Mark. 1985. "The Austrian Mind in Exile: Kelsen, Schumpeter, and Hayek." In M. Francis (ed.), *The Viennese Enlightenment* (pp. 63–87). London: Croom Helm.

Frankfurt, Harry. 2005. *On Bullshit*. Princeton, NJ: Princeton University Press.

Friedman, Jeffrey. 2014. "Political Epistemology." Special issue, *Critical Review*, 26, 1–2.

Friedman, Milton and Anna Schwartz. 1987. "Has Government Any Role in Money?" In *Money in Historical Perspective* (pp. 289–314). Cambridge, MA: National Bureau of Economic Research, Inc.

Gamble, Andrew. 2006. "Hayek on Knowledge, Economics, and Society." In E. Feser (ed.), *The Cambridge Companion to Hayek* (pp. 111–131). Cambridge: Cambridge University Press.

Garrison, Roger. 2000. *Time and Money: The Macroeconomics of Capital Structure*. London: Routledge.

Gettier, Edmund L. 1963. "Is Justified True Belief Knowledge?" *Analysis*, 23, 121–123.

Gontier, Nathalie. n.d. "Evolutionary Epistemology." *The Internet Encyclopedia of Philosophy*, ISSN 2161-0002. Retrieved from www.iep.utm.edu. Accessed September 24, 2019.

Gossen, Hermann, H. 1854. *Entwicklung der Gesetze des Menschlichen Verkehrs und der daraus-fliessenden Regelnjur menschliches Handeln*. Braunschweig.

Gregory, Theodore E., Friedrich A. Hayek, Arnold Plant, and Lionel Robbins. 1932. "Spending and Saving." *The Times*, 19 October 1932, p. 11. Op-ed.

Haberler, Gottfried. 1986. "Reflections on Hayek's Business Cycle Theory." *Cato Journal*, 6(2), 421–435.

Hampshire, Stuart. 1951. "Symposium: Freedom of the Will." *Aristotelian Society Supplementary*, 25, 161–178.

Hare, R. M. 1951. "Symposium: Freedom of the Will." *Aristotelian Society Supplementary*, 25, 201–216.

Hare, R. M. 1963. *Freedom and Reason*. Oxford: Clarendon Press.

Hatfield, Gary. 1990. *The Natural and the Normative: Theories of Spatial Perception from Kant to Helmholtz*. Cambridge, MA: The MIT Press.

Hayek, F. A. [1920] 2017. "Contributions to a Theory of How Consciousness Develops." In V. Vanberg (ed.), Grete Heinz (trans.), *The Collected Works of F. A. Hayek, Volume 14, The Sensory Order and Other Writings on the Foundations of Theoretical Psychology* (pp. 321–347). Chicago, IL: University of Chicago Press.

Hayek, F. A. [1925] 1984. "The Monetary Policy of the United States after the Recovery from the 1920 Crisis." In R. McCloughry (ed.), *Money, Capital, and Fluctuations: Early Essays* (pp. 5–32). Chicago, IL: University of Chicago Press; originally published as "Die Währungspolitik der Vereinigten Staaten seit der Überwindung der Krise von 1920." *Zeitschrift für Volkswirtschaft und Sozialpolitik*, new series, 5, 1 and 2, 25–63 and 254–317.

Hayek, F. A. [1928] 1984. "Intertemporal Price Equilibrium and Movements in the Value of Money." In R. McCloughry (ed.), *Money, Capital, and Fluctuations: Early Essays* (pp. 71–117). Chicago, IL: University of Chicago Press; originally published as "Das intertemporale Gleichgewichtssystem der Preise und die Bewegungen des 'Geldwertes'." *Weltwirtschaftliches Archiv*, 28, 33–76.

Hayek, F. A. [1929] 1984. "The Exchange Value of Money: A Review." In R. McCloughry (ed.), *Money, Capital, and Fluctuations: Early Essays* (pp. 190–194). Chicago, IL: University of Chicago Press; A review of H. Neisser. 1928. *Der Tauschwert der Geldes*. Jena: Fischer; originally published in *Weltwirtschaftliches Archiv*, 29, 103–106.

Hayek, F. A. [1931, 1935] 2012a. "Prices and Production." In H. Klausinger (ed.), *The Collected Works of F. A. Hayek, Volume 7, Business Cycles, Part I* (pp. 167–283). Chicago, IL: University of Chicago Press.

Hayek, F. A. [1931a] 1995. "Reflections on the Pure Theory of Money of Mr. J. M. Keynes." In *The Collected Works of F. A. Hayek*, Stephen Kresge (ed.), *Volume 9, Contra Keynes and Cambridge: Essays, Correspondence*, Bruce Caldwell (ed.) (pp. 121–146). Chicago, IL: University of Chicago Press.

Hayek, F. A. [1931b] 1995. "A rejoinder to Mr. Keynes." In *The Collected Works of F. A. Hayek*, Stephen Kresge (ed.), *Volume 9, Contra Keynes and Cambridge: Essays, Correspondence*, Bruce Caldwell (ed.) (pp. 159–164). Chicago, IL: University of Chicago Press.

Hayek, F. A. [1932] 1995. "Reflections on the Pure Theory of Money of Mr. J. M. Keynes (continued)." In *The Collected Works of F. A. Hayek*, Stephen Kresge (ed.), *Volume 9, Contra Keynes and Cambridge: Essays, Correspondence*, Bruce Caldwell (ed.) (pp. 174–197). Chicago, IL: University of Chicago Press.

Hayek, F. A. [1933] 1939. "Price Expectations, Monetary Disturbances, and Malinvestments." In *Profits, Interest, and Investment* (pp. 135–156). New York: Augustus M. Kelley; originally a lecture delivered in Copenhagen on December 7, 1933 in the *Sozialökonomisk Samfund* and published as "Preiserwartungen, monetare Storungen und Fehlinvestionen." *Nationalökonomisk Tidsschrift*, 73, page numbers unavailable.

Hayek, F. A. [1933] 1984. "On 'Neutral Money'." In R. McCloughry (ed.), *Money, Capital, and Fluctuations: Early Essays* (pp. 159–162). Chicago, IL: University of Chicago Press; originally published as "Über 'neutrales Geld'." *Zeitschrift für Nationolökonomie*, 4, 659.

Hayek, F. A. [1933] 2012a. Monetary Theory and the Trade Cycle. In H. Klausinger (ed.), *The Collected Works of F. A. Hayek, Volume 7, Business Cycles, Part I* (pp. 47–165). Chicago, IL: University of Chicago Press.

Hayek, F. A. 1935. *Collectivist Economic Planning* (F. A. Hayek, ed.). London: Routledge.

Hayek, F. A. [1935a] 1997. "The Nature and History of the Problem." In B. J. Caldwell (ed.), *The Collected Works of F. A. Hayek, Volume X: Socialism and War* (pp. 53–78). Chicago, IL: The University of Chicago Press.

Hayek, F. A. [1935b] 1997. "The Present State of the Debate." In B. J. Caldwell (ed.), *The Collected Works of F. A. Hayek, Volume X: Socialism and War* (pp. 79–116). Chicago, IL: The University of Chicago Press.

Hayek, F. A. [1937] 2014. "Economics and Knowledge." In B. J. Caldwell (ed.), *The Collected Works of F. A. Hayek, Volume XV, The Market and Other Orders* (pp. 57–77). Chicago, IL: University of Chicago Press.

Hayek, F. A. 1939. *Profits, Interest, and Investment*. London: Routledge & Kegan Paul.

Hayek, F. A. [1940] 1997. "Socialist Calculation: The Competitive 'Solution'." In B. J. Caldwell (ed.), *The Collected Works of F. A. Hayek, Volume X: Socialism and War* (pp. 117–140). Chicago, IL: The University of Chicago Press.

Hayek, F. A. [1941] 2007. "The Pure Theory of Capital." In L. H. White (ed.), *The Collected Works of F. A. Hayek, Volume 12, The Pure Theory of Capital*. Chicago, IL: University of Chicago Press; originally published in 1941, Chicago, IL: University of Chicago Press.

Hayek, F. A. [1942] 1948. "The Ricardo Effect." In *Individualism and Economic Order* (pp. 220–254). Chicago, IL: University of Chicago Press; originally published in *Economica*, 9, 34 new series, 127–152.

Hayek, F. A. [1944] 1991. "On Being an Economist." In W. W. Bartley and Stephen Kresge (eds.), *The Collected Works of F. A. Hayek, Volume III, The Trend of Economic Thinking:*

Essays on Political Economists and Economic History (pp. 35–48). Indianapolis, IN: Liberty Fund.

Hayek, F. A. [1944] 2007. *The Road to Serfdom.* In B. J. Caldwell (ed.), *The Collected Works of F. A. Hayek, Volume II, The Road to Serfdom: Text and Documents – The Definitive Edition.* Chicago, IL: University of Chicago Press.

Hayek, F. A. [1945] 2014. "The Use of Knowledge in Society." In B. J. Caldwell (ed.), *The Collected Works of F. A. Hayek, Volume XV, The Market and Other Orders* (pp. 93–104). Chicago, IL: University of Chicago Press.

Hayek, F. A. [1946] 2014. "The Meaning of Competition." In B. J. Caldwell (ed.), *The Collected Works of F. A. Hayek, Volume XV, The Market and Other Orders* (pp. 105–116). Chicago, IL: University of Chicago Press.

Hayek, F. A. [1949] 1997. "The Intellectuals and Socialism." In B. J. Caldwell (ed.), *The Collected Works of F. A. Hayek, Volume X: Socialism and War* (pp. 221–237). Chicago, IL: The University of Chicago Press.

Hayek, F. A. [1952] 2010. "Scientism and the Study of Society." In Bruce Caldwell (ed.), *The Collected Works of F. A. Hayek, Volume 18, Studies on the Abuse and Decline of Reason, Text and Documents.* Chicago, IL: The University of Chicago Press.

Hayek, F. A. [1952] 2017. "The Sensory Order." In V. Vanberg (ed.), *The Collected Works of F. A. Hayek, Volume 14, The Sensory Order and Other Writings on the Foundations of Theoretical Psychology* (pp. 113–316). Chicago, IL: University of Chicago Press.

Hayek, F. A. [1955] 2014. "Degrees of Explanation." In B. J. Caldwell (ed.), *The Collected Works of F. A. Hayek, Volume XV, The Market and Other Orders* (pp. 195–212). Chicago, IL: University of Chicago Press.

Hayek, F. A. [1956] 1967. "The Dilemma of Specialization." In *Studies in Philosophy, Politics, and Economics* (122–132). Chicago, IL: University of Chicago Press.

Hayek, F. A. [1960] 2011. *The Constitution of Liberty. The Collected Works of F. A. Hayek,* Bruce Caldwell (ed.), *Volume 17, The Constitution of Liberty: The Definitive Edition,* Ronald Hamowy (ed.). Chicago, IL: The University of Chicago Press.

Hayek, F. A. [1961] 2014. "A New Look at Economic Theory." In B. J. Caldwell (ed.), *The Collected Works of F. A. Hayek, Volume XV, The Market and Other Orders* (pp. 373–426). Chicago, IL: University of Chicago Press.

Hayek, F. A. [1962] 2014. "Rules, Perception and Intelligibility." In B. J. Caldwell (ed.), *The Collected Works of F. A. Hayek, Volume XV, The Market and Other Orders* (pp. 232–253). Chicago, IL: University of Chicago Press.

Hayek, F. A. [1964a] 2014. "Kinds of Rationalism." In B. J. Caldwell (ed.), *The Collected Works of F. A. Hayek, Volume XV, The Market and Other Orders* (pp. 39–53). Chicago, IL: University of Chicago Press.

Hayek, F. A. [1964b] 2014. "The Theory of Complex Phenomena." In B. J. Caldwell (ed.), *The Collected Works of F. A. Hayek, Volume XV, The Market and Other Orders* (pp. 257–277). Chicago, IL: University of Chicago Press.

Hayek, F. A. [1966] 1978. "Personal Recollections of Keynes and the 'Keynesian Revolution'." In *New Studies in Philosophy, Politics, Economics, and the History of Ideas* (pp. 283–289). Chicago, IL: University of Chicago Press; originally published in the *Oriental Economist,* 34(663), 78–80.

Hayek, F. A. [1967] 1992. "Ernst Mach (1838–1916) and the Social Sciences in Vienna." In P. G. Klein (ed.), *The Collected Works of F. A. Hayek, Volume IV, The Fortunes of Liberalism: Essays on Austrian Economics and the Ideal of Freedom* (pp. 172–175). London: Routledge.

Hayek, F. A. [1967a] 2014. "Notes on the Evolution of Systems of Rules of Conduct: The Interplay between Rules of Individual Conduct and the Social Order of Actions." In B. J.

Caldwell (ed.), *The Collected Works of F. A. Hayek, Volume XV, The Market and Other Orders* (pp. 278–292). Chicago, IL: University of Chicago Press.

Hayek, F. A. [1967b] 2014. "The Results of Human Action but Not of Human Design." In B. J. Caldwell (ed.), *The Collected Works of F. A. Hayek, Volume XV, The Market and Other Orders* (pp. 293–303). Chicago, IL: University of Chicago Press.

Hayek, F. A. [1968] 1992. "The Austrian School of Economics." In P. G. Klein (ed.), *The Collected Works of F. A. Hayek, Volume IV, The Fortunes of Liberalism: Essays on Austrian Economics and the Ideal of Freedom* (pp. 42–60). London: Routledge.

Hayek, F. A. [1968] 2014. "Competition as a Discovery Procedure." In B. J. Caldwell (ed.), *The Collected Works of F. A. Hayek, Volume XV, The Market and Other Orders* (pp. 304–313). Chicago, IL: University of Chicago Press.

Hayek, F. A. [1969] 2014. "The Primacy of the Abstract." In B. J. Caldwell (ed.), *The Collected Works of F. A. Hayek, Volume XV: The Market and Other Orders* (pp. 314–327). Chicago, IL: The University of Chicago Press.

Hayek, F. A. [1970] 2014. "The Errors of Constructivism." In B. J. Caldwell (ed.), *The Collected Works of F. A. Hayek, Volume XV, The Market and Other Orders* (pp. 338–356). Chicago, IL: University of Chicago Press.

Hayek, F. A. 1973. *Law, Legislation and Liberty, Volume 1: Rules and Order.* Chicago, IL: University of Chicago Press.

Hayek, F. A. [1975] 2014. "The Pretence of Knowledge." In B. J. Caldwell (ed.), *The Collected Works of F. A. Hayek, Volume XV, The Market and Other Orders* (pp. 362–372). Chicago, IL: University of Chicago Press.

Hayek, F. A. 1976. *Law, Legislation and Liberty, Volume 2: The Mirage of Social Justice.* Chicago, IL: University of Chicago Press.

Hayek, F. A. [1976, 1978] 1990. *The Denationalization of Money,* 2nd edn. London: Institute of Economic Affairs; originally published in October 1976, London: Institute of Economic Affairs.

Hayek, F. A. [1977] 2017. "*The Sensory Order* after 25 years." In V. Vanberg (ed.), *The Collected Works of F. A. Hayek, Volume 14, The Sensory Order and Other Writings on the Foundations of Theoretical Psychology* (pp. 382–389). Chicago, IL: University of Chicago Press.

Hayek, F. A. 1978a. *Interview with Axel Leijonhufvud.* Retrieved from https://ia801407.us.archive.org/18/items/nobelprizewinnin00haye/nobelprizewinnin00haye.pdf

Hayek, F. A. 1978b. *Interview with Leo Rosten.* Retrieved from https://ia801407.us.archive.org/18/items/nobelprizewinnin00haye/nobelprizewinnin00haye.pdf

Hayek, F. A. 1979. *Law, Legislation and Liberty, Volume 3: The Political Order of a Free People.* Chicago, IL: University of Chicago Press.

Hayek, F. A. 1991. *The Fatal Conceit: The Errors of Socialism.* In W. W. Bartley (ed.), *The Collected Works of F. A. Hayek, Volume I, The Fatal Conceit.* Chicago, IL: University of Chicago Press.

Hayek, F. A. 1994. *Hayek on Hayek: An Autobiographical Dialogue* (Stephen Kresge and Leif Wenar, eds.). Chicago, IL: University of Chicago Press.

Hayek, F. A. 2006. *Die sensorische Ordnung: Eine Untersuchung der Grundlagen der theoretischen Psychologie* (M. Streit, trans.). Tübingen: Mohr Siebeck.

Hayek, F. A. 2012a. "Business Cycles, Part I." In H. Klausinger (ed.), *The Collected Works of F. A. Hayek, Volume 7, Business Cycles, Part I.* Chicago, IL: University of Chicago Press.

Hayek, F. A. 2012b. "Business Cycles, Part II." In H. Klausinger (ed.), *The Collected Works of F. A. Hayek, Volume 8, Business Cycles, Part II.* Chicago, IL: University of Chicago Press.

Hebert, David J. 2019. "The Spontaneous Order of Politics." In *Austrian Economics: The Next Generation, Advances in Austrian Economics* (Vol. 23, pp. 131–144). Bingley, UK: Emerald.

Helmholtz, Hermann. 1896. *Vorträge und Reden*, 4th edn., 2 Vols. Braunschweig: Vieweg und Sohn.

Helmholtz, Hermann. 1921. *Schriften zur Erkenntnistheorie* (Paul Hertz and Moritz Schlick, eds.). Berlin: Springer.

Helmholtz, Hermann. 1924–25. *Treatise on Physiological Optics*, 3 Vols. (James P. C. Southall, trans.). Milwaukee, WI: Optical Society of America.

Hollis, Martin and Edward J. Nell. 1975. *Rational Economic Man*. Cambridge: Cambridge University Press.

Hoover, Kevin D. 2006. "Doctor Keynes: Economic Theory in a Diagnostic Science." In R. E. Backhouse and B. W. Bateman (eds.), *The Cambridge Companion to Keynes* (pp. 78–97) Cambridge: Cambridge University Press.

Horwitz, Steven. 2000. "From *The Sensory Order* to the Liberal Order: Hayek's Non-rationalist Liberalism." *Review of Austrian Economics*, 13, 23–40.

Hume, David. 1739–1740. *A Treatise of Human Nature*. London: John Noon.

Hume, David. [1741, 1777, 1889] 1987. "Of the Independency of Parliament." In *Essays Moral, Political, Literary*, edited and with a Foreword, Notes, and Glossary by Eugene F. Miller, with an appendix of variant readings from the 1889 edition by T. H. Green and T. H. Grose, revised edn. Indianapolis, IN: Liberty Fund.

Hutchison, Terence W. 1981. *The Politics and Philosophy of Economics: Marxians, Keynesians, and Austrians*. New York: New York University Press.

Ivanova, Maria. 2016. "Hayek, Mach, and the Re-Ordering of Mind." *European Journal of the History of Economic Thought*, 23(5), 693–717.

Johnson, Paul. 1983. *Modern Times: A History of the World from the 1920s to the 1980s*. London: Weidenfeld & Nicolson Ltd.

Kautsky, Karl. [1902] 1907. *The Social Revolution and on the Morrow of the Social Revolution*. London: Twentieth Century Press.

Keynes, John Maynard. [1930] 1971. "A Treatise on Money: The Pure Theory of Money." In Donald Moggridge (ed.), *The Collected Writings of John Maynard Keynes*, Vol. 5. London: Macmillan.

Keynes, John Maynard. [1931] 1973. "The Pure Theory of Money: A Reply to Hayek." In *The Collected Writings of John Maynard Keynes*, Donald Moggridge (ed.), *Volume 13, The General Theory and After, Part I: Preparation* (pp. 243–256). London: Macmillan.

Keynes, John Maynard. ([1936] 1973). "The General Theory of Employment, Interest, and Money." In D. Moggridge and E. Johnson (eds.), *The Collected Writings of John Maynard Keynes*, Vol. 12. London: Macmillan.

Keynes, John Maynard. 1939. "Professor Tinbergen's Method." *Economic Journal*, 49(194), 558–568.

Keynes, John Maynard. 1940. *How to Pay for the War*. London: Macmillan.

Keynes, John Maynard. [1944] 1971. "Letter to Hayek." In E. Johnson and D. Moggridge (eds.), *The Collected Writings of John Maynard Keynes* (Vol. 27, pp. 385–388). Cambridge: Cambridge University Press.

Klausinger, Hansjörg. 2012a. "Introduction." In H. Klausinger (ed.), *The Collected Works of F. A. Hayek, Volume 7, Business Cycles, Part I* (pp. 1–51). Chicago, IL: University of Chicago Press.

Klausinger, Hansjörg. 2012b. "Introduction." In H. Klausinger (ed.), *The Collected Works of F. A. Hayek, Volume 8, Business Cycles, Part II* (pp. 1–43). Chicago, IL: University of Chicago Press.

Knight, Frank. 1935. "Economic Theory and Nationalism." In *The Ethics of Competition and Other Essays*. London: George Allen & Unwin Ltd.

Koppl, Roger. 2018. *Expert Failure*. New York: Cambridge University Press.

Kukathas, Chandran. 2003. *The Liberal Archipelago: A Theory of Diversity and Freedom*. Oxford: Oxford University Press.

Kusch, Martin. 1995. *Pscyhologism: A Case Study in the Sociology of Philosophical Knowledge*. London and New York: Routledge.

Laer, Wolf von. Manuscript. "Patterns of Crisis: Legislative Voting, Urgency, and Errors – An Empirical Analysis of Law Making during the Great Recession".

Landemore, Hélène. 2012. *Democratic Reason: Politics, Collective Intelligence, and the Rule of the Many*. Princeton, NJ: Princeton University Press.

Lange, Oskar and Fred M. Taylor. 1938. *On the Economic Theory of Socialism* (B. E. Lipincott, ed.). Minneapolis, MN: University of Minnesota Press.

Lavoie, Don. [1985] 2015. *Rivalry and Central Planning*. Arlington, VA: Mercatus Center.

Lavoie, Don. [1985] 2016. *National Economic Planning: What Is Left?* Arlington, VA: Mercatus Center.

Leeson, Peter and Robert Subrick. 2006. "Robust Political Economy." *Review of Austrian Economics*, 19, 107–111.

Lenin, V. I. [1917] 1923. *Moskovsky Rabocy*.

Lenin, V. I. [1917] 1960. *Collected Works*. London: Lawrence and Wishart.

Lerner, Abba. 1937. "Statics and Dynamics in Socialist Economics." *Economic Journal*, 47, 253–270.

Lerner, Abba. 1938. "Theory and Practice in Socialist Economics." *Review of Economic Studies*, 6, 71–75.

Lerner, Abba. 1944. *The Economics of Control: Principles of Welfare Economics*. New York: Macmillan.

Lewis, Paul A. 2017. "Ontology and the History of Economic Thought: The Case of Anti-Reductionism in the work of Friedrich Hayek." *Cambridge Journal of Economics*, 41, 1343–1365.

Littlejohn, Clayton. 2009. "'Ought', 'can', and practical reasons." *American Philosophical Quarterly*, 46(4), 363–373.

Lorenz, Konrad. (1941). "Kant's Doctrine of the A Priori in the Light of Contemporary Biology." In H. Plotkin (ed.), *Learning, Development and Culture* (pp. 121–143). Chichester: John Wiley and Sons.

Mach, Ernst. [1886] 1959. *The Analysis of Sensations*. New York: Dover.

Markie, Peter. 2017. "Rationalism vs. Empiricism." In Edward N. Zalta (ed.), *The Stanford Encyclopedia of Philosophy*, Fall 2017 edn. Retrieved from https://plato.stanford.edu/archives/fall2017/entries/rationalism-empiricism/

Marsh, Leslie. 2010. "Hayek: Cognitive Scientist *Avant la Lettre*." In *The Social Science of Hayek's 'The Sensory Order', Advances in Austrian Economics* (Vol. 13, pp. 115–155). Bingley, UK: Emerald.

Martin, Wayne (2009). Ought but cannot. *Proceedings of the Aristotelian Society* 109 (2): 103–128.

Mauthner, Fritz. 1901–1903. *Beiträge zu einer Kritik der Sprache*, 3 Vols. Stuttgart: J.G. Cotta.

McCloskey, Deirdre. 2007. *The Bourgeois Virtues: Ethics for an Age of Commerce*. Chicago, IL: University of Chicago Press.

McCloskey, Deirdre. 2011. *Bourgeois Dignity: Why Economics Can't Explain the Modern World*. Chicago, IL: University of Chicago Press.

McCloskey, Deirdre. 2017. *Bourgeois Equality: How Ideas, Not Capital or Institutions, Enriched the World*. Chicago, IL: University of Chicago Press.

McGinn, Robert E. 1990. *Science, Technology, and Society*. New York: Pearson.

McQuade, Thomas J. 2010. "Science and The Sensory Order." *Advances in Austrian Economics*, 13, 23–56.

McQuade, Thomas J. and W. N. Butos. 2003. "Order-Dependent Knowledge and the Economics of Science." *Review of Austrian Economics*, 16(2/3), 133–152.

Meadowcroft, John. 2011. "Nozick's Critique of Rawls: Distribution, Entitlement, and the Assumptive World of *A Theory of Justice*." In R. M. Bader and J. Meadowcroft (eds.), *The Cambridge Companion to Nozick's Anarchy, State, and Utopia* (pp. 168–196). Cambridge: Cambridge University Press.

Mises, Ludwig von. [1920] 1935. "Economic Calculation in the Socialist Commonwealth." In F. A. Hayek (ed.), *Collectivist Economic Planning*. London: Routledge.

Mises, Ludwig von. [1922] 2009. *Socialism: An Economic and Sociological Analysis*. Auburn, AL: Ludwig von Mises Institute.

Mises, Ludwig von. [1933] 2003. *Epistemological Problems of Economics*. Auburn, AL: Ludwig von Mises Institute.

Mises, Ludwig von. [1949] 1998. *Human Action: A Treatise on Economics*. Auburn, AL: Ludwig von Mises Institute.

Mises, Ludwig von. 1962. *The Ultimate Foundation of Economic Science*. Princeton, NJ: D. Van Nostrand.

Mizrahi, Moti. (2015). "Ought, Can, and Presupposition: An Experimental Study." *Methode*, 4(6), 232–243.

Munk, Nina. 2014. *The Idealist: Jeffrey Sachs and the Quest to End Poverty*. New York: Anchor.

Myrdal, Gunnar. 1933. "Der Gleichgewichtsbegriff als Instrument des geldtheoretischen Analyse." In F. A. Hayek (ed.), *Beiträge zur Geldtheorie* (pp. 361–487). Vienna: Julius Springer; English translation, 1939, *Monetary Equilibrium*. London: William Hodge.

Neurath, Otto. 1919. *Durch die Kriegswirtschaft zur Naturalwirtschaft*. Munich: G. D. W. Callwey.

North, Douglass. 1982. *Structure and Change in Economic History*. New York: W. W. Norton.

North, Douglass. 1990. *Institutions, Institutional Change and Economic Performance*. Cambridge: Cambridge University Press.

North, Douglass. 2010. *Understanding the Process of Economic Change*. Princeton, NJ: Princeton University Press.

Nozick, Robert. [1974] 2013. *Anarchy, State, and Utopia*. New York: Basic Books.

O'Driscoll, Gerald P. 1977. *Economics as a Coordination Problem*. Menlo Park, CA: Institute for Humane Studies.

Oberdan, Thomas. 2017. "Moritz Schlick." In Edward N. Zalta (ed.), *The Stanford Encyclopedia of Philosophy*, Winter 2017 edn. Retrieved from https://plato.stanford.edu/archives/win2017/entries/schlick/

Oppenheim, Felix E. 1987. "National Interest, Rationality, and Morality." *Political Theory*, 15(3), 369–389.

Pareto, Vilfredo. 1927. *Manuel d'économie politique*, 2nd edn. Paris: Giard.

Pennington, Mark. 2011. *Robust Political Economy: Classical Liberalism and the Future of Public Policy*. Cheltenham, UK: Edward Elgar.

Pierson, Nicolaas G. [1902] 1935. "The Problem of Value in the Socialist Society." In F. A. Hayek (ed.), *Collectivist Economic Planning*. London: Routledge.

Plato. 1991. *The Republic* (Benjamin Jowett, trans.). New York: Penguin Random House.

Polanyi, Michael. 1966. *The Tacit Dimension*. Garden City, NY: Doubleday & Company, Inc.

Quine, W. V. O. [1951] 1961. "Two Dogmas of Empiricism." In *From a Logical Point of View*, 2nd revised edn. New York: Harper and Row. Originally published in *The Philosophical Review*, 60(1951), 20–43.

Quine, W. V. O. 1969. "Epistemology Naturalized." In *Ontological Relativity and Other Essays*. New York: Columbia University Press.

Ralston, Shane. 2012. "Dewey and Hayek on Democratic Experimentalism." *Contemporary Pragmatism*, 9(2), 93–116.

Rawls, John. [1971] 2005. *A Theory of Justice: Original Edition*. Cambridge, MA: Belknap Press.

Rawls, John. [1993] 2005. *Political Liberalism*. New York: Columbia University Press.

Rawls, John. 1999. *A Theory of Justice: Revised Edition*. Cambridge, MA: Belknap Press.

Rawls, John. 2001. *Justice as Fairness: A Restatement*. Cambridge, MA: Belknap Press.

Repapis, Constantinos. 2011. "Hayek's Business Cycle Theory during the 1930s: A Critical Account of Its Development." *History of Political Economy*, 43(4), 699–742.

Roper, Crosby W. 1929. *The Problem of Pricing in a Socialist State*. Cambridge, MA: Harvard University Press.

Rothbard, Murray. 1982. *The Ethics of Liberty*. Atlantic Highlands, NJ: Humanities Press.

Ryle, Gilbert. 1946. "Knowing How and Knowing That." *Proceedings of the Aristotelian Society*, 46(1945–1946), 1–16.

Sachs, Jeffrey. 2006. *The End of Poverty: Economic Possibilities for Our Time*. New York: Penguin.

Saka, Paul. 2000. "Ought Does Not Imply Can." *American Philosophical Quarterly*, 37(2), 93–105.

Scheall, Scott. 2015a. "Lesser Degrees of Explanation: Some Implications of F. A. Hayek's Methodology of Sciences of Complex Phenomena." *Erasmus Journal for Philosophy and Economics*, 8(1), 42–60. https://doi.org/10.23941/ejpe.v8i1.183

Scheall, Scott. 2015b. "Hayek's Epistemic Theory of Industrial Fluctuations." *History of Economic Ideas*, 23(1), 101–122.

Scheall, Scott. 2015c. "A Hayekian Explanation of Hayek's 'Epistemic Turn'." *Economic Thought*, 4(2), 32–47

Scheall, Scott. 2015d. "Hayek the Apriorist?" *Journal of the History of Economic Thought*, 37(1), 87–110.

Scheall, Scott. 2015e. "Slaves of the Defunct: The Epistemic Intractability of the Hayek–Keynes Debate." *Journal of Economic Methodology*, 215–234. https://doi.org/10.1080/1350178X.2015.1024875

Scheall, Scott. 2016. "A Brief Note Concerning Hayek's Non-Standard Conception of Knowledge." *Review of Austrian Economics*, 29(2), 205–210.

Scheall, Scott. 2017a. "'What Is Extreme about Mises' Extreme Apriorism?" *Journal of Economic Methodology*, 24(3), 226–249.

Scheall, Scott. 2017b. "Review of Alexander Linsbichler's *Was Ludwig von Mises a Conventionalist? A New Analysis of the Epistemology of the Austrian School of Economics*." *Erasmus Journal for Philosophy and Economics*, 10(2), 110–115.

Scheall, Scott. 2019a. "Ignorance and the Incentive Structure confronting Policymakers." *Cosmos + Taxis*, 7(1–2), 39–51.

Scheall, Scott. 2019b. "On the Method Appropriate to Hayek Studies." *Œconomia – History/Methodology/Philosophy*, 9(1), 29–35.

Scheall, Scott. 2019c. "Review of Peter J. Boettke's *F.A. Hayek: Economics, Political Economy, and Social Philosophy*." *History of Political Economy*, 51(5), 970–973.

Scheall, Scott. Manuscript. "Kinds of Scientific Rationalism: The Case for Methodological Liberalism".

Scheall, Scott, William N. Butos, and Thomas McQuade. 2019. "Social and Scientific Disorder as Epistemic Phenomena, or the Consequences of Government Dietary Guidelines." *Journal of Institutional Economics*, 15, 431–447. https://doi.org/10.1017/S1744137418000358

Scheall, Scott and Parker Crutchfield. Forthcoming. "The Priority of the Epistemic". *Episteme*, Volume and Issue TBD.

Schlick, Moritz. 1918. *Allgemeine Erkenntnislehre*. Berlin: Springer.

Schmidtz, David. 2012. "Friedrich Hayek." In Edward N. Zalta (ed.), *The Stanford Encyclopedia of Philosophy*. Retrieved from http://plato.stanford.edu/archives/fall2012/entries/friedrich-hayek/

Schuck, Peter H. 2014. *Why Government Fails So Often and How It Can Do Better*. Princeton, NJ: Princeton University Press.

Sigmund, Karl. 2017. *Exact Thinking in Demented Times: The Vienna Circle and the Epic Quest for the Foundations of Science*. New York: Basic Books.

Sinnott-Armstrong, Walter. 1984. "'Ought' Conversationally Implies 'Can'." *The Philosophical Review*, 93, 249–261.

Smith, Adam. [1759] 1853. *The Theory of Moral Sentiments*. London: Henry G. Bohn.

Smith, George H. 2013. *The System of Liberty: Themes in the History of Classical Liberalism*. Cambridge: Cambridge University Press.

Smith, Vernon L. [2002] 2016. "Constructivist and Ecological Rationality in Economics." In P. Boettke and S. Haeffele-Balch, V. H. Storr (eds.), *Mainline Economics: Six Nobel Lectures in the Tradition of Adam Smith* (pp. 101–190). Arlington, VA: Mercatus Center.

Smith, Vernon L. 2008. *Rationality in Economics*. Cambridge: Cambridge University Press.

Spencer, Herbert. 1870–1872. *Principles of Psychology*. London: Williams and Norgate.

Spufford, Francis. 2010. *Red Plenty*. Minneapolis, MN: Graywolf Press.

Steele, David Ramsay. 1992. *From Marx to Mises: Post-Capitalist Society and the Challenge of Economic Calculation*. La Salle, IL: Open Court.

Steele, Gerald R. 1992. "Hayek's Contribution to Business Cycle Theory: A Modern Assessment." *History of Political Economy*, 24(2), 477–491.

Stöhr, Adolf. 1910. *Lehrbuch der Logik in psychologisierender Darstellung*. Vienna: Deuticke.

Stöhr, Adolf. 1921. *Wege des Glaubens*. Vienna and Leipzig: Braumüller.

Strawson, P. F. 1985. *Skepticism and Naturalism: Some Varieties*. New York: Columbia University Press.

Sulzer, Georg. 1899. *Die Zrikunft des Sozialismus*. Dresden.

Sumner, William Graham. [1881] 1992. "Sociology." In Robert C. Bannister (ed.), *On Liberty, Society, and Politics: The Essential Essays of William Graham Sumner*. Indianapolis, IN: Liberty Fund.

Taylor, Fred M. 1929. "The Guidance of Production in a Socialist State." *American Economic Review*, 19(March 1929), 1–8.

Turner, R. S. [1994] 2016. *In the Eye's Mind: Vision and the Helmholtz-Hering Controversy*. Princeton, NJ: Princeton University Press.

Vallentyne, Peter. 1989. "Two Types of Moral Dilemmas." *Erkenntnis*, 30, 301–318.

Vallentyne, Peter. 2011. "Nozick's Libertarian Theory of Justice." In R. M. Bader and J. Meadowcroft (eds.), *The Cambridge Companion to Nozick's Anarchy, State, and Utopia* (pp. 145–167). Cambridge: Cambridge University Press.

Vanberg, Viktor. 2017. "The 'Knowledge Problem' as the Integrating Theme of F. A. Hayek's Oeuvre." In V. Vanberg (ed.), *The Collected Works of F. A. Hayek, Volume 14, The Sensory Order and Other Writings on the Foundations of Theoretical Psychology* (pp. 1–111). Chicago, IL: University of Chicago Press.

Vaughn, Karen I. 1994. *Austrian Economics in America: The Migration of a Tradition*. Cambridge: Cambridge University Press.

Vaughn, Karen I. 1999. "Hayek's Implicit Economics: Rules and the Problem of Order." *Review of Austrian Economics*, 11(1), 129–144.

Vaughn, Karen I. 2013. "Hayek, Equilibrium and the Role of Institutions in Economic Order." *Critical Review*, 25(3–4), 473–496.

Vogelstein, Eric. 2012. "Subjective Reasons." *Ethical Theory and Moral Practice*, 15, 239–257.

Weber, Max. 1921. *Wirtschaft und Gesellschaft*. Tübingen.

Weimer, Walter B. 1980. "For and against Method: Reflections on Feyerabend and the Foibles of Philosophy." *Pre/Text*, 1–2, 161–203.

Weimer, Walter B. 1982. "Hayek's Approach to the Problems of Complex Phenomena: An Introduction to the Theoretical Psychology of The Sensory Order." In W. B. Weimer and D. A. Palermo (eds.), *Cognition and the Symbolic Processes* (Vol. 2, pp. 241–285). Hillsdale, NJ: Lawrence Erlbaum.

White, Lawrence H. 1999a. "Hayek's Monetary Theory and Policy: A Critical Reconstruction." *Journal of Money, Credit, and Banking*, 31(1), 109–120.

White, Lawrence H. 1999b. "Why Didn't Hayek Favor Laissez-Faire in Banking?" *History of Political Economy*, 31(4), 753–769.

Wikipedia contributors. 2019, September 17. "2019 College Admissions Bribery Scandal." *Wikipedia, The Free Encyclopedia*. Retrieved 15:41, September 23, 2019, from https://en.wikipedia.org/w/index.php?title=2019_college_admissions_bribery_scandal&oldid=916221729

Witt, Ulrich. 1997. "The Hayekian Puzzle: Spontaneous Order and the Business Cycle." *Scottish Journal of Political Economy*, 44(1), 44–58.

Wittgenstein, Ludwig, 1922. *Tractatus Logico-Philosophicus* (C. K. Ogden, trans.). London: Routledge & Kegan Paul.

Wundt, Wilhelm. 1873–1874. *Grundzüge der physiologischen Psychologie*. Leipzig: W. Engelmann.

Zappia, Carlo. 1999. "The Assumption of Perfect Foresight and Hayek's Theory of Knowledge." *Revue d'economie politique*, 109(6), 833–846.

Zingales, Luigi. 2012. *A Capitalism for the People: Recapturing the Lost Genius of American Prosperity*. New York: Basic Books.

Index

Allgemeine Erkenntnislehre (General Theory of Knowledge) (Schlick 1918) 114
American Institutionalist economists 170
a priori knowledge 112, 124–125, 129–130, 135n38, 136n41, 172, 179, 181; as pre-sensory linkages 122–123
argument for the logical priority of the epistemic 22–24
Arrow, Kenneth 26, 156–157n9
association, psychological 119–122
Austrian Institute of Business Cycle Research 108
Austrian School of economics 1–2, 4, 30; and crony capitalism 97; epistemic burdens of liberalism 77–98
Austrians' political-epistemological approach, underlying reasoning of 63–65

Barry, Norman 104n10
Bateman, Victoria 73–74n59
Bauer, Otto 35
Berkeley, George 112, 120
Boettke, Peter 14, 92, 108–111, 131n4
Böhm-Bawerk, Eugen 35, 109
Boltzmann, Ludwig 113
Brentano, Franz 113
Brutzkus, Boris 69n21, 70n34
Buchanan, James 31n7, 93
Bush, George W. 180
business cycle, theory of 34–35, 37, 54–55, 72n47, 108, 159, 163
Butos, William 137, 139–140, 147–148, 165

calculation problem 42–48
"carbohydrate hypothesis" 150–151
causation 119
central bank and natural rate 72–73n51
central planning: burden of achieving a consensus 51–53; and the mathematical solution 42–47; problem of 13–14

ceteris paribus 182n1
Coase, Ronald 102n2, 108
collective, central planning for 35–36
Collectivist Economic Planning (Hayek 1935, 1997) 41–42
commutative vs. distributive justice 102n6
"Competition as a Discovery Procedure" (Hayek 1968, 2014) 49, 59–60
complexity 38–41, 109, 119
consciousness, theory of 114
consensuses 139
consensus for central plan 51–53
constituent, definition of 15
constituent disappointment 25–27
constitutional approach 9, 10n6, 158–159, 170, 174–175
constitutional design 176n1
Constitution of Liberty, The (Hayek 1960, 2011) 85–86, 90, 103–104n9, 172
constructivist thinking 89
"Contributions to a Theory of How Consciousness Develops" (Hayek 1920, 2017) 114–115
countercyclical economic policymaking 53–63
credit expansion 54–58
Crutchfield, Parker 19
currency: denaturalization of 85; over-issue of 84–85

Darwin, Charles 39
data, subjective and objective 127–128
data problem 39–40, 42, 49, 55, 68n19, 69n21, 119, 162, 166–167
DeCanio, Samuel 31n11–32n11
"dekulaked" peasants 71–72n41
deliberate political action, limits of 174–175; constitutional approach to the problem of policymaker ignorance 170–174; overview 158–159

Descartes, René 112, 116
Dickinson, H. D. 42, 48–49
Die Gemeinwirtschaft: Untersuchungen über den Sozialismus (*Socialism: An Economic and Sociological Analysis*) (Mises 1922) 108
"Dilemma of Specialization, The" (Keynes 1956, 1967) 40
do-nothing policies 98–100, 104n16, 163–166, 177n4

Easterly, William 78
econometrics 170
"Economic Calculation in the Socialist Commonwealth" (Mises 1920) 36, 107–108
economic disorder 84, 139, 146, 163, 168
economic freedom and solution of the calculation problem 47–48
economic order ("equilibrium") 58–59, 160
economic order, theory of 58, 93, 109, 137–139, 142, 159–160, 163–164, 168
"Economics and Knowledge " (Hayek 1937, 2014) 58
empirism and rationalism, conjunction of 133n24
empiristic theory of spatial perception 120
epistemic burdens 19–22; of achieving consensus concerning a central plan 51–53; of the administrator in a socialist oasis 35–37; of the central planner under market socialism 48–51; of countercyclical economic policymaking and Keynesian demand management 54–63; defined 3; of policy inaction 76, 97–99; of realizing effective liberal order, problem of epistemic requirements of liberal transitions 76, 77–98; of socialist administrators in other contexts 41–53
epistemic institutionalism 92–93
epistemic-mechanistic approach 8–9, 10n6, 137, 155–156, 174; *see also* political order and disorder
equality of opportunity 97
equilibrium state 67n9
evolution, theory of 39
explanations of the principle 39

"fat hypothesis" 150–151
Fermi, Enrico 108
Freud, Sigmund 113
Friedman, Milton 89, 108
functional omniscience and omnipotence 170–174
"full-employment equilibrium" 160, 177n2
"full" explanation 68n18

general equilibrium theory, Walrasian 42, 48–49, 59–60, 73n55
General Theory of Employment, Interest, and Money (Keynes 1936, 1973) 41, 177n2
German Historicist economists 170
governmental assembly 86–88
Great Depression/Great Recession 159
Greater Certainty thesis 124, 135–136n40
Green New Deal 101–102

Hampshire, Stuart 22
Hare, R. M. 22
Hayek, F. A.: association as the principle that explains the complex phenomena of mental life 119–122; on central planning 13–14; epistemic justification and Hayek's non-standard conception of knowledge 126–128; and government intervention in economy 4–5; vs. Mises on matters epistemological 107–112, 123–125; political epistemology, Hayekian 128; problem of policymaker ignorance 30; *radical empiricism* 125–126; social order 8; theoretical psychologist and epistemological naturalist 112–122; theory of knowledge 7–8; understanding 10n4
Hayek versus Keynes: general schema for empirical political epistemology 160–163; Hayek-Keynes debate through the lens of political epistemology 163–170; overview 159–160
Helmholtz, Hermann von 113–114, 120–121, 132n12, 133n25, 133n27, 133n28, 136n45
Herbert, David 32n11
Humboldt, Wilhelm von 135–136n40
Hume, David 15–18, 112, 134n35
Hume's maxim 15–18

ignorance, first and second order 3
"Ignorance and the Incentive Structure confronting Policymakers" (Scheall 2019a) 19
illiberal policymaking 5
"impossibility theorem" 156–157n9
incentives, policymaker *see* policymaker incentives
income inequality 97
"Of the Independency of Parliament" (Hume) 15–16
industrial fluctuations, epistemic theory of 54–56, 58–63, 72n53–73n53, 84, 139, 146, 160; role of ignorance in 54–58

introspective argument for the logical
    priority of the epistemic 21–22
"Intuition/Deduction Thesis" 135–136n40

James, William 114
"Jeffersonian, market-guided society" 104n11
justified true belief 116

Kant, Immanuel 112, 121
Keynes, John Maynard 41, 54, 69n22,
    73–74n59, 73n57, 108, 177n2
Keynesian demand management 53–63, 92
Knight, Frank 108
knowing 138
knowledge: definition of 15; and epistemic
    mechanisms 137–140; first and second
    order 27–28, 82; kinds of 4–5
knowledge, concept of, Hayek 114–116
knowledge, theory of 107, 131n5

Lange, Oskar 48–49
Lavoie, Don 31n7, 67n4, 69n25, 100,
    104n17, 109–110, 131n6
Law, Legislation and Liberty (Hayek 1973,
    1976, 1979) 85–86, 90, 103–104n9,
    131n3, 172
Leeson, Peter 14, 94
legislative assembly 86–88
Leibniz, Gottfried 112
Lenin, V. I. 34
liberalism and policymaker ignorance: epistemic
    burden of policy inaction 97–99;
    epistemic burdens of realizing liberal
    order 77–98; overview 75–77
liberal order: artificiality of the assumption
    of the committed liberalizer 81–82;
    Hayek's failure to see the problem of
    liberal transitions 82–92; overview
    77–81
liberalization 78
liberal transitions 82–98
limited altruism 93
limited knowledge 93
Locke, John 112
logical priority of the epistemic 19–27
Lorenz, Konrad 134n36
Lysenko, Trofim 156n7

Mach, Ernst 113–114, 121
macroeconomic theory 54, 59–62, 73n52,
    100, 159, 165–167, 177n2
market socialism 48–51
market socialists 70n33, 70n35

Marx, Karl 35, 67n4–5
mathematical solution 42–47, 68n20,
    69n25, 70n31, 70n32
Mauthner, Fritz 113
McCloskey, Deirdre 78
McQuade, Thomas 137, 139–140, 147–148,
    165
Menger, Carl 109
Mises, Ludwig von 1–2; on central
    planning 13–14; and government
    intervention in economy 4; problem of
    policymaker ignorance 30; theory of
    knowledge 7–8
monetary-neutrality theory 57
Müller, Johannes 114

nativism 132–133n23, 133n25
"in natura" economic reckoning 35, 42
naturalism, epistemological vs.
    normativism, epistemological 116–122
naturalized falsificationism 134n35
"natural rights" 79
Neurath, Otto 35, 42, 67n3
New Institutionalist schools of economics 78
normativism, epistemological vs.
    naturalism, epistemological 116–122
North, Douglass 78

Obamacare 180
Ocasio-Cortez, Alexandria 101–102
omniscience and omnipotence 31n4, 158–159
order and disorder, epistemic theory 137
ought implies can 2, 19–20, 22–24;
    ought conversationally implicates can 22; *ought
    implies knows enough to* 24, 102; *ought makes
    plausible can* 23; *ought presupposes can* 22

pattern predictions 39
planning and epistemic mechanisms
    137–140
Plato 29, 112, 116
policy, definition of 15
policy effectiveness 31n5
policy goal 4–5
policy inaction 98–99
policymaker, definition of 15
policymaker ignorance: constitutional
    approach to 170–174; effects of the
    problem 10n6; overview 13–14,
    19–20; and constituent disappointment
    24–25; and political theory 161–162;
    problematic nature of political
    decision-making 24–25; problem of

1–10, 14; the problem of policymaker incentives 15–19; taxonomy of ignorant policymakers 27–29; terminological clarifications 15
policymaker incentives 2–4, 9, 15–19, 27–30, 32n11, 159, 171–172, 175–176, 178
policymaking: in liberal environments 96–98; *in medias res* 79
political epistemology 1, 10n2, 92–93
political epistemology, Hayekian 107; overview 128
political order and disorder 151–155; knowledge, planning, social order and epistemic mechanisms 137–140
Polyani, Michael 123
Popper, Karl 108
"pretence of knowledge" 13, 62–64, 73n52, 84, 139–140, 149, 169, 180
"Pretence of Knowledge, The" (Hayek 1975, 2014) 13, 29, 54, 168
price *elasticities* 145–146
price-level stabilization argument 72n47
Prices and Production (Hayek 1931,1935) 55
price theory 58
pricing 139, 142–146
"Primacy of the Abstract, The" (Hayek 1969, 2014) 38
Privatseminar, Mises 108
problem of ignorance 31n8
profit and loss 36
propositional/non-propositional knowledge 15
"publication-citation-reputation" (PCR) 148–151
public interests 51–52
Pure Theory of Capital, The (Hayek 1941, 2007). 58

Quine, W. V. O. 117

radical empiricism 125–126
rationalist apriorism 124
Reason without Experience thesis 124
reputation 146–151
resources, distribution of 70–71n37
The Road to Serfdom (Hayek 1944, 2007) 170–171, 173
Robbins, Lionel 98, 108
robust political economy (RPE) 93–96, 104n12
Roper, W. C. 42
Rothbard, Murray 79
rule of law 6, 76–81, 94, 96–98, 101, 103

rules of conduct 140
Rumsfeld, Donald 27, 180

Scheall's maxim 18, 179–180
Schlick, Moritz 113–114, 132n12
Schwartz, Anna 89
scientistic methodology 60–61
Sensory Order, The: An Inquiry into the Foundations of Theoretical Psychology (Hayek 1952, 2017) 38–39, 115, 131n3, 132n14
Sinnott-Armstrong, Walter 22
Smith, Adam 16–17
Smith, Vernon 78
"Social and Scientific Disorder as Epistemic Phenomena, or the Consequences of Government Dietary Guidelines" (Scheall, Butos, and McQuade 2019) 150
social clubs 103n8
Social Democratic Party, Austria 35
social goals 70n36, 89, 178
socialism 1, 13–14
socialist calculation argument 41, 129
social justice 71n38
social morality by coercive law 72n42
social order 8, 17, 66, 82–84, 130, 137–144, 149–150, 156n1, 156n3, 165
spatial perception 120
"spontaneous orders" 140
Stigler, Geroge 108
Stöhr, Adolf 113, 131n7, 136n41
study of social cooperation 109
Subrick, Robert 14, 94
Sumner, William Graham 13
supply and demand, equilibrium 37, 67n7
surrogate decision making 25
system of rules 140–141

tabula rasa 119, 121
taxonomy of ignorant policymakers 27–29
Taylor, Fred 42, 48
"theory problem" 40–41, 50, 60, 68n19–20, 69n21, 161, 166
"tin example" 142–144
trade cycle, epistemic theory of 55, 72n44, 85, 139
Treatise on Money, A (Keynes, 1930, 1971) 41, 69n22

unconscious inference, theory of 121, 125, 133–134n29, 136n43, 139, 168
"unknown unknowns" 180
Utopia, political-epistemological 91–92

Vanberg, Viktor 131n3
Vienna Circle of Logical Positivism 113
vision, theory of 120–121
voting mechanisms 8, 151–152, 155,
    156n8

Weimer, Walter 68n11, 110
Witt, Ulrich 57
Wittgenstein, Ludwig 108, 113
Wolff, Christian 135–136n40
Wundt, Wilhelm 113–114, 133–134n29

Printed in the United States
by Baker & Taylor Publisher Services

Printed in the United States
by Baker & Taylor Publisher Services